The Fundamentals
of Jewish Mysticism

The Fundamentals of Jewish Mysticism

The Book of Creation and Its Commentaries

LEONARD R. GLOTZER

JASON ARONSON INC.
Northvale, New Jersey
London

This book was set in 11 point Bem by Lind Graphics of Upper Saddle River, New Jersey, and printed by Haddon Craftsmen in Scranton, Pennsylvania.

10 9 8 7 6 5 4 3 2 1

Library of Congress Cataloging-in-Publication Data

Glotzer, Leonard R.
   The fundamentals of Jewish mysticism : the Book of creation and
its commentaries / by Leonard R. Glotzer.
      p. cm.
   Includes bibliographical references and index.
   ISBN 0-87668-437-1
   1. Sefer Yeẓirah. 2. Cabala—History. 3. Mysticism—Judaism—
History. I. Title.
BM525.A419G56   1992
296.1'6—dc20   92-11018

Manufactured in the United States of America. Jason Aronson Inc. offers books and cassettes. For information and catalog write to Jason Aronson Inc., 230 Livingston Street, Northvale, New Jersey 07647.

To the beloved memory
of my father,
Benjamin Glotzer,
and my father-in-law,
Rabbi Hyman Kahn,
Aleihem HaShalom

Contents

Preface

While the actual writing of this book took much time and effort, the greatest part of the work took place in the years of study before a word was penned. In a sense, it represents a lifetime effort and is certainly the fulfillment of a dream. It has given me the opportunity to make available to the public an important part of Jewish thought that was not previously very accessible. That I am so privileged provides me with much satisfaction.

Of the many people I would like to thank, two come most to mind: first, my grandfather, Harry Weiner, who more than anyone stimulated my interest in Jewish scholarship; second, my wonderful Rebbe, Rabbi Yehuda Gershuni, who influenced me with his enlightened approach to learning and his love for not just Talmud but Jewish philosophy as well.

No one contributed more to this work than my sister, Anita Roll. She spent many hours editing the book and ensuring its clarity and readability. I would also like to thank my wife, Shirley, for tolerating the many hours I disappeared to write and for serving as a sounding board for many of my ideas.

Finally, thanks goes to my children, Esther, Sara, Dror, and Yossie, for believing in me, and to my grandson, Yitzchak Tzvi, for his great inspiration.

I pray this book interests some readers enough to further pursue the fascinating study of Jewish philosophy and Kabbalah.

Introduction: Overview of the Principles of Kabbalah

The ultimate absurdity is that anything exists.

Certainly, for the atheist, the existence of the world is an irresolvable paradox. This is because there are only two logical possibilities for the origin of the world. Either Being arose out of nothingness, or something has always existed. Neither of these alternatives seems possible, however.

The problem with the first alternative is that it seems illogical for something to be produced by nothing. It flies in the face of all our experience. Even the findings in quantum physics that suggest that randomness governs the subatomic universe do not account for matter arising from an absolute void.

The claim that matter always existed does not help either. The question of its origin and cause will forever pull at the human heart. Why did matter always exist? What was its cause? These questions will never find emotionally satisfying resolution.

The Scottish philosopher David Hume explored whether questions of this type can be addressed at all. He claimed they are based on the presumption that cause and effect operate in nature. He stated that this belief in causation cannot be proven. We can never observe that something is caused, only that one event follows another.[1] Therefore, according to Hume, it would follow that any questions about what *caused* the existence of the universe cannot be successfully addressed.

While Hume is correct that we do not directly observe causation, it is nonetheless true that all empirical thought is based on it. Man cannot exist without this assumption. Philosophy, science, and reason would be impossible. Man, therefore, stubbornly clings to his belief in causation. To be human is to reason based on cause and effect.

For the theist, the situation is somewhat different. The universe exists as a result of God's existence. Belief in God, however, is not sufficient to fully explain existence. Why should the concept of God imply the existence of a universe? Why does God need the universe? Why does He need man? Thus, even for the theist, existence is a mystery.

While it seems to make no sense that anything exists, we know for certain that it does. We feel and we think. As Rene Descartes once taught, "Cognito Ergo Sum."[2] The fact that I think proves beyond a doubt that I exist.

This brings us to the subject of this book. *Sefer Yetzirah* is an attempt to understand existence. It concerns itself with how the world came to exist. It addresses the question of "how" rather than "why." In explaining the "how," however, the myriad of questions as to the purpose and meaning of existence cannot help but arise. Thus, the commentaries often incorporate discussions about the underlying purpose of the Creation, a purpose that is perhaps implied but not explicitly addressed by the work itself.

HISTORY OF *SEFER YETZIRAH*

Sefer Yetzirah is probably the oldest known kabbalistic work. Its origins are lost in antiquity. It is mentioned in the Talmud (*Sanhedrin* 65b), although some scholars question whether the book referred to there is identical to the current version of *Sefer Yetzirah*. Rabbi Moses Cordovero (Ramak), in his masterpiece *Pardes Rimonim*, states, "There are those who attribute it (*Sefer Yetzirah*) to Abraham our father and those who attribute it to Rabbi Akiva, but the latter is not the accepted opinion."[3] Cordovero goes on to claim that even those who attribute it to Rabbi Akiva only mean that he put the book into its current form; they admit that Abraham is the author.

There are a few other major kabbalistic works that are allegedly from as far back as the mishnaic period. The most famous, aside from the *Zohar*, is *Sefer HaBahir*,[4] attributed to the *Tanna* Nachunia ben HaKaneh. However, it is difficult to believe that all of *Sefer HaBahir* is that ancient, as vowel points (*nikudot*) are discussed in it. There are strong indications that these vowel points were not invented until the eighth century, when the Massorites decided that vowel points were necessary to preserve the traditional biblical pronunciations. A fascinating discussion of this subject is the central theme of the sixteenth-century classic *Masoret HaMesoret*,[5] by Eliyahu Bachur.

Sefer Yetzirah has been held in great reverence throughout the ages. Cordovero writes of *Sefer Yetzirah* in the beginning of *Pardes Rimonim* as follows: "The words of this book (*Sefer Yetzirah*) are deep, high and hidden from the stare of those who study it, notwithstanding that many have tried to explain it."[6]

There are commentaries on *Sefer Yetzirah* from as early as the Gaonic period. We have parts of a commentary by the most renowned of the Gaonim, Rav Saadia himself (800 C.E.). The great thirteenth-century rabbi, Naimonides, wrote a commentary on *Sefer Yetzirah* that is as mysterious as the book it tries to explain. So did the Raivad[7] and many other rabbis.

Major rabbis of the more recent period have also written commentaries and have held the book in awe. An especially beautiful and erudite work is that of Rabbi Eliyahu, Gaon of Vilna.

Name of the Book

The book's name, *Sefer Yetzirah*, is somewhat difficult to translate. In Hebrew, there are various synonyms for "creation," and "*yetzirah*" is one of them. Another one is "*briyah*." An ancient tradition differentiates between the two synonyms. According to this tradition, which is discussed by Maimonides in his *Guide to the Perplexed*,[8] "*briyah*" refers to the creation of being from nonbeing, while "*yetzirah*" connotes being arising from other being. This has led some to translate "*yetzirah*" as "formation" rather than "creation." It seems to me, however, that translating "*yetzirah*" as creation is correct, for the English word "creation" is applied to the creation of things from other things more often than to the creation of "being from nothingness."

It is common in Kabbalah to refer to the existence of four major worlds. Each world is named after a different type of "creation." The first type of creation is emanation (*atzilut*), and implies light being given off from a preexisting source. The second world is that of "*briyah*," which results from a change in the intensity and quality of this light, rather than the creation of light from nothingness. This

differs from the pure Maimonidean use of the word "*briyah*." Afterward are the worlds of *Yetzirah* and *Asiyah* ("making"). These, too, are
the result of light from the upper worlds being transformed rather
than being created anew. Thus, the source of all creation is God, not in
the sense of His creation of objects outside Himself, but in the sense
that all existence is but a transformation of the light of Him Himself!

Sefer Yetzirah is about the forms the divine light takes. It studies the
heavenly sources of the spatial and temporal worlds. Some have noted
that its main focus is the creation of "*Yesh MiYesh*"—being from
other being—and that this fact is emphasized by the book's name, *Sefer
Yetzirah*. I have not, however, found the differentiation between the
terms "*yetzirah*" and "*briyah*" in any literature as early as *Sefer Yetzirah*.
Therefore, I question whether this special meaning was intended by
the book's author.

Influence of the *Zohar* on the Commentaries

There is a striking difference between the earlier and later commentaries on *Sefer Yetzirah*. This difference is attributable in the main to the
influence of one great work, the *Zohar*,[9] which made its appearance in
Europe during the thirteenth century.

The *Zohar* revolutionized Kabbalah. From somewhat diverse concepts and cosmologies, it established a framework for all subsequent
Kabbalah. Certainly, many of the ideas in the *Zohar* preceded it. Many
were, in fact, first formulated in *Sefer Yetzirah*. However, the *Zohar*
was so powerful in its approach, and developed the existing concepts
so beautifully and thoroughly, that its influence is apparent in all
subsequent Kabbalah.

It is precisely the lack of Zoharic influence that is so interesting
about the early commentaries on *Sefer Yetzirah*. There are not too
many existing examples of pre-*Zohar* Kabbalah, and thus *Sefer Yetzirah* and its commentaries are important sources. They stand out in
their independence and lack of uniformity. Post-*Zohar* Kabbalah universally incorporates the *Zohar*'s concepts, cosmology, and often even
its language.

Sefer Yetzirah and the *Zohar* have themselves become foundations
for differing kabbalistic systems. Systems like those of Meir Gabbai,
Moses Cordovero, and Yitzchak Luria all quote from these sources in

a manner similar to that in which the Talmud and *Midrashim*[10] quote from the Bible. They justify their theories based on these early works and sometimes read much more into them than seems to be present.

THE BASIC CONCEPTS
OF *SEFER YETZIRAH*

Numbers, Letters, and *Sefirot*

Sefer Yetzirah is a book of numbers and letters. The world was created with ten numbers and twenty-two letters. The numbers are associated with the ten emanations of God's light, known as *Sefirot*. The letters represent basic forces of nature. They are derived from flows of light between the *Sefirot*.

If all this sounds quite mystical and obscure, it is only because in reality it is. The concepts of Kabbalah are couched in everyday physical terms like light and flows, but they refer to spiritual ideas of a completely different nature. There is a parallelism, though, between the worlds. The physical world, being a result of the higher spiritual spheres, retains much of their structure. Thus, for example, the ten emanations are said to manifest in the physical world as actual spheres surrounding the earth.

The creation of the world began by God emanating the *Sefirot* (plural of *Sefirah*). They are known also as "God's attributes." They are spiritual entities and are not at all physical. Their exact nature has been a matter of much kabbalistic debate.

In the *Zohar*, the positions the ten *Sefirot* assume in relation to each other are described in at least three seemingly incompatible ways.

1. *Each* Sefirah *is directly above the next.* God emanated the first *Sefirah*, and the first emanated the second, and so forth. This setup implies that the first *Sefirah* is closest to the source (God) and is thus holier than the second. The tenth is the furthest from the source and is thus the least spiritual.
2. *They are like the skin of onions.* The outer sphere encloses the inner. The outer is like a peel (*klipah*) to the inner. The inner is like the marrow (*mo'ach*) to the outer. In this metaphor, the inner is the greater (more spiritual).

3. *They form the shape of a man.* They stand in three columns—three *Sefirot* represent the right side of the body, three the left, and four the middle. (See Appendix A.) The different kabbalistic schools deal differently with the reconciliation of these differing structures.

Moses Cordovero says that all three are valid ways of describing different aspects of the *Sefirot*.[11] Thus, one above the other stresses the superiority of the emanator over the emanated. The prior *Sefirah* is the cause of the others and is thus represented as higher. The second is emanated from the first and is thus lower. At the same time it is the cause of the third and is consequently higher.

The second structure (the Onion Model) is meant to show that the same *Sefirah* can be described as important (marrow) or less important (peel), depending on the relationship. Each is marrow to the other skins at the same time as they are peel to the inner layers. Finally, the third structure (three-column man-shaped model) stresses the individual aspects of each *Sefirah* in relationship to the others.

Thus, to Moses Cordovero, there is no contradiction between these three models. The *Sefirot* are not physical, and the different models are just a way to convey spiritual relationships. Sometimes one model is more appropriate for explaining a specific relationship than another. Lurian Kabbalah adopts a different approach. Chaim Vital, the main expounder of Lurian Kabbalah, says in his main work, *Etz Chaim*,[12] that in different worlds different structures apply. Thus, in the world known as the World of Dots, the *Sefirot* are one above the other; in other worlds they are in circles and in columns.

The model that has been used most frequently is the three-column man-shaped one. The *Sefirot* on the right represent attributes of kindness (*chesed*), those on the left represent strictness (*din*), and the middle ones mediate between the left and right.[13] The ten *Sefirot* have flows of spiritual matter between them, flowing through what are known in the kabbalistic physical metaphor as "pipes" (*tzinorot*). There are twenty-two of these "pipes," from which are derived the twenty-two letters of the Hebrew alphabet.

The first *Mishnah* in *Sefer Yetzirah* states, "He created his world with book, number, and story." By this is meant that the elements of language and math were combined in such a way as to create a story—not any story, but the story of creation.

It must be pointed out that what is meant by letters is clearly more than mere elements of language. The Raivad says in his glosses to *Mishneh Torah*[14] that all languages are translations of reality, except for the Holy Tongue, which is the language of reality itself, that is, the Hebrew letters for "chair" represent the powers that give chairs their real world existence. The English word "chair," on the other hand, is merely a convenient way to refer to a chair. So it is these powers, represented by the Hebrew alphabet, that are referred to by *Sefer Yetzirah* as the basic building blocks with which the world was created.

Perhaps even more esoteric is the other main group of elements in *Sefer Yetzirah*, the numbers. The source for the numbers are the *Sefirot*. The word "*Sefirah*" in Hebrew comes from the same root as number, "*sefor*." It refers to the ten emanations of God's light. It is these emanations that are responsible for the diversity in the world.

Sefirot—Vessels or Essence

Discussions as to exactly what the *Sefirot* are took place among the early Kabbalists. Perhaps the most basic debate is that discussed by Moses Cordovero in *Pardes Rimonim*. He quotes two Kabbalists, Rabbi Menachem Mayrakanati and Rabbi David. One states that the *Sefirot* are vessels, not the actual essence of God. The latter states that they are essence.[15]

Cordovero reached the conclusion that they were both right. The *Sefirot* are composed of both vessels and essence. All subsequent Kabbalists adopted this approach.

While this resolved the question of the composition of the *Sefirot*, it leaves a very great theological difficulty. The idea of God's essence being split into different *Sefirot* seems to challenge the basic Jewish belief of pure monotheism. On the surface, it contradicts the concept that God is an "undifferentiated one," as expounded by Maimonides and most of the other great religious philosophers.[16]

Monotheism and Ten *Sefirot*

There is a well-known debate between Maimonides and the Raivad as to whether a Jew may believe in a physical God. Maimonides states in *Mishneh Torah* that believing in a corporal God is heresy. The Raivad, in his glosses, states that while he himself does not believe that God is physical, it should nevertheless not be considered heresy since "greater and better Jews than us did in fact believe this."[17]

The theological problem that Maimonides had with believing in a corporal God is that a physical body can be subdivided. A subdividable entity is potentially not one. Therefore, a person with such a belief is a heretic, because saying God can be potentially split into parts is not monotheistic and is against the basic tenets of the Torah.

The Kabbalists were well aware that the doctrine of ten *Sefirot* posed similar problems. The *Sefirot* were not considered to be merely God's creations, out of the borders of the divine. Rather, most Kabbalists believed they consisted of God's "essence" (*atzmut*), with the possible additional element of "vessels" (*Keilim*).

Evolution of Kabbalistic Thought

Many of the ideas in Kabbalah seem to have developed in time. The earlier works were simpler and lacked some of the structures, concepts, and problems that are found in later works.

For instance, early books, such as *Sefer Yetzirah*, only discuss one set of ten *Sefirot*. There is no discussion as to whether the *Sefirot* are actually divine.

All major kabbalistic schools after the *Zohar*'s appearance believe in at least four sets of ten *Sefirot*. Meir Gabbai (fifteenth century), in *Avodat HaKodesh*, states that there are exactly forty *Sefirot*, ten in each of four worlds. Most later Kabbalists believed that there were many more sets.

The *Zohar* itself refers to the four worlds as follows:

1. *The World of the Emanations (Atzilot)*—This world is considered "within the boundary of the divine."
2. *The World of Creation (Briyah)*—This is the world of the "Holy Throne," also described as the chariot (*Merkavah*) of God. (See the first chapter of Ezekiel.)
3. *The World of Creation (Yetzirah)*—This is the world of the angels.
4. *The World of Making (Asiyah)*—This is the lower world, its *Sefirot* being the ten firmaments that surround the physical earth.

These worlds represent "the side of holiness" and are paralleled by the worlds of "the other side" (evil). It is a well-known kabbalistic doctrine that everything that is in the "side of holiness" has a corresponding entity in "the other side," as it states in Ecclesiastes 7:14, "Each to the level of each God created."

Later Kabbalists have said there are many higher worlds in the holy side, all with sets of ten *Sefirot*. This is especially emphasized in Lurian Kabbalah. Isaac Luria states that there are higher worlds beyond number.

That each world contains a set of exactly ten *Sefirot* and no other amount is of utmost necessity and is greatly stressed in early works like *Sefer Yetzirah*. The reason is based on the relationship of the number ten to the number one in the decimal system. That is, the number ten "reverts" to one (when the digits of ten are added together, they equal one). The numbers greater than ten start from one again. Eleven in Hebrew is ten and one. The point being emphasized is that there are ten *Sefirot* only from the vantage point of man. For God, there is only the One, i.e., the undifferentiated God.

The ten *Sefirot* have been said to represent the fingers of God with which He molded the world.[18] The entire first third of Maimonides' *Guide to the Perplexed* is spent in explaining that biblical references to God's fingers and other physical parts are meant symbolically and not literally. Maimonides felt that the belief that God has parts, even nonphysical spiritual parts, is heretical.[19]

Many explanations have been offered by Kabbalists to bring them more in line with Maimonides' monotheism. Most explanations are based on the idea that the *Sefirot* are ten in the way their influence is felt in the world. From God's perspective, there is only Himself. His essence flowing through all the *Sefirot* is the same. It is God's one undifferentiated essence. His essence takes on different aspects and appearances depending on the particular host vessel through which it is flowing. It is as if we see Him through colored glass. The colors of the glass make Him appear to have various aspects. These ten vessels of colored glass are what we called the vessels of the *Sefirot*. His essence within these vessels is but one. Thus, the dual vessel-essence nature of *Sefirot* allows them to be ten yet one.

Why the Concept of *Sefirot*

The *Sefirot* represent an answer to a fundamental theological problem. If God is one inseparable being, why do we find such a diversity in the world? How can kindness and strictness, good and evil, all be derived from the same undifferentiated benevolent unity that is God?

The *Sefirot* serve to insulate the pure Maimonidean concept of an undifferentiated God from the multifaceted universe. Before God created the world, the ten *Sefirot* did not exist. There was only God and His name (i.e., His will).[20] After the creation, God remained unchanged. However, the divine attributes (*Sefirot*) from which the world's diversity flows were created to administer the world. From them come the dichotomies we see in the world, strictness and kindness, masculinity and femininity, and so on.

In order to accomplish their task, the *Sefirot* are organized into groups of threes (except for the last). One *Sefirah* of each group is of "kindness" (*chesed*), one of "strictness"(*din*), and a third *Sefirah* reconciles the differences between them. They are described as a human body, the right side representing kindness (*chesed*), the left representing strictness (*din*), and the middle representing arbitration (*rachamim*). These primary attributes are all good in themselves. However, indirectly from strictness, the existence of evil is made possible. This is not all negative, however, for evil creates the possibility of free choice. Without it, man could choose no evil. Thus, his existence would be trivialized.

Are the *Sefirot* Really God's Essence?

It appears, at least on the surface, that when the works of Moses Cordovero and Chaim Vital (Lurian Kabbalah) say that the *Sefirot* contain "essence," they mean it quite literally. Cordoveo writes: "At the start of the emanation, the *Ein Sof* (infinite light), King of all kings, the Holy One, blessed be He, emanated ten *Sefirot*, which are from His essence, are one with Him, and He and They are all one complete unity."[21]

He goes on to explain that these ten "*Sefirot* of essence" constitute the soul of the ten "*Sefirot* of vessels." He states that the names and images found in Kabbalah apply only to the vessels, not to the essence.

The idea of ten *Sefirot* of "essence" may be shocking to many Jews. It sounds too similar to the Christian idea of "three yet one." It seems far removed from Maimonides' idea of monotheism. Many explanations have been offered by the Kabbalists to make this concept compatible with the traditional tenet of God being "An Undifferentiated

One." Nevertheless, it probably remains Kabbalah's greatest departure from normative Judaism.

Perhaps, for this reason, some prominent Kabbalists have explicitly denied that the "essence" in the Sefirot is God as He exists unto Himself. Rather, they say that it is God only in the sense of His manifestation to the world. Thus, the famous eighteenth-century Kabbalist, Moses Chaim Luzzatto, states that the infinite light is God's unbound will, while His limited will is the Sefirah of Keter.[22] A similar opinion is held by Rabbi Yehuda Leib Ashlag, the most prolific of the more recent Lurian Kabbalists. He states in Talmud Esser Sefirot that Kabbalah does not discuss God's essence at all, but rather the light that is given off from Him. To him, the essence flowing through the Sefirot is God's radiance, but not God Himself.[23] Aryeh Kaplan, in his work on Sefer HaBahir, brings some support for this viewpoint.[24]

However, notwithstanding the attempted explanations, the words of Moses Cordovero retain their startling impact. They contrast sharply with Maimonides' second principle that God is a unity and there is no unity as pure as His, which has no parts or subdivisions of any sort.

Description of the Individual Sefirot

Let me describe briefly the ten Sefirot. I will use the standard post-Zohar names for the Sefirot. It should be noted that the names of the Sefirot found in The Book of Creation differ from these and will be discussed in the body of this book.

The following are the ten Sefirot:

1. *Keter* (Crown)
2. *Chachmah* (Wisdom)
3. *Binah* (Understanding)
4. *Chesed* (Kindness)
5. *Gevurah* (Courage)
6. *Tiferet* (Glory)
7. *Netzach* (Eternity)
8. *Hod* (Beauty)
9. *Yisod* (Foundation)
10. *Malchut* (Kingdom)

The *Sefirot* are often described as being in the shape of a man. Actually, according to Kabbalah, man was created in their shape, that is, "in the Image of God" (Genesis 1:27). The highest three *Sefirot* correspond to the head. They are known as the *Sefirot* of Reason (*Sichliyim*). The next three *Sefirot* are the *Sefirot* of Feeling. They correspond to the heart and the two arms. The lowest group of *Sefirot* are known as the *Sefirot* of Life (*Chiyunim*) and correspond in man to the elements needed to sustain life. They represent the two lower sides of the body and the sex organ. The lowest *Sefirah* is usually considered the female partner to the male. Occasionally this lowest *Sefirah* is considered part of the male body, specifically, the crown of the male reproductive organ (*atarah*). Which model applies depends on the particular context and the thought being conveyed.

Sefirah 1—Keter (Crown, Will)

In Kabbalah, intelligence is made up of various components. The highest aspect of intelligence is Will. Some would argue that Will is distinct from intelligence, but it is considered in Kabbalah as its source. Clearly, exactly what Will is and how it operates is elusive. Kabbalah acknowledges the difficulty in understanding Will, and one frequently finds warnings in kabbalistic literature about trying to delve into this subject. Kabbalists never tire of repeating the admonition, *"B'mufla mimcha al tidrosh"*—"Do not delve into that which is too far above you."

Keter is the first *Sefirah* emanated, and thus closest to the source. It is in this sense the highest, holiest *Sefirah*. It represents God's Will. There is a *Midrash* that has been interpreted by Kabbalists to mean that before the creation of the world, only God and His Will (i.e., the *Sefirah* of *Keter*) existed. After all, God had to will the creation of the world.

The question of the identity of the emanator of this first *Sefirah* has been a matter of kabbalistic discussion. The clearest description is found in the beginning of *Etz Chaim*, the central work of Lurian Kabbalah. It states that at the beginning there was God's light everywhere. The world could not be created because any creation would be immediately obliterated by the intensity of this light. In order to create the world, therefore, the light receded from the middle of this infinity.

A line of light penetrated this newly created void and reached its center. From this line the *Sefirot* were emanated. All creation, including the *Sefirot*, exist only within this void.

Rabbi Moses Cordovero, in *Pardes Rimonim*, offers various proofs to show that *Keter* and the Infinite Light (*Ein Sof*) are not the same.[25] It is clear that some earlier Kabbalists had considered them synonymous. Isaac Luria and all later Kabbalists are unanimous in their opinion that *Keter* is not the Infinite Light (*Ein Sof*).

Thus, according to Luria, the Emanator of *Keter* was the line of light that entered the circular void. This line is known as the Line of the Infinite Light (*Kav Ein Sof*). It is the basis for the concept of "The Primal Man" (*Adam Kadmon*).

This concept is fully developed only in the Lurian school.[26] Most earlier Kabbalists seem to consider the "undifferentiated One God," or the *Ein Sof*, the emanator.

Like Luria, Moses Cordovero believed in the existence of intermediate worlds below the *Ein Sof* (The Infinite) but above *Keter*. He explains the *Zohar*'s allusion to "the thirteen glimmerings (*Tzachtzachot*) on the Crown (*Keter*)" as a reference to the existence of these worlds. These, in a sense, are the immediate emanator of *Keter*. However, it has become customary to include them in the term *Ein Sof*, even though they are clearly distinct from it.

Sefirah 2—Chachmah (Wisdom)

After the *Sefirah* of *Keter* (Will) comes *Chachmah*, primal unformed wisdom. This is the second *Sefirah*. Wisdom is a difficult *Sefirah* to explain. It has been described as "matter without form." This concept comes from the ancient Greeks, whose term "*heyuli*" has been adapted by the Kabbalists to refer to primal, unformed thought, as well as to unformed matter. It is associated with the *Sefirah* of Wisdom, which represents the beginning of thought. The completion of the thought is not until later, in the *Sefirah* known as Understanding (*Binah*).

Chachmah is symbolized in the Tetragrammaton (see Appendix C) by its first letter, *Yud*. This letter looks like little more than a dot, unshaped, which is appropriate, since the *Yud* represents unshaped Wisdom. *Sefer Yetzirah* begins with a feature of this *Sefirah*—the thirty-two paths of Wisdom. This will be discussed later.

Sefirah 3—Binah (Understanding)

Binah, the last of the "*Sefirot* of the head," is where thought takes a concrete shape. After *Binah*, all that remains is for thought to be put into action, which is done by the lower *Sefirot*. *Binah* is known by many aliases and performs many interesting functions.

The *Sefirot* all have specific Hebrew vowels and letters associated with them (see Appendix C). The vowel of *Keter* is the *Kamatz* because *Kamatz* in Hebrew means "closed." It emphasizes that *Keter*, the highest of the *Sefirot*, is like a closed book about which very little is known. The vowel of *Chachmah* is the *Patach*, from the Hebrew root meaning "to start," because *Chachmah* is the start of thought. Finally, *Binah*'s vowel is *Tzeirei*, since this means "form." It is here that amorphous thought is shaped.

Binah is known as the upper Garden of Eden. The lower Garden of Eden is the last *Sefirah*, *Malchut*. The feminine aspect of both of these *Sefirot* is often stressed. They are often compared, and the *Zohar* spends much time showing their similarity. They are both represented in God's name (Tetragrammaton) by the same letter, *Hey*—*Binah* by the first *Hey* and *Malchut* by the second. They are sometimes called "the upper *Shechinah*" and "the lower *Shechinah*." Sometimes the name Leah is applied to *Binah* and the name Rachel to *Malchut*. It should be remembered that the biblical Leah had six sons and one daughter. There are six masculine *Sefirot* and one feminine *Sefirah* (*Malchut*) beneath *Binah*.

There is a tradition that there are fifty gates of understanding (*Binah*). Therefore, the number fifty is generally associated with this *Sefirah*. It is also called *Yovel* (Jubilee) (the biblical Jubilee has fifty years). It is associated with repentance (*Teshuvah*) because the Hebrew word for repentance means return, and the Jews returned to their ancestral plots in the Jubilee year.

Binah is considered the mother of the lower *Sefirot*. *Chachmah* is their father. A prominent feature of Lurian Kabbalah is the emphasis put on the pregnancy of *Binah* with the lower *Sefirot* and her nursing them. Finally, it is to the level of *Binah* that *Malchut* must ultimately ascend, when in the end of days *Malchut* becomes a "crown to the head of her husband" (who is composed of *Sefirot* four through nine, as explained below).

Sefirot 4–9—The Six Extremes

As a group, *Sefirot* four through nine are known as "The Six Extremes" (*Shesh HaKetzavot*). When described in this manner, they represent east, west, north, south, up, and down. These are the six sides of cubic space and define the concept of "place." It should be noted that it is common in religious circles to refer to God in Hebrew as "*HaMakom*"—The Place. The rabbis tell us, "The world is not *the place* of God, but rather God is *the place* of the world."[27] These six *Sefirot* are also known as the six days of creation. They are represented, therefore, in the Tetragrammaton by the letter *Vav*, whose numerical value is six. (See Appendix B for an explanation of the numerical values of the letters.)

Together these six *Sefirot* combine to make up what is called in Kabbalah a *Partzuf*. "*Partzuf*" literally means "a face." It refers to a complete, separate object, one with its own ten *Sefirot*. That is, the six original *Sefirot* together form another object, which has a complete set of *Sefirot*.

The *Partzuf* of these six *Sefirot* is of prime importance in the *Zohar* and is known by many names. The most common is *Zair Anpin* (the short face). (There is also a *Partzuf* known as the "long face," which contrasts to this. It is associated with the *Sefirah* of *Keter*.)

Zair Anpin is also known as "*Kudsha Brich Hu*"—the Holy One, blessed is He. He is the male suitor that appears in the biblical Song of Songs. He appears in the same capacity in Alkabitz's famous prayer *Lecha Dodi*. The female is the last *Sefirah*, *Malchut*, also known as the *Shechinah*. In addition, *Malchut* is known as the Sabbath. It should be noted that the six *Sefirot* comprising *Zair Anpin* represent the six workdays.

One cannot talk about *Zair Anpin* without also including *Malchut*. It is these two who are referenced in the prayer "*Leshem Yichud Kudsha Brich Hu U'Shechintei*" ("In order to unite the Holy One Blessed be He and his *Shechinah*"). It is their union that brings blessings on the lower worlds. They are *not* always united, in contradistinction to another pair of *Sefirot*—*Chachmah* and *Binah* (also known as *Abba* [father] and *Imma* [mother]). The *Zohar* tells us that "father and mother do not ever separate." *Zair Anpin* and *Malchut* do, however, and thus many of the *mitzvot* are meant as a help in getting them to

xxviii   Introduction

unite. *Zair Anpin* and *Malchut* are also referred to as the sun and moon. The sun sends light to the moon. The male gives the seed and the female receives.

This pair is at times referred to by the *Zohar* as the Son and Daughter (*Brah U'Barta*). This notion was not intentionally similar to Christian thought, although Christian theologians found it attractive. In the sixteenth century, when the Christians were publicly burning the Talmud, they were actually printing the *Zohar*. Among the early fathers of the reformation, there were some who considered themselves Kabbalists and actually produced works of "Christian Kabbalah."[28]

Sefirah 4—Chesed (Kindness)

This is the first of the *Sefirot* of the Six Extremes. It corresponds to Sunday in the time model. It is the right arm in the body model. It refers to the attribute of Abraham among the Ancestors.

The *Partzuf* of *Zair Anpin* is also known as "The World." *Chesed* is the beginning of this world, just as Sunday is the beginning of creation, as the Scripture says, "*Olam Chesed Yibaneh*" (Psalms 89:3)— the world will be built from kindness (*Chesed*). *Chesed* is also known as "Water"; on the first day the land was still covered with water.

Sefirah 5—Gevurah (Courage)

This *Sefirah* is the left arm of the "heavenly man" and represents strict law. It is the attribute of Isaac. It is called *Aish*—fire. It is in a sense the antithesis of *Chesed* (Kindness). They are opposed in the same sense that fire and water, kindness and strictness are opposed. They are extremes that must be mixed or "sweetened" (*Hamtakat HaDinim*).

Meir Gabbai, in his classic *Avodat HaKodesh*, states that when one prays, one should deliberately concentrate on this "sweetening" process. When one says the first blessing in the *Amidah*, which represents *Chesed* (Kindness) (Abraham's attribute), he should think of Isaac, too (whose attribute was Courage). In the second blessing, which represents *Gevurah* (Courage), one should likewise try to include *Chesed*.

Sefirah 6—Tiferet (Glory)

This *Sefirah* is midway between *Chesed* and *Gevurah*, and a little lower. The position has symbolic significance (see Appendix A).

In Kabbalah, the words "to the right" mean "toward kindness." Likewise "to the left" means "toward strictness." Although Kabbalah uses physical terms, what is meant is in no way physical. The Kabbalists continually warn us not to err and think that above, in the world of the *Sefirot*, there is actually a right and left, an up and a down.

It must be pointed out that the term *up* refers to increases in kindness, whereas *down* refers to more strictness (similar to right and left). These directions also have sexual significance. Kindness is associated with masculinity and strictness with femininity. The male gives the seed, and giving is considered kindness toward the woman, who is the recipient. Also, Leah (*Binah*) had six sons and a daughter, which correspond to *Zair Anpin* and his mate, *Malchut*. Leah's daughter's name was *Dinah*. In Hebrew, the word for "strict law" is Din, and so Kabbalah adopted the usage of femininity as representing strictness.

The *Sefirah* of *Tiferet* resolves the antitheses of *Chesed* and *Gevurah*. The mix of these two extremes results in an intermediate quality, *Rachamim* (Mercy). At first, one might object that *Rachamim*'s meaning is almost the same as *Chesed* (Kindness). However, the root of *Rachamim* is *Rechem*, womb. This is to stress its feminine aspect. While *Chesed* is masculine, *Rachamim* represents a feminine modification of this *Chesed*. Love involves a desire both to give and take, and thus love is the mixing of *Chesed* and *Din*, masculine and feminine.

It should be noted that the relationship of *Chesed*, *Gevurah*, and *Tiferet* is reminiscent of a basic concept of the German philosopher George Hegel. Hegel believed that history advances because of the opposition of antithetical ideas and their ultimate resolution or synthesis.[29] The resulting synthesis, he believed, is of a higher nature than the original opposing ideas. Thus history advances.

In Kabbalah, there is the basic antithesis of Kindness and Strictness. It is resolved by the next *Sefirah*, representing *Rachamim* (Mercy). However, the *Sefirah* of resolution is beneath the opposed pair (see Appendix A). In this model, history does not advance. The Talmud's theory of *Yiredat HaDorot*—the decline of the generations—is fully incorporated into Kabbalah. Each generation is worse than its predecessor. Although the last generation may have resolved some of the antithetical conflicts of previous generations, these resolutions are not without a price. The original energy and intensity of the opposing ideas may be lost in the synthesis. There is a loss of energy, as when opposing electric charges cancel each other out.

That is not to say that the original antithesis ceases to exist after its resolution. Both Hegel and Kabbalah agree that "the blossom does not refute the bud"[30]; and the original opposition exists even afterward. It is only within the resultant synthesis itself that something is lost.

The *Sefirah* of *Tiferet* is symbolized by Jacob. It is known as the tree of life and also as the sun. It is the main *Sefirah* of the Six Extremes and often symbolizes all six. It has the number twelve associated with it, since Jacob had twelve sons. There are twelve different ways in which the letters of God's name (Tetragrammaton) can be ordered. This name of God (Tetragrammaton), is thus closely associated with the *Sefirah* of *Tiferet*.

Sefirah 7—Netzach (Eternity)

This *Sefirah* is to the right, below *Tiferet*. It is the attribute of Moses. It represents Wednesday. Together with *Hod* and *Yisod*, it forms a triple (*Segol*) that closely parallels the triple of *Chesed*, *Gevurah*, and *Tiferet*.

Sefirah 8—Hod (Beauty)

This is the attribute of Aaron. It is to the left (*Din*). Together, *Netzach* and *Hod* are known as *Tray Palgay Gufa*—the two sides of the body. One of God's names applies to them both—*Tzvaot*. Sometimes *Elohim Tzvaot* is used to signify *Hod* and Tetragrammaton *Tzvaot* to specify *Netzach*.

Sefirah 9—Yisod (Foundation)

Yisod is a key *Sefirah*, as it is the *Sefirah* through which *Zair Anpin* and *Malchut* mate. It is, therefore, symbolized as the reproductive organ. It resolves the opposition of *Netzach* and *Hod*. It symbolizes life and is called *Chaim*. It is also called *Tzadik*—righteous—for the verse states, "*Tzadik yisod olam*" (Proverbs 10:25)—"The righteous (*tzadik*) are the Foundation (*Yisod*) of the world." Souls are sent through this *Sefirah* to the lower worlds.

Sefirah 10—Malchut (Kingdom)

Malchut is a key *Sefirah*. It represents the *Shechinah* (God's presence). It is feminine in that it is the last *Sefirah* and receives the light of the others, but since it is the last *Sefirah*, it does not give to the others. This is like a woman, who receives man's seed but does not give. For the same reason it is called the moon, since the moon has no light of its own but merely receives that of the sun.

It is known also as the Bride, as Sabbath, as the lower *Gan Eden*, and as the Tree of Knowledge. When referring to it in its *Partzuf* form (containing a full set of *Sefirot* within), it is usually called "the female of *Zair Anpin*."

There is a famous *Midrash* that states that Adam and Eve were created attached. God separated them (*Nesirah*) so they could reproduce. This was taken by Kabbalists to refer to *Zair Anpin* and *Malchut*. The object was to enable them to mate and thus supply abundance to the worlds beneath.

There is another *Midrash* that states that the sun and the moon were created equal, but the moon complained that two rulers could not rule with the same one crown, so the moon was ordered to become dimmer. In the future, however, there would be a time when the light of the moon would grow to that of the sun.[31] This *Midrash* is heavily used in Kabbalah and is said to refer to *Zair Anpin* and *Malchut*.

While both Cordoverian and Lurian Kabbalah use both models (Adam and Eve as *Zair Anpin* and *Malchut*; the sun and the moon as *Zair Anpin* and *Malchut*), the former is stressed by Lurian and the latter by Cordoverian. In fact, the eventual elevation of *Malchut* is a central theme in Cordoverian Kabbalah, and perhaps can even be said to constitute the goal of creation. It represents the end of days, the messianic era. The famous Cordoverian Kabbalist, Shabbetai Horowitz, in his book *Shefa Tal* (Abundance of Dew), greatly stresses this theme.[32] In Lurian Kabbalah, on the other hand, the emphasis is more on the reelevation of 288 fallen sparks. These sparks were originally part of higher spheres that "broke" because they were unable to hold the intense light of the Infinite. In their fallen state, they give life to the shells (Evil). Reelevating them results in the destruction of evil.

There is one more extremely important name for *Malchut*. That is *Knesset Yisroel*—the collection of Israel. It represents all of Israel. The well-known statement of the *Zohar*, "Israel and God are one," applies here. Thus, the elevation of *Malchut* is the elevation of Israel and the hope of the messianic period.

Sefirah 11—Daat (Knowledge)

There are only ten *Sefirot*. Why then is an eleventh mentioned here? It seems that another *Sefirah* often appears in kabbalistic writing. This

Sefirah is alluded to even in *Sefer Yetzirah*. The question of how there can be an eleventh is dealt with by both Cordovero and Luria. While their approaches differ somewhat, they do agree that there are, in fact, only ten *Sefirot*. *Sefer Yetzirah* says this clearly in the first chapter, fourth *Mishnah*: "The ten *Sefirot* of naught, they are ten and not nine, ten and not eleven."

The place of *Daat*, when it is present, is between *Chachmah* and *Binah*. *Daat* is similar to *Keter*, which is also between *Chachmah* and *Binah*. The difference is that *Keter* is above them while *Daat* is beneath them (see Appendix A). In a sense, *Daat* is not a separate *Sefirah*, but rather the presence of *Keter* below. Cordovero changes this formula slightly. "*Daat*," he says, "is the presence of *Tiferet* above."

Isaac Luria offers another explanation. He states that each *Sefirah* consists of a inner and an outer part. The inner ten *Sefirot* include *Keter* but not *Daat*, while the outer *Sefirot* begin with *Chachmah*, not *Keter*, and include *Daat*.

Complications of this sort are the trademark of Lurian Kabbalah, and they are meant to serve a purpose. In order to better understand why all this complexity is needed, the function of *Daat* must be examined.

Daat comes into play after the thought has already been formed in *Binah*. It represents putting the thought into action. It links the thought process with the body that acts.

The *Sefirot* of the head (*Sefirot* 1–3) are all above time. The first *Sefirah* within time is *Chesed*, which represents the first weekday. *Daat* is intermediary, the link between thought and action.

It is the same *Sefirah* as *Keter* in at least two ways. *Keter* represents Will. *Daat* adds the *will* to perform an action to the thought that was completed in *Binah*. Thus, like *Keter*, it is a form of Will. In addition, it is a mediator between *Chachmah* and *Binah*. *Keter*, too, is between *Chachmah* and *Binah*.

Daat has other special functions as well. It is a collecting place for what are known as "the five kindnesses" (*Chasadim*) and "the five courages" (*Gevurot*). These are elements used in the creation of the lower world—that of *Zair Anpin*.

One last thought about *Daat*. The first three *Sefirot* form a triangle. The apex points up when *Keter* is included and points down when *Daat* replaces *Keter*. This is because *Keter* must be alone on top of the triangle, for it is the closest to the source. As God is an undifferentiated one, there can only be a single point of liaison between Him and the creation. *Keter* represents the resolution of the *Chachmah–Binah* antithesis in advance of their creation. The Talmud says, "God prepares the remedy before creating the sickness." *Keter*, God's Will, is the ultimate resolution of all antitheses.

After the opposing attributes (*Chachmah–Binah*) have come into being, however, they must once again be resolved. This represents "resolution in action," while the earlier resolution through *Keter* was a "resolution in potential." This second resolution is represented by the *Sefirah* of *Daat*, which is lower than the attributes being resolved. It connects the upper and lower worlds, the world that is above time to the one that defines time (time is defined by the *Sefirot* of *Zair Anpin*, which are also known as *Sidrei Zemanim*, the orders of time).

STRUCTURE OF *SEFER YETZIRAH*

Sefer Yetzirah contains six chapters. Each chapter is subdivided into what are called *Mishnayot*. They are not *Mishnayot* in the sense of talmudic *Mishnayot*, which were written in the period of 100 B.C.E.–200 C.E. and deal with religious law. Whether *Sefer Yetzirah*'s *Mishnayot* are from the period of the *Mishnah* at all is a matter of debate. According to some, Rabbi Akiva authored *Sefer Yetzirah*, and he did, in fact, live in the time of the *Mishnah*. However, even bonafide mishnaic material that Rabbi Yehuda HaNasi chose to omit from the official codification of the "Six Orders of *Mishnah*" are not properly called *Mishnayot* but rather *Beraitot*. *Beraita* means "outside." It usually refers only to material that is of the same basic origin as the *Mishnah*, but for some reason was left outside. It is questionable whether the term *Beraita* is appropriate for *Sefer Yetzirah*.

The first chapter of *Sefer Yetzirah* deals with the *Sefirot*. Most of the remainder of the book is about the letters of the Hebrew alphabet. The last chapter ties the previous material together and ascribes the authorship.

The book is concerned with showing how actions of God with the letters (i.e., the powers of creation) have manifestations in multiple aspects of creation. Many manifestations are traced on three levels—

the physical world, time, and the soul. Thus, for example, there is a common source for the twelve constellations in the physical universe, the twelve months in time, and the twelve functions of the soul (such as thought, anger, and so on). Often other levels are added as well, such as the twelve combinations of the four letters in God's name, the twelve sons of Jacob, and so on.

Sefer Yetzirah is written in a mystical style. It does not attempt to make comprehension particularly easy. It seems to want the reader to wonder. It stimulates thought, wonder, and even awe. One feels that there is much beyond a simple understanding, much that the author is purposely hiding. It stimulates the desire to search and go beyond the given—to address the eternal secrets.

The language is not very difficult. While most of it is in simple Hebrew, it does not sound particularly biblical. Some of the terms and even some of the concepts seem to be from a later period. For instance, it speaks about *Tlee*. This is a term used in medieval astrology to refer to a great snake that turns the circle of the constellations. Some think it is intended to denote the constellation Draco. I don't believe the term appears anywhere in talmudic literature, and it is certainly not biblical.

CONCLUSION

A complete understanding of *Sefer Yetzirah* might well be impossible, because the book was intended to reveal and yet to hide. As the book itself warns, "Close your mouth from talking and your heart from thinking, and if your heart runs, return to the place (from where you started), as it says (in Ezekiel), 'The Angels (*Chayot*) run and return,' and on this matter (not to go beyond one's limits) a convenant was executed (i.e., the *brit*, the covenant of Abraham)."[33] It further states, "And God's word in them (the angels) runs and returns."[34] That is, even the angels glimpse but a little of God's word but cannot stay with that insight—they must return to their prior state.

1

Paths of Wisdom
and Sefirot

PATHS OF WISDOM
AND HEAVENLY BOOKS

Sefer Yetzirah, Chapter 1, Mishnah 1

מִשְׁנָה א בשלשים ושתים נתיבות פליאות
חכמה חקק יה יהוה צבאות
אלהי ישראל אלהים חיים ומלך עולם אל שדי
רחום וחנון רם ונשא שוכן עד מרום וקדוש
שמו וברא את עולמו בשלשה ספרים בספר
וספר וספור:

**With thirty-two wondrous paths of wisdom, He
engraved "*Yah*," "*YaHoVaH*," "Hosts," "God
of Israel," "Living God and King of the World,"
"*El Shaddai*," "Merciful and Pitying," "High
and Elevated," "He Who Dwells Eternally,"
"Aloof and Holy is His Name," and created his
world with three books, with number and book
and story.**

The essence of the mystical experience is awe and wonder. The
obscure nature of Kabbalah is essential, rather than coincidental, to its
existence. The difficulty in comprehending Kabbalah, the need to
stretch the imagination as well as the intellect, are necessary elements
in the generation of the mystic emotions—the marvel, longing, and

3

fear that are at the heart of the mystic experience. Yet obscurity in itself explains nothing. It is only on the border—where that which is known abuts the infinite unknown—that mysticism is born.

Kabbalists strive for knowledge of God while knowing full well that they are doomed to ultimate failure. They content themselves, however, with trying to catch a fleeting glimpse of the infinite, a reflection or spark of God's unfathomable grandeur. Just as the finite cannot encompass the infinite, man cannot understand God. Even Moses was rebuffed when he asked to be shown God's essence: "My back you will see, but my face will not be seen" (Exodus 33:18). Maimonides, in his *Guide to the Perplexed*, explains this verse as meaning that man can never know God as He really is, but can only comprehend the manifestations of His being.[1]

In the introduction of the *Zohar*, a similar idea as to the limitation of human understanding is described with the following beautiful mystic imagery:

> The edge of heaven is called "who." There is another lower place called "what." What is the difference between these two? Only that the first one, the one called "who," we can ask about. However, once a person asks and investigates and looks to understand from level to level till the ultimate level, once one reaches there—then "what?"—what do you now know, for what did you look, what did you investigate, for all is sealed and unknown as before.

The first *Mishnah* of *Sefer Yetzirah* reflects the sublime interaction between the knowable and the infinite. We are not told the source of the thirty-two paths of wisdom or their exact nature. We are told merely that they were used by God to create the world.

The commentaries state that the reason *Sefer Yetzirah* calls the paths of wisdom "wondrous" is to emphasis their unknowable nature. Wondrous is understood as a reference to the highest *Sefirah*, *Keter*, a *Sefirah* that is said to be totally above any human understanding. *Keter* represents God's will, which humans cannot fathom. By stating that the paths of wisdom are "wondrous," *Sefer Yetzirah* implies that they originated in God's unknowable Will (*Keter*) and, therefore, they cannot be fully understood. It is for this reason that they are called the paths of "wisdom" rather than "will." It is only at the level beneath *Keter*, that of the second *Sefirah*, *Chachmah* (Wisdom)—that they can be discerned at all—discerned but not understood.

It is important to understand the difference between what is meant by God's will and His wisdom. Basically, wisdom is a tool of will. If you want something, wisdom helps you obtain it. Wisdom is not, however, the determinant of the original raw desire.

It may not be possible to address questions as to why something is "willed." Who can say why they want to be happy or why they want to avoid pain? It is a basic feeling that we all share, and no reason is possible or necessary. It is *above* logic. That is what Kabbalists mean when they say that the *Sefirah* of *Keter* (Will) is above *Chachmah* (Wisdom).

We, of course, do not have any grasp of God's will. However, it is so intrinsic to God's essential being that it is believed to have existed before any creation took place. After all, God had to will the Creation. This is what is meant by the statement in *Pirke DeRabbi Eliezer,* "Before God created the world, only He and his *Name* existed." "Name" (*Shemo*) has the same numerical value as Will (see Appendix B for an explanation of the numerical values of letters). Will, in turn, is understood by the Kabbalists as a reference to its representative *Sefirah, Keter.*

It is at the level of *Chachmah* (Wisdom) that laws of creation first appear. It is here where the paths take on substance—substance, but not definite form (which does not occur until the third *Sefirah, Binah*).

The paths of wisdom are the ramifications of the existence of Wisdom, the results of God's emanation of the *Sefirah* of Wisdom. They are laws with which the world was created and by which it runs. They are the powers represented by the letters and vowels of the Hebrew alphabet.

These paths are said to run through the Torah. They are the thread with which its fabric is woven. They are hinted at by the first and last letters in the Torah, *Bet* and *Lamed,* whose numerical values equal thirty-two.

The *Sefirah* of *Chachmah* (Wisdom) is known by Kabbalists by the name *yesh* (being). The first *Sefirah, Keter,* is called *ayin* (nonbeing). God created the world "*Yesh MeiAyin*"—being from nonbeing. Therefore, creation is said to have begun with the *Sefirah* of *Chachmah* (Wisdom), the beginning of *being.* Since the purpose of the thirty-two paths is their manifestations below, their main existence is from the *Sefirah* of *Chachmah* (Wisdom, Being) rather than from *Keter,* which is their root.

It must be pointed out that the term *nonbeing* used in reference to *Keter* is not true nonbeing. It is called nonbeing because of *Keter*'s incomprehensible nature, not because of its lack of reality. On the contrary, it is closer to the Infinite than *Chachmah* (Wisdom) and is thus greater. The Raivad[2] puts it this way: "*Keter* is known as *ayin* (nonbeing) since it is different from the Infinite only in that it is a result and the Infinite is its cause."[3] Since it is so similar to its cause, it is sometimes thought to lack separate existence.

The Talmud tells us that the search for leavened bread before Passover must be done at night by candlelight.[4] The reason why it cannot be done during the daytime is "*Shraga beteihara mai ahanei*"— What good is a candle at noon?" That is to say, the light of the candle has no effect due to the much greater light of the sun. For the same reason *Keter* is called *ayin* (nonbeing), for it is the closest *Sefirah* to the Infinite, and although its light is the greatest of all the *Sefirot*, it is as naught compared to the boundless light of the Infinite.

The idea that creation begins with *Chachmah* (Wisdom), rather than *Keter*, is alluded to in another classical Kabbalist text, *Sefer HaBahir*.[5] It states: "The Torah said, 'Two thousand years I was a plaything in God's lap, as it is written, *I was with Him as a craftsman, I was his delight for a day, a day, frolicking before him at every time*' (Proverbs 8:30)."

The six *Sefirot* of *Zair Anpin* represent the six days of creation. The two *Sefirot* above them are *Chachmah* and *Binah*, alluded to above by the phrase "two thousand years." The Torah was a plaything only 2,000 years before the era of creation. The third thousand, *Keter*, is excluded, since the creation does not begin until the emanation of *Chachmah* (Wisdom).

The Torah begins with the verse "In the *beginning* . . . " (Genesis 1:1). Another biblical verse states, "The *beginning* of *wisdom* (is to) purchase wisdom" (Proverbs 4:7). Kabbalists therefore associate the word "beginning" (*reishit*) with the *Sefirah* of Wisdom. The first sentence of Genesis is thus reinterpreted by Kabbalists to state, "With the *Sefirah* of Wisdom, God created the heavens and the earth." Wisdom was the beginning of creation.

Thus, it appears that the thirty-two paths are called "Paths of Wisdom" because the *Sefirah* of Wisdom is the source of the Laws of Creation. But why are they thirty-two? Many reasons have been given.

The most fundamental reason is implied in the second *Mishnah* of *Sefer Yetzirah*. It reads, "The ten *Sefirot* of nothing and the twenty-two letters of foundation, three mothers, seven doubles, and twelve singles." Most commentaries conclude from this that the thirty-two paths are composed of the ten *Sefirot* and twenty-two letters. Many Kabbalists, including Rabbi Eliyahu (the Gaon of Vilna), have noted that in Hebrew there are ten vowels (*Nekudot*) in addition to the twenty-two letters, and each vowel is associated with a *Sefirah*.[6] Therefore, the paths represent the letters and vowels of the Hebrew alphabet, that is, the powers associated with each.

The Raivad, in the introduction to his commentary on *Sefer Yetzirah*, states that there is a tradition that supplies the names and descriptions of each path. He then proceeds to list them. (The list is given in Appendix E.)

It is well known in Kabbalah that God's name, *Elohim*, appears thirty-two times during the story of creation, from the beginning of Genesis through the sixth day. These represent the powers of the thirty-two paths in creation.

The *Idra Rabba*, one of the subdivisions of the *Zohar*, states, "Wisdom, the beginning of all—from it stretch thirty-two paths and the Torah is filled with them, in twenty-two letters and ten statements."[7] The letters are the Hebrew alphabet; the ten statements are the ten times God said "Let there be" during the creation.[8] These ten statements are associated by Kabbalists with the ten *Sefirot*.

It has been pointed out that the numerical value of the Hebrew word for Heart, "*Lev*," is 32. These paths are thus considered the heart of creation.

Aside from the questions of the source and composition of these paths, the Kabbalists have discussed their ramifications in the world. They have pointed out, for instance, that human beings have thirty-two teeth. This is said to be a result of the paths. They also have thirty-two spinal nerves.

The Vilna Gaon explains this in an unusually scientific manner for an eighteenth-century Kabbalist:

> The thirty-two paths are such that the first path is from the gap between the neck and the first vertebrae, and the thirty-one others are eighteen paths in the eighteen gaps between the nineteen vertebrae, and five paths at the end of the nineteenth vertebrae exit together but then split into five. Afterward, another two paths leave, and in the buttocks another three, from the two sides, and then another three.[9]

Another manifestation is in geometry. It is not accidental, according to the Gaon, that a diameter of ten yields a circumference of thirty-two. It is the manifestation of the relationship of the ten *Sefirot* and the thirty-two paths. The Gaon goes on to state that the ten *Sefirot* are divided into three upper *Sefirot* and seven lower *Sefirot*. The circumference of a circle with a diameter of 3 is 10 and with a diameter of 7 is 22—hence the *Sefirot* and the letters. Consequently, geometry and language are seen as a result of the spiritual structure of the universe.

Kabbalah is an associative process. It ties together many diverse concepts. The association of ideas, enhanced by active imagination and intellect, are vital tools for the Kabbalist. Perhaps the most important emotion this process produces is the feeling of unity. As a result, the world seems truly one, and everything appears somehow related to everything else. All is the consequence of the one law and has but one source.

The *Mishnah* speaks of paths. The Hebrew word for path, *netiv*, has special significance. The numerical value is 462 (see Appendix B). In the second chapter of *Sefer Yetzirah*, combinations of the letters of the alphabet are discussed. Each of the twenty-two Hebrew letters is combined with each of the others, which results in 22 x 21 combinations, equaling 462. For instance, the first letter, *Aleph*, is combined first with *Bet* to form *Aleph Bet*, then with *Gimel* to form *Aleph Gimel*, and so on. This results in twenty-one pairs of two letters. This is then done for *Bet*, then *Gimel*, and so forth. The result is 462, the numerical value of *netiv*—path.

The Bible states, "With the word of the Lord the heavens were created" (Psalms 33:6). This is taken literally. By combining the powers represented by the Hebrew letters, the creation took place. These combinations are implied in the Hebrew term for the path—*netiv*.

The *Mishnah* states that God engraved the paths. The term *engraved* is also used by *Sefer Yetzirah* in connection with the creation of the letters. In chapter two, *Sefer Yetzirah* describes the alphabet as being engraved in the "Sphere of the Letters." The *Mishnah* here uses the term *engraved* to stress identification of the paths with the letters. Letters are given permanence by being engraved. Similarly, the permanence of the creation is stressed by describing the paths as engraved. The laws of the universe, so to speak, are chiseled in stone.

The next part of the *Mishnah* is particularly perplexing. It mentions many different names for God. It is unclear why all these names are mentioned.

Rabbi Eliezer of Garmisha states in his commentary that there are ten names mentioned in the *Mishnah* and that they represent the ten statements of God in the biblical story of creation (*Pirke Avot* 5:1). (From the text of *Sefer Yetzirah*, Chapter 1, *Mishnah* 1, it is not clear that there are exactly ten names. However, I have put quotation marks around what are considered to constitute the ten.)

The ten statements of creation are identified by Kabbalists with the ten *Sefirot*. This *Mishnah* is the first source to tie names of God to *Sefirot*. However, even in nonkabbalistic Jewish literature, the different names of God are said to reflect His different aspects. In Kabbalah, the study of God's names has taken on giant proportions. The *Zohar* says that all of the Torah is a name of God. In addition to studying the biblical names of God, Kabbalists have produced various other combinations, permutations, and transformations of divine names.

In later kabbalistic literature, specific names of God are associated with each *Sefirah*. There are basically three levels of names. The highest group contains the names of "essence" (*Shemot HaAtzmut*). They refer to what God *is*. All the other names refer only to what He *does*. The holiest name in this group is the Tetragrammaton—*Yud Hey Vav Hey*. According to Abraham Ibn Ezra, there are two other names in this group—*Yah* and *EhHehYeh*.[10] All three are composed of letters from the Hebrew root "to be." They refer to God's existence, past, present, and future. After all, the only knowledge we have of God's essence is that it exists forever.

The lower levels are the names that apply to God's actions. These fall into two categories, the formal names that may not be erased[11] and descriptive names. Examples of the formal names applying to God's actions are *Adonai* and *Shaddai*. The first literally means that God is the *Adon*—the master. *Shaddai* implies that He places limits on the world, "*SheAmar LeOlamo Dai.*"[12] The nonformal descriptive names are terms like *merciful, slow to anger,* and *truthful.*

This *Mishnah* uses all three levels of names. The order of the names is not in accordance with the usual symbolism. For instance, the Tetragrammaton is generally associated in Kabbalah with the sixth *Sefirah, Tiferet.* Here, however, it is the second name mentioned. Differing explanations have been offered by various commentaries.

Discussions of God's names ultimately translate into discussions of

His essence and His attributes. One is reminded of the opposing theories of Maimonides and Yosef Albo on this subject.

Maimonides is known as "*Sholel HaTaarim*"—"the negator of descriptive names." According to him, what is meant by "God is merciful" is that He is not not merciful. Positive terms are used for convenience, but we really can only know what God is not, not what He is. More than ten chapters in Maimonides' *Guide to the Perplexed* are spent on this subject.[13]

On the other hand, Yosef Albo, in his *Sefer HaIkarim*, emphasizes that rather than none of the descriptive terms applying to God, the positive terms may indeed apply. These terms are truly part of Him, but in the sense of descriptions of His essence and *not* additions to it. He is good, merciful, slow to anger, and so on. It has been said that Spinoza was greatly influenced by Albo's work and that many of his pantheistic ideas were modifications of Albo's theory.

The conclusion of the *Mishnah* is particularly interesting. It states that God "created the world with three books, with number and book and story." This is one of the most often quoted parts of *Sefer Yetzirah*. It is discussed by many famous early rabbis, including those known more as rationalists than Kabbalists, such as Yehuda Halevi and Avraham Ibn Ezra. What are the books to which this phrase alludes?

First, it must be noted that my translation of this phrase reflects a prejudice. I translated the *Mishnah*'s description of the first book as "number" (*Sefor*). The Hebrew letters can also be read as "*Sefer*"—book. If that were correct, the *Mishnah* would read, "He created the world with book and book and story." The commentaries use both readings, and perhaps the ambiguity is not accidental.

Yehuda Halevi, in the *Kuzari*, says the following:

Sefor means the calculation and weighing of the created bodies. The calculation which is required for the harmonious and advantageous arrangement of a body is based on a numerical figure. Expansion, measure, weight, relation of movements and musical harmony, all these are based on the number expressed by the word "*Sefor*." No building emerges from the architect unless its image first existed in the soul. *Sippur* (Story) signifies the language, the divine language, the voice and words of the living God. This produced the existence of the form which this language assumed in the words "Let there be light," "Let there be a firmament." The words were hardly spoken when the thing came into existence. This is also *sefer* (book), by which writing is meant. The writing of God means His creatures, the speech of God is His writing, the will of God is His speech. In the nature of God, therefore, number, story and book are a unity, while they are three in human reckoning.

Supporting this translation of the *Mishnah* is the fact that the *Sefer Yetzirah* deals with exactly these elements—the first chapter with numbers (*Sefirot*) and most of the rest with letters and words.

The alternative translation of the *Mishnah* as "book and book and story" is also very common. One of the interpretations offered by the Vilna Gaon is as follows: The first two books are the two tablets of stone that contained the ten commandments. The third, the story, is the oral recitation of these ten commandments by God at Sinai. On another level, however, the Vilna Gaon states that they are the three *Sefirot* of *Chachmah*, *Binah*, and *Daat*. The Ramban states a similar idea in different words. He says that the three books are the first three letters of the Tetragrammaton. These three letters, in turn, represent *Sefirot* (see Appendix D).

Mystic phrases generally have multiple meanings. The same commentators do not refrain from offering several alternative explanations. They consider all the explanations valid and all of them related.

The first *Mishnah* of *Sefer Yetzirah* tells of the thirty-two paths. The rest of the book is dedicated to supplying the details of these paths, that is to say, the details of the ten *Sefirot* and twenty-two letters.

THE *SEFIROT* AND THE LETTERS
OF CREATION

Sefer Yetzirah, Chapter 1, Mishnah 2

מ"ב עשר ספירות בלי מה ועשרים ושתים
אותיות יסוד שלש אמות ושבע כפולות
ושתים עשרה פשוטות:

Ten *Sefirot* of nothing and twenty-two letters of foundation, three mothers and seven doubles and twelve singles.

This *Mishnah* is the earliest source where the term "*Sefirot*" is used. There have been various opinions as to the origin of this term. Among the theories that have been offered are the following:

1. *Sefirah* comes from the same root as "*Sefor*," number. It signifies that the *Sefirot* are the source of the mathematical relationships that we find in the world.

   Among the early commentators who give this definition was the Ramban,[14] who wrote, "They are called *Sefirot* because they are the power of all that is enclosed in the enclosure of ten."[15] This implies that all that was created and is subject to the rules of mathematics is empowered by these *Sefirot*. A similar definition was also used by Yehuda HaLevi, Baal HaMaarechet, and others.

2. *Sefirah* is derived from the Hebrew word *Sapir*, meaning sapphire or gem. The Torah says in Exodus 23:10, "And they saw the God of Israel, and under his legs was like the whiteness of '*Sapir*,' and like the aspect of heaven in purity." Thus, this definition stresses the purity and brilliance of the *Sefirot*.

   Rabbi Moses Botarel quotes an earlier Kabbalist, Rabbi Yitchak bar Shmuel, as follows: "It was coined from the concept of sapphire and diamond, like (in the verses) 'the whiteness of *Sapir*' (Exodus 23:10) and 'their aspect was like *Sapir*' (Lamentations 4:7)." Moshe bar Yaakov HaGoleh brings a similar quotation.

3. The Book of Psalms states, "The heavens tell the honor of the Lord, and the deeds of His hands are related by the firmament" (Psalms 19:1). The Hebrew word for "tell" is *Mesaprim*, whose root contains the same letters (*Samech, Peh, Resh*) as the root of *Sefirah*. Thus, some say they are called *Sefirot*, because, in a sense, they "tell the honor of the Lord."

   This opinion is brought by the *Zohar* itself. It says, "They are called '*Sefirim*' because they tell the honor of the Lord. Since they tell the honor of the Lord they are called the ten *Sefirot* of nothing. The ten letters of God's name, *Yud, Vav, Dalet, Hey, Aleph, Vav, Aleph, Vav, Hey*, and *Aleph* descend and shine in them, since they are called by His name."[16]

4. Some modern scholars have suggested that the word has the same origin as the English word "sphere." It has been said that

the concept was perhaps originally Greek. I have known of no Kabbalist that concurred with this opinion.

The *Mishnah* calls the *Sefirot*, "*Sefirot* of nothing." This phrase presents difficulties regarding translation and explanation. The Hebrew for "nothing" is "*Bli Mah*." If taken as two separate words, "*Bli*" means "without" and "*Mah*" means "anything," that is, without anything, or "of nothing." If taken as one word, however, "*Blimah*" means shutting, as in shutting one's mouth and not talking.

Both of these opinions are common in the commentaries. For instance, the Lurian Kabbalist Yitzchak Isaac, author of books *Bair Yitzchak* and *Pree Yitzchak*, states:

> The definition of the word (*Blimah*) comes from the verse "his mouth to close" (Psalms 12:9). It is the language of closing the mouth and not speaking about the *Sefirot*, since they are covered and hidden. It is proper for us to close our mouth as to their essence, because the *Sefirot* are without an understood essence. In addition, the term "*Blimah*" also is from the verse, "He hangs the earth on nothing (*BliMah*)" (Job 26:7), on *Tohu*, that which bewilders, that which cannot be understood.[17]

In actuality, both of these definitions are quite similar. They stress the difficulty in understanding the *Sefirot*. The Ramban puts it this way: "Since they (the *Sefirot*) are the door to the Infinite (*Ein Sof*), and the Lord cannot be understood and does not have content (that can be understood), and He is '*Blimah*,' they are also called '*Blimah*.'"[18]

It will be remembered that the first *Sefirah*, the one closest to the Infinite, *Keter*, is sometimes called "*Ayin*," nothing, to emphasize its unfathomable nature. The term *Blimah* is used here in a similar manner, but refers to all the *Sefirot*. Kabbalistic terms are relative. When the object is to express that *Keter* is much higher than *Chachmah* (Wisdom), Kabbalists call *Keter* "*Ayin*" (Nothing) and Wisdom "*Yesh*" (Being). When describing the difficulty in understanding the true essence of any of the *Sefirot*, all the *Sefirot* are called "*Sefirot* of nothing."

At this point the *Mishnah* turns its attention to the letters. It has been said that the letters compose the body of the *Sefirot*, the vessels. Their soul is the inner light that flows through them. This light is sometimes symbolized by the vowel points (*nikudot*). Just as the vowels give life to the letters and allow them to be pronounced, so does the inner light of the *Sefirot* constitute their soul, while the letters form their outer body.

There is some question as to whether Kabbalists are permitted to discuss this inner light at all. After all, this is the divine light, the essence of God.

Moses Cordovera says in *Pardes Rimonim* that all the names and attributes of the *Sefirot* are only from the perspective of the created. The names do not apply to the essence of God in relation to itself. Only in relationship to the lower worlds, which is through the vessels, do any of God's names or descriptions apply.

This implies that any kabbalistic reference to a *Sefirah*'s inner light should be understood as applying to their reflection below. In relationship to God Himself, there is no syllable that applies, not the vowels, not the letters—not even the Tetragrammaton, the holiest of God's names.

To better understand this, let us consider the functions of "names" in general. They are a handle, a means of referring to something. They are a description. They point to objects. Something that we have no grasp of at all cannot be described. Something that is not limited in time and space cannot be pointed at.

It is a kabbalistic principle that all of God's names are descriptive; they say something about Him. What they say is from the human perspective, how His being appears to us. However, there is an infinite aspect of God that cannot be understood at all. There is the aspect of God unto Himself, as He really is. This aspect is never addressed in Kabbalah, and none of God's names applies to it.

The *Mishnah* states that there are twenty-two letters of *foundation*. As explained above, they are the *foundation* of the body of the *Sefirot*. In the words of the Vilna Gaon, they are called *letters of foundation* "because the body was created from many letters and these are the base."[19] Details as to what developed from this base are given in Chapter 2, where the "231 Gates" are discussed.

Other reasons have been offered as to why the twenty-two letters are called "letters of foundation." In Hebrew, there are twenty-two basic letters. However, five of them have a special form when they appear at the end of a word. They are called *Sofeyot*, end letters. Thus, although these five letters have two forms, there are, nevertheless, only twenty-two basic foundation letters.

It has been said that the twenty-two basic foundation letters come from the seed of the male, the *Partzuf* of Wisdom, known as *Abba*-Father. The five end letters come from *Imma*, the *Partzuf* of Understanding (*Binah*). From the combination of both, the child is produced. However, the main part of the child, the foundation, is from the twenty-two letters of the male.

In the words of Chaim Vital, the main expounder of Lurian Kabbalah:

> Why are they always called in *Sefer Yetzirah* "twenty-two letters of foundation?" Because the drop of matter that constitutes the seed of the father, the secret of *Chachmah* (Wisdom), that he put in mother, *Binah*, at the beginning, is from the twenty-two letters. In these twenty-two letters are 248 bones, all of which are from the male, who emits white seed. However, from the red drop of the woman, which is the five end letters, the only things that get shaped in the mother's womb afterward is the skin, flesh, hair, black in the eyes, and the blood in the veins.[20]

Without getting too deeply into Lurian Kabbalah, we can conclude that it considers that the main part of the creation is due to the twenty-two basic letters.[21]

The *Mishnah* says that these twenty-two letters are composed of three mothers, seven doubles, and twelve singles. These three groupings are important to the understanding of *Sefer Yetzirah*.

The mother letters are *Aleph*, *Mem*, and *Shin*. They are the basis for the three columns in which the *Sefirot* are arranged. The *Mem* stands for *Mayim* (water), the *Shin* for *Aish* (fire), and the *Aleph* for *Avir* (air). Water and fire are opposites and are assigned the right and left sides, respectively. Air is in between, the mediator, and is associated with the middle column. Whenever the *Sefirot* are spoken about in the structure of a man, these three columns apply. Right means Kindness, left means Strictness, and the middle is a mix of the two (sometimes called *Rachamim*).

These three mother letters are associated with the first three *Sefirot*, the ones above time. They are mothers in that they are the cause of the seven lower *Sefirot*. These lower *Sefirot* form what is often called the Son and Daughter. The Son, *Zair Anpin*, is the "child" to which Chaim Vital was referring in the quote above.

The seven double letters are as follows: *Bet*, *Gimel*, *Dalet*, *Kaf*, *Peh*, *Resh*, and *Tav*. Those familiar with Hebrew grammar will recognize all but the *Resh* as belonging to a well-known grammatical group. These are the letters that have two different pronunciations. At the beginning of a word they are pronounced as hard consonants (for instance, *Bet* is "Ba"). In the middle of a syllable, however, they often are pronounced soft (*Bet* becomes *Vet* and is pronounced "Ve").

Therefore, these letters are ideal to represent hard law and soft kindness, the attributes of the *Sefirot*. They represent the seven lower *Sefirot* that change from Strict Law to Mercy.

Although the Hebrew letter *Resh* normally does not have a hard form, and it is not dotted, there are several places in the Scriptures where it has a strong dot (1 Samuel 1:6). Therefore, it, too, is considered in this grouping by Kabbalists, although not by grammarians.

Finally, there remain the twelve single letters. They are pronounced the same wherever they appear. They are all said to be aspects of the *Sefirah* of *Tiferet* and are associated with the sons of Jacob. (*Tiferet* is the *Sefirah* associated with Jacob.) *Tiferet* is represented in the Tetragrammaton by the letter *Vav*. The name "*Vav*" spelled out as a word in Hebrew is *Vav Vav*. The numerical value of *Vav* is six. *Vav Vav* is thus twelve, symbolizing these twelve letters.

Also symbolized is a group of lines known as the "twelve boundaries." A cube in physical space has six sides and twelve edges (boundary lines). The Six Extremes in the world of the *Sefirot* are similar. They are six that generate twelve. The twelve *edges* of the *Sefirot* are the spiritual qualities represented by Jacob's twelve sons. This is another example of the physical world paralleling the spiritual world.

The purpose of this *Mishnah* is to introduce us to the subject matter of the remainder of the book. The rest of the first chapter deals predominantly with *Sefirot*. In subsequent chapters, letters are the main topic.

THE BODILY COVENANTS

Sefer Yetzirah, Chapter 1, Mishnah 3

מ"ג עשר ספירות בלימה מספר עשר
אצבעות חמש כנגד חמש וברית יחיד
מכוונת באמצע כמלת הלשון וכמילת מעור:

> **Ten *Sefirot* of nothing, the number of the ten fingers, five opposite five, and the single covenant is in between, as in the circumcision of the tongue and the circumcision of the penis.**

There is a parallelism among the worlds. The physical world contains man with his body of physical matter, the spiritual world God with his "body" of *Sefirot*. The essence of man is his soul; the essence of the *Sefirot* is the light of God.

Whatever we see in our physical bodies has a parallel above. This *Mishnah* discusses the fingers because they are objects that have a similar structure to the *Sefirot*. It in no way intends to imply that there is a spatial dimension to the *Sefirot* themselves. However, the relationships in the spiritual realm are seen as the cause for what we find below. They are the root of the spatial aspects of the physical universe. They are the source of the laws of nature.

The *Sefirot* stand in three columns. The right is kindness; the left is strictness; the middle mediates. This *Mishnah* suggests that the *Sefirot* are like the fingers. Fingers are all on the right and left hands, with none in the middle. How then can the analogy between fingers and *Sefirot* be maintained? To understand this, one must realize that mediators are not necessarily impartial. Even the mediators lean toward one of the sides. Some of the mediator *Sefirot* lean toward kindness, some toward strictness.

The *Pree Yitzchak* says that *Binah*, *Gevurah*, *Hod*, *Yisod*, and *Malchut* are toward the left. The other five are toward the right. Thus, of the four *Sefirot* in the middle, *Keter* and *Tiferet* lean toward the right, while *Yisod* and *Malchut* lean toward the left.[22]

When discussing hands in the realm of the *Sefirot*, they refer to the hands of God. Often in the Bible, reference is made to the hand of God or the finger of God. Maimonides spent the first third of his *Guide to the Perplexed* explaining what these anthropomorphisms really mean. Kabbalah explains them also, but in an entirely different manner. Nevertheless, all the major Kabbalists have concluded, like Maimonides, that there is no physical aspect of the divine.

This *Mishnah* is problematic in several ways. It seems to suggest twenty *Sefirot*, ten represented by the fingers and ten by the toes. Furthermore, it is not clear what the tongue and the penis represent in the *Mishnah*. Are they additional *Sefirot*?

The commentators have addressed these questions in various ways. All agree that there are only ten *Sefirot* in the realm of the divine (the World of Emanations—*Atzilot*). These *Sefirot* are represented by the fingers of the hand. They are reflected in the world below, the World of Creation (*Briyah*). This reflection is represented by the toes. Just as the fingers of the right and left hands are united above through what the *Mishnah* describes as the mediation of the tongue, so are the toes of the right and left feet united below by a mediator between the legs.[23]

The Vilna Gaon states that the fingers represent the first ten commandments and the toes the second. There were five commandments on each stone, like the fingers on each hand. The commandments were also recited verbally, symbolized by the tongue.

Furthermore, the Gaon points out, the hands and tongue of this *Mishnah* correspond to the books mentioned in the first *Mishnah*. The last book was called "story" since it refers to the concept that is here called "the tongue." *Tongue* and *story* represent speech, specifically, the oral recitation of the ten commandments.[24]

The ten commandments are composed of the letters of the Hebrew alphabet. The bodies of the ten *Sefirot* are likewise composed of letters. Letters are combined by the tongue during speech. They are also what is passed from *Abba* (Father, *Partzuf* of Wisdom) to *Imma* (Mother, *Partzuf* of Understanding) through the reproductive organ (*Yisod*) to produce *Zair Anpin*.

Thus, the term "circumcision of the penis" in the *Mishnah* is usually taken to refer to the *Sefirah* of *Yisod* (Foundation). The reproductive organ, after all, is in a sense the *foundation* of the world. It is a mediator in that its function is to mediate between male and female and unite them.

The word *circumcision* is interesting. In Hebrew the same term, *milah*, means both "word" and "circumcision." The tongue speaks words and the penis is circumcised. Both involve cutting (*articulation* in the case of the tongue). Both the tongue and sex organ are important in uniting and relating.

The *Sefirah* symbolized by the tongue is somewhat more difficult to determine. It is sometimes said to be *Daat* and sometimes *Tiferet*. The Vilna Gaon mentions both.[25] As *Daat*, its position in the body seems correct. *Tiferet*, however, is below the head and usually symbolizes the heart. Since the tongue expresses what the heart feels, however, they are used interchangeably. In addition, since the tongue controls the quality of sounds, it is said to mediate between the palate and the throat. The more guttural a sound, the more the mediator favors the throat.

What is meant by saying the tongue is circumcised? The Torah speaks of circumcising the heart. "And God will circumcise your heart and the heart of your seed to love the Lord thy God with all your heart and all your soul, for the sake of your life" (Deuteronomy 30:6). That is, circumcision means purification, cutting off that which is impure. Purification of the tongue is similar. It involves choosing wholesome thoughts for the tongue to express.

The point this *Mishnah* is making is that there is peace in heaven—the conflicting attributes of the ten *Sefirot* are always resolved. The mediators mentioned do not represent an eleventh *Sefirah*, since *Sefer Yetzirah* clearly states that the *Sefirot* are "ten and not eleven."[26] Nonetheless, the text is somewhat difficult, as it appears to indicate that the mediators are in addition to the ten *Sefirot*.

Commentators that follow the Lurian system resolve this in a unique fashion. Lurian Kabbalah represents an extremely complex system that deals with many interrelated worlds of ten *Sefirot*. Some of these worlds overlap. Some are the cause of others and have a parent--child relationship. Some are siblings. Sometimes the lower world is thought of as a garment for the higher.

An extremely high world is that of *Arich Anpin* (The Long Face). It is a complete *Partzuf* of ten *Sefirot* in the shape of a man. Its arms are covered with two other complete *Partzufim*. The right is "clothed" by the *Partzuf* of *Abba*-father and the left by *Imma*-mother. The *Sefirah* of *Daat* in *Arich Anpin* is represented by its tongue. It is this tongue that mediates between the worlds of *Abba* and *Imma*.[27]

Different kabbalistic systems explain *Sefer Yetzirah* on completely different planes. Most Kabbalists would probably say, "*Eilu VeEilu divrei Elohim Chaim*" ("All varying legitimate interpretations are the words of the living God"). The Ramban and the Raivad both consider the first three *Mishnayot* of Chapter 1 to constitute a unit. In the words of the Ramban, "The first *Mishnah* explained that they (the thirty-two paths) are all in Wisdom, the second all in Understanding, and the third all in *Daat*."[28] Thus, according to him, these three *Mishnayot* trace the Paths through the first three *Sefirot*. The Raivad states that the entire *Sefer Yetzirah* is built on three levels. Creation is traced by *Sefer Yetzirah* first to the world, then to the year, and finally to the soul. By world, not only physical, spatial relationships are meant, but also relations in the higher worlds that we allegorically describe in spatial terms. By year, time is meant. Finally, soul refers to the human being, including his body.[29] The Raivad concludes that the first *Mishnah* discusses the thirty-two paths in the world, the second discusses the paths in the year, and the current *Mishnah*, which refers to the fingers, refers to the level of the soul.

THE SIGNIFICANCE OF
THE NUMBER TEN

Sefer Yetzirah, Chapter 1, Mishnah 4

מ"ד עשר ספירות בלימה עשר ולא תשע,
עשר ולא אחת עשרה , הבן בחכמה
וחכם בבינה, בחון בהם וחקור מהם והעמד
דבר על בוריו והשב יוצר על מכונו :

Ten *Sefirot* of nothing, ten and not nine, ten and not eleven, understand in wisdom and be wise in understanding, contemplate them, and study of them, and establish the matter clearly, and seat the Creator on His place.

Central to the Jewish concept of God is His unity. There is only one, indivisible, infinite being. By fully understanding this, we are "seating the Creator on His place," that is, we are accepting Him as Master of the universe.

The author of *Sefer Yetzirah* was aware that the doctrine of ten *Sefirot* could easily be misunderstood. It could easily be misconstrued to undermine true monotheism, to imply a God of multiple parts. That is why this *Mishnah* stresses the symbolism of "ten" so much.

Ten is closely associated with one in the decimal system. It is indicated in our writing by a 1 and a 0, which add up to 1. The decimal system, which has only ten symbols for numbers, is universally used. The next higher number must use 1 again.

In the Hebrew language the situation is similar. After the term for ten (*esser*), the terms for higher numbers are formed by combining *esser* with the names of the lower numbers. For example, in Hebrew, 11 is 1 and 10 (*achad-assar*).

There is a special type of religious calculation known as *Prat Katan*. It calculates numerical values of letters by ignoring the zeroes. For instance, the value of *Shin*, which is usually taken to be 300, would be 3 under this system, and the value of 10 would be 1 (see Appendix B). Thus, ten is stressed by *Sefer Yetzirah* to emphasize that the essence of the *Sefirot* is one unity. The *Sefirot* are ten only as far as they relate to the worlds below. The inner light that constitutes their soul is the essence of God, which is the same unity everywhere. The vessels of the *Sefirot* merely filter this light, and this filtering produces the various particular qualities of the individual *Sefirot*. Although there are ten *Sefirot*, their essence in reality is only one. It is the undifferentiated essence of God. This is hinted at by the fact that the *Sefirot* are ten and no other number.

In counting the *Sefirot*, there has been some debate as to which *Sefirot* constitute the ten. The inclusion of three *Sefirot*—*Keter, Daat,* and *Malchut*—has sometimes been questioned. *Sefer Yetzirah* begins with the Paths of Wisdom. *Keter* is not explicitly mentioned. It has been called *Ayin*, nonbeing. Even the Torah itself begins with an allusion to Wisdom rather than *Keter*. It will be remembered that the phrase "In the beginning" refers to Wisdom, as it says in Proverbs, "The *beginning* of *wisdom*" (Proverbs 4:7). *Daat* is often not mentioned in the list of *Sefirot*. It only appears at times when *Keter* is neglected. Its status is somewhat elusive. *Malchut* is the last of the *Sefirot*. It has no light of its own and is a recipient of the light of the other *Sefirot*. It is, therefore, compared to the moon, while *Zair Anpin* is the sun. Since *Malchut* does not have its own light, perhaps it should not be counted.

Rabbi Moses Cordovero, in *Pardes Rimonim*, states, "Ordinary *Daat* refers to the *Sefirah* of *Tiferet*."[30] According to this, *Daat* is not an eleventh *Sefirah*. We sometimes find that it is associated with *Keter* and is considered to be the presence of *Keter* below. It is the mediating aspect of *Keter* and helps unite Wisdom and Understanding. Since *Tiferet* is also a mediator, *Daat* may be considered either *Tiferet* above or *Keter* below. The idea is the same. It resolves the Wisdom–Understanding antithesis.

Other explanations have been offered. For instance, it has been said that *Daat* is not counted because it is always concealed. This is because it serves to unite *Chachmah* and *Binah*. The *Zohar* states that *Chachmah* and *Binah* never separate. Therefore, *Daat*, which is between them, is always concealed in their union. The *Sefirah* of *Yisod* serves the same function for *Zair Anpin* and *Malchut*. However, the union of *Zair Anpin* and *Malchut* is only occasional, so *Yisod* is not always covered. Therefore, it is counted.[31]

Another theory offered by the Ari is that *Daat* does not have its own inner content, but rather holds the light to be passed to the lower *Sefirot*. Therefore, it is not counted separately when the inner aspect of the *Sefirot* is counted. *Keter* is counted instead. However, the opposite is true when counting the outside of the *Sefirot*. The outside is for the purpose of creation, and creation begins with Wisdom (being). Therefore, *Daat* is included, and not *Keter*.[32]

Finally, as far as *Malchut* is concerned, it is usually counted despite the lack of its own light. It is considered a key *Sefirah* in that its elevation is a central theme in Kabbalah. However, building on the Lurian model, the Vilna Gaon states that in certain cases *Malchut* is not counted. For instance, within the *Partzuf* of *Arich Anpin*, two aspects of *Keter* exist and each is counted separately. *Malchut*, which would be the eleventh *Sefirah*, is therefore excluded.[33] This substitution of an aspect of *Keter* for *Malchut* is based on the very special relationship between *Malchut* and *Keter*, which will be examined in a later *Mishnah*. For now, suffice it to say that the *Sefirah* of *Malchut* of one world is the main "ingredient" in the *Keter* of the world beneath.

The *Mishnah* continues by telling us to "understand in wisdom and be wise in understanding." In other words, it is advising us to mix these attributes. Each *Sefirah* contains aspects of all the rest. By looking at the wisdom in Understanding and the understanding in Wisdom, each of these *Sefirot* incorporates the attributes of both. This is what the Kabbalists call "uniting the *Sefirot*."

Much has been made of the interrelationship of *Sefirot* by Shabbetai Horowitz[34] in his famous work, *Shefa Tal*. He states that every dot of each *Sefirah* contains all the *Sefirot*. For instance, Wisdom is itself composed of ten *Sefirot*, and each of them is composed of ten *Sefirot*, ad infinitum. Thus, the *Sefirot* are all one, and God's unity is uncompromised.[35]

Meir Gabbai stresses the importance of "uniting" the *Sefirot* during prayer. In the *Amidah*, the first three blessings represent the forefathers, Abraham, Isaac, and Jacob. They also symbolize the three *Sefirot* of *Chesed* (Kindness), *Gevurah* (Courage), and *Tiferet* (Glory). According to him, when one says the first blessing, which represents Abraham's trait of kindness, he should think of Isaac's courage as well. While saying the second blessing, representing Courage, one should try to include Kindness. Both Kindness and Courage should be mixed in the third blessing.[36]

It has been pointed out that this combining of Wisdom and Understanding is present in the letters of God's name. It is well accepted in Kabbalah that the letters of the Tetragrammaton represent *Sefirot*. The first letter, *Yud*, represents Wisdom. The second letter, the *Hey*, represents Understanding. Each of these letters can be spelled out as words, just like in English the letter "b" can be written in word form "bee." *Hey* is spelled *Hey Yud*. [Please note that *Yud* is the letter that represents *Chachmah* (Wisdom).] Thus, Wisdom is included in Understanding. Similarly, *Yud* (י) is spelled *Yud Vav Dalet* (יוד). The two letters *Vav* (ו) and *Dalet* (ד), however, form a *Hey* (ה) (put the *Dalet* first and the *Vav* beneath it (ד,). Thus Wisdom, too, contains Understanding.[37]

The *Mishnah* continues with "contemplate them, and study of them." All the *Sefirot* are to be contemplated so that their existence and number are clear. However, only some of them may be studied in any depth. These are the seven lower *Sefirot*, which are within time. The first three are beyond the scope of human understanding, and studying them is prohibited.[38]

THE INFINITE DEPTHS

Sefer Yetzirah, Chapter 1, Mishnah 5

מ"ה עשר ספירות בלי מה מדתן עשר שאין
להם סוף עומק ראשית ועומק אחרית
עומק טוב ועומק רע עומק רום ועומק תחת
עומק מזרח ועומק מערב עומק צפון ועומק
דרום אדון יחיד אל מלך נאמן מושל בכולם
ממעון קדשו ועד עדי עד :

Ten *Sefirot* of nothing, their measure is ten that have no end:

The depth of the beginning,
The depth of the end,
The depth of good,
The depth of bad,
The depth of the heights,
The depth of the bottom,
The depth of the east,
The depth of the west,
The depth of the north,
The depth of the south,

and one master, God faithful King, rules them all, from His holy place till forever and ever.

This *Mishnah* is known as "*Mishnat HaAmakim*"—The *Mishnah* of the Depths. The ten depths correspond to the ten *Sefirot*. However, the description of them in this *Mishnah* is unusual. Not all commentators agree as to which *depth* corresponds to which *Sefirah*.

The standard names for the *Sefirot*, the ones we have been using until now, are not mentioned anywhere in *Sefer Yetzirah*. It is uncertain when they came into common usage. In addition to this *Mishnah*, which describes the *Sefirot* in terms of depths, *Sefer Yetzirah* assigns them names, beginning in the ninth *Mishnah* of this chapter. These differ from the names generally used by all later Kabbalists.

The *Mishnah* begins with the unusual phrase, "their measure is ten that have no end." We know the Kabbalists use the term "*Ein Sof*"— ("without end") to refer to the infinite, boundless light of God. This is the light that is too great to be contained in any vessel, including the vessels of the *Sefirot*. Nevertheless, *Sefer Yetzirah* tells us that even the bounded light contained in the vessels is infinite.

Thus, we are faced with two levels of infinity. The first is the *Ein Sof*, which surrounds all the worlds and stretches forever and ever. However, the infinite light not only surrounds the creation, but fills it. That is, it enters the vessels of the *Sefirot* and gives them life. The very souls of the *Sefirot* are, in fact, comprised of this light. In the capacity of soul, the light is bounded within the body of each particular *Sefirah*.

A purpose of this *Mishnah* is to inform us that although the light of the *Sefirot* is bounded by their vessels, it is nonetheless without end. That is, the *Sefirot* constitute "limited infinities."

That is why the *Mishnah* speaks of "their measure." Measure implies limit. The *Sefirot* are called *Midot* (measures), to differentiate them from the *Ein Sof*, the Infinite, surrounding light. However, even though they are bounded in comparison with the *Ein Sof*, they are still infinite.

This concept is not foreign to modern mathematics, which recognizes infinite sets of various sizes. For instance, the sets of "all positive numbers" and "all even numbers" are both infinite, but the first is twice the size of the second.

It is clear that even within a limited space, various infinities exist. Thus, a room may be cut in half an infinite number of times. Although the size of each cut *approaches* zero, it does not *reach* zero until an infinite number of cuts have been completed. Thus, any bounded space is, itself, an example of a limited infinity.

Based on this *Mishnah*, it has become a common practice for Kabbalists to use the term *"Midot"* as a synonym for *"Sefirot."* The word has a double meaning. It means "measure," but it also means "attributes." Both meanings apply here. They are measures because they are confined to vessels, but they also represent the *attributes* of God. As specific attributes, they are limited in relation to the *Ein Sof*, which is an undifferentiated, limitless unity.

This *Mishnah* seem to be saying that the *Sefirot* are the source of various dimensions. While each of these dimensions is distinct from the others and is thus limited in its scope, each is infinite in its own realm.

Three types of dimensions are discussed:

1. Time
2. Morality
3. Space

The "depth of the beginning and the depth of the end" represent time. The *Mishnah* says they have no end. Time stretches forever in both directions.

The moral dimension is represented by "the depth of good and the depth of bad." These, too, have no end. There is no limit to how good or bad one can be.

The final six depths are those of the heights, the bottom, the east, the west, the north, and the south. These are spatial dimensions. Space stretches out limitlessly in all directions.

It is interesting that *Sefer Yetzirah* sees the world in terms of these particular three dimensions. Other dimensions could have been used, such as intelligence and beauty. In fact, these other dimensions are used in later Kabbalah. [The names of the *Sefirot* in the *Zohar* and later Kabbalah, for example, include *Chachmah* (Wisdom) and *Hod* (Beauty) (see Appendix A).]

It is probable that *Sefer Yetzirah* considers the dimensions of space, time, and morality primary. The attributes represented by the later names somehow result from these primary dimensions. It is also possible that the dimensions found in *Sefer Yetzirah* merely represent an alternative way of thinking about the *Sefirot*. It is common throughout kabbalistic literature to give the ten *Sefirot* many different interpretations and appellations. They all have meaning in their particular contexts. One set does not invalidate an alternate set, even if, on the surface, the elements appear contradictory.

It appears from the Torah that time itself was created. Then how can we say that "the depth of the beginning" is limitless? We also speak of "*Acharit HaYomim*" (the end of time), so how can we say that "the depth of the end" is unbounded?

It seems to me that the "dimensions" mentioned in *Sefer Yetzirah* must be understood in terms of potentials. While the world as we find it has a beginning and an end, has a particular amount of good and evil, and a particular spatial extent, it has the potential to be different. There is no theoretical limit on the extent these dimensions may assume. Thus, man can strive to expand the limits of his reality, for the limits that currently exist are not absolute.

The whole of *Sefer Yetzirah* is written on three *levels*, that of world, year, and soul. The three types of *dimensions* in this *Mishnah* correspond exactly to these three *levels*. The spatial dimension corresponds to the world, the temporal dimension to the year, and the moral dimension to the soul.

The *Mishnah* continues, "And one master, God faithful King, rules them all, from His holy place till forever and ever." Most of the commentaries agree that the one master is a reference to the Infinite (*Ein Sof*). The *Ein Sof* is the source of the light that enters the vessels of the *Sefirot* and becomes their soul. Just as the soul rules the body, so does the light of the Infinite rule the vessels of the *Sefirot*.

The phrase "from His holy place till forever and ever" is taken by many commentaries to refer to all ten *Sefirot*. For instance, the Vilna Gaon says:

> "His holy place" is *Keter*, since the light of the *Ein Sof* is hidden in *Keter*. From there onward, all is by way of the "clothing of the light,"[39] as is known. "Till forever and ever" are *Binah*, the six extremes and *Malchut*, respectively (*till* is *Binah*, *forever* is the extremes, *and ever* is *Malchut*).[40]

It should be understood that *Sefer Yetzirah* has no explicit reference to "vessels" at all, and certainly not to the differentiation made by later Kabbalists between them and "essence." Nor does *Sefer Yetzirah* mention the *Ein Sof* as an entity. When it states, "Their measure is ten that have *no end* (*ein sof*)," it is referring to the *Sefirot*, not the unbounded surrounding light.

Following is a list of the *Sefirot* that correspond to the "depths." The correspondence, according to the Ramban,[41] is as follows:

The depth of the beginning—*Chachmah* (Wisdom)
The depth of the end—*Binah* (Understanding)
The depth of good—*Chesed* (Kindness)
The depth of bad—*Gevurah* (Courage)[42]
The depth of the heights—*Keter* (Crown)★
The depth of the bottom—*Malchut* (Kingdom)★
The depth of the east—*Tiferet* (Glory)★
The depth of the west—*Yisod* (Foundation)
The depth of the north—*Netzach* (Eternity)
The depth of the south—*Hod* (Beauty)

The asterisks (★) are the correspondences that the Ramban implies but does not explicitly state. An alternative list is offered by Rabbi Yitzchak Isaac in his commentary, *Pree Yitzchak*:

The depth of the beginning—*Keter* (Crown)
The depth of the end— *Malchut* (Kingdom)
The depth of good—*Chesed* (Kindness)
The depth of bad—*Gevurah* (Courage)
The depth of the heights—*Netzach* (Eternity)
The depth of the bottom—*Hod* (Beauty)

The depth of the east—*Tiferet* (Glory)
The depth of the west—*Yisod* (Foundation)
The depth of the north—*Binah* (Understanding)
The depth of the south—*Chachmah* (Wisdom)

A third list is given by the Vilna Gaon, who says, for instance, that the depth of bad is *Malchut*, rather than *Gevurah*. In addition to these lists, other possibilities exist.

The reason for the many opinions is that Kabbalah is full of indirect references, hints, and symbolism. The same symbol may refer to different objects depending on the context. The Ramban's list implies that the *Mishnah* uses the phrase "the heights" to refer to *Keter*. This is logical, since *Keter* is the first *Sefirah* and the *highest*. The Ramban says that "the depth of the beginning" means Wisdom, since the Book of Proverbs associates "wisdom" and "beginning" in the verse, "The beginning of Wisdom"(Proverbs 4:7). As *Wisdom* and *Understanding* are antitheses, *Wisdom* as the beginning implies that *Understanding* is the end.

In *Pree Yitzchak*'s list, however, *beginning* refers to the first *Sefirah* (*Keter*) and *end* to the last (*Malchut*). This is a perfectly reasonable alternate hypothesis. This leaves the *Pree Yitzchak* the problem of what to do with "the heights" and "the bottom." He chose *Netzach* and *Hod*, since they are described in the *Zohar* as two millstones that grind manna for the righteous, the upper millstone being *Netzach* and the lower one, *Hod*.

The Vilna Gaon's association of *Malchut* with bad is based on the fact that it is closest to the *Klipot*, the shells of "the side of uncleanliness." It is universally accepted that the *Sefirot* themselves contain no bad. Saying that they include bad would be tantamount to associating God Himself with evil, since they are His attributes. The Vilna Gaon emphasizes that while *the depth of bad* is a reference to *Malchut*, *Malchut* itself is all good.

There are various kabbalistic theories as to the existence of evil. While all major Kabbalists agree that the *Sefirot* themselves contain no evil, most feel that the attributes associated with strictness (*din*) are an indirect source for evil. The two main *Sefirot* associated with strictness are *Gevurah* and *Malchut*. *Gevurah* is often called "the harsh attribute of strict law" and *Malchut* "the soft attribute of strict law." Therefore, these two are the obvious choices to be associated with "the depth of bad." *Gevurah* seems the better candidate because it is "harsher" than *Malchut*. However, *Malchut* also has a claim, since it is lower on the tree of *Sefirot* and thus closer to the *Klipot* (shells of uncleanliness). Consequently, the Ramban picked the former, the Gaon the latter.

The idea that evil does not issue directly from God is supported in the philosophical sphere by Maimonides. He says in *The Guide to the Perplexed* that evil is an absence rather than a positive creation.[43] This is because evil cannot proceed from a totally good God. Maimonides compares it to darkness, which is an absence of light. Likewise, evil is the absence of good. God created the world incompletely. All that He did was good, but He *left room* for the bad. He did not create it.

Nevertheless, without positive existence there would be no evil. There would merely be nothing. Thus, in a sense, even according to Maimonides, evil is indirectly a product of good. God did not create it, but He made its existence possible. Ultimately, evil is in the world for positive reasons. It makes choice possible, allowing existence to be meaningful. Without it, decisions would be without moral import and would become trivial. Thus, all is ultimately for the good.[44]

This idea plays a central role in Lurian Kabbalah. Evil, according to Rabbi Luria, is given life by the "sparks of holiness." These sparks fell into the *Klipot* (World of Evil; literally, *shells*) when the vessels broke in the upper world (known as the World of *Tohu*) due to the inability of the vessels to stand the intensity of the light from above. With the reelevation of the sparks, the *Klipot* are left without their life source, and they die. This elevation of the sparks is the main purpose of man. Without the light of holiness, nothing can exist, not even evil itself.[45]

THE ASPECT AND ACTION
OF THE *SEFIROT*

Sefer Yetzirah, Chapter 1, Mishnah 6

מ"ן עשר ספירות בלי מה צפייתן כמראה
הבזק ותכליתן אין להן קץ ודברו בהן
ברצוא ושוב ולמאמרו כסופה ירדופו ולפני
כסאו הם משתחוים:

> **Ten *Sefirot* of nothing, their look is like the aspect of lightning, and their end is without bound. His word in them is running and returning and to His words they hurry like a storm, and before His throne they bow.**

The *Sefirot* are not physical. Why, then, is the *Mishnah* speaking about "their look"? The reference to the "look" of the *Sefirot* in the *Mishnah* has been understood, by all the commentators, on a purely metaphorical level.

This *Mishnah* is trying to convey the idea that very little is known of the *Sefirot*. The term *their look* means that which is "seen intellectually" of the *Sefirot*. The ability to intellectually understand the *Sefirot* is very limited.

In certain aspects, learning of the *Sefirot* can be compared to lightning. Lightning is a very powerful event that takes place in a very short time. So is spiritual enlightenment. You merely can catch a glance of the splendor, not fully understand it. If one gets too close to lightning, one can get burned or even killed. Spiritual knowledge can be dangerous, too. There is a famous story in the Talmud about four scholars in the time of the *Mishnah* who entered upon the study of Kabbalah. Of them, only Rabbi Akiva entered and left unharmed.[46]

The word "lightning" in the original Hebrew is *"bazak."* "Lightning" is the most common translation, probably because of its similarity to the more common word for lightning, *"barak."* Not everyone agrees that the word *"bazak"* in the *Mishnah* should be translated "lightning." Some say it means "spread," as when fuel is spread in a stove and momentarily flares up.[47] Others say it refers to the appearance of fire through a hole in an earthenware vessel.[48] Whatever the translation, the idea is similar. One may only momentarily glance the strong fire, and then it disappears from sight. One cannot maintain a steady stare at the fire or at the *Sefirot*. Eternity may be glimpsed but not captured.

In the same vein, the *Mishnah* then tells us that the end of the *Sefirot* is without bound. The *Sefirot* are infinite and cannot be fully fathomed. The Vilna Gaon points out that the previous *Mishnah* stated that the *Sefirot* have no end (*Sof*). Here it says that they lack bound (*Keitz*). The first, according to the Gaon, means that they are infinite in the direction of the surrounding *Ein Sof*, that is, from them and above. The latter means that they extend through all the lower worlds. Even our lowly physical world is given its life force through the *Sefirot*. There is no place devoid of God's presence.[49]

The *Mishnah* continues, telling us that God's word runs and returns in the *Sefirot*. That is, God's actions are seen through the *Sefirot*, which He uses to run the affairs of the world. They are His vessels and do His bidding. Yet, His presence in the *Sefirot* is not understood, nor are the reasons for His actions. We glimpse, through God's manifestations in the world, His presence and His will, but we do not understand. It is as if His words run and quickly return. We cannot truly understand Him.

Pree Yitzchak states that the phrase, "His word in them is running and returning," is a warning against studying that which is too far above us, specifically, the first three *Sefirot*. It says in the Torah:

> If a nest of birds chanced to be before you in the way, in any tree or on the ground, with young ones or eggs, and the mother sitting on the young or the eggs, take not the mother with the children. Send away the mother, but the children you may take for yourselves, so it may be well with you and you may live long (Deuteronomy 22:6–7).

The term *the children* has been taken by the Kabbalists to mean the seven lower *Sefirot*, while by *the mother* is meant *Binah* and the higher *Sefirot*. The Torah says that we may take the children, that is, we may study the lower *Sefirot*, but we must "send away the mother," *Binah* and above.[50]

The *Mishnah* continues by telling us that the *Sefirot* hurry like a storm to his words. The commentators widely differ as to *whose* words. The simplest explanation is that the *Sefirot* obey the orders of the Infinite (*Ein Sof*).

Some alternate possibilities are as follows: The Raivad says that "his words" refers to *Malchut*. *Pree Yitzchak* says it refers to *Chachmah*. The Gaon says it refers to the "six extremes" of Primal Man—*Adam Kadmon* (the concept of the Primal Man is developed in the Lurian kabbalistic system and refers to the earliest set of emanations). Saadia Gaon, one of the earliest of the commentators on *Sefer Yetzirah*, interprets the phrase "his words" on a different level entirely. He states, in a particularly strange style, "To the words of the ten *Sefirot*, just like a storm that runs after the wind that chases it, so will they who think and speak of those ten *Sefirot* be pursued and destroyed." Thus, according to Saadia, the *Mishnah* is referring to people being pursued as a punishment for studying what is forbidden, rather than the *Sefirot* pursuing obediently the orders of the Infinite.

The final phrase of the *Mishnah*, "before His throne they bow," also has varied interpretations. The simplest is found in *Pree Yitzchak*, which states that *Keter* is the first *Sefirah* beneath the Infinite and is considered the Infinite's throne. Consequently, that which is before the throne is the Infinite himself (*Ein Sof*). According to this interpretation, the *Mishnah* is merely telling us that the *Sefirot* bow before the Infinite. The Ramban very simply states that the outer bows to the inner. The spiritual world is hierarchical. Saadia understands this phrase to refer to man rather than the *Sefirot*. According to him it means, "Anyone who studies this *Sefer Yetzirah* and this *Mishnah* has an obligation to bow to the Creator of all."[51]

What is abundantly clear is that this one book, *Sefer Yetzirah*, has been interpreted in many very different ways. The particular kabbalistic system with which the commentator identifies is a major determinant as to which type of explanation he will choose. Affiliation with Lurian or Cordoverian Kabbalah, as well as pre-*Zohar* kabbalistic thought, is often easy to detect. Later Kabbalists tend to be somewhat eclectic and do not shy away from integrating concepts from the different schools and periods.

THE UNITY OF THE DIVINE

Sefer Yetzirah, Chapter 1, Mishnah 7

מ״ז עשר ספירות בלי מה נעוץ סופן בתחלתן
ותחלתן בסופן כשלהבת קשורה בגחלת
שאדון יחיד ואין לו שני ולפני אחד מה
אתה סופר:

> **Ten *Sefirot* of nothing, insert their end in their beginning and their beginning in their end, like a flame bound to a coal, that a single master who has no second [rules], and before one what do you count?**

God is one. His attributes and actions all flow from His unity. The ten *Sefirot* are not ten separate items, but rather are related in the most fundamental way.

This *Mishnah* has a salient theme, the unity of God. Kabbalists have always been very sensitive about the subject of God's oneness. The doctrine of ten *Sefirot* has been interpreted by some as an abandonment of the pure monotheism of philosophical Judaism. Much time has been spent in kabbalistic writing trying to show that this is not the case. This *Mishnah* is often quoted to support the idea that Kabbalah does not dilute the notion of God's unity.

The *Mishnah* begins by telling us to "insert their end in their beginning and their beginning in their end." Like most mysterious statements in *Sefer Yetzirah*, the meaning of this phrase is open to different interpretations by the various kabbalistic systems.

Most commentators agree that this part of the *Mishnah* is concerned with stressing that the *Sefirot* are not unrelated entities. As the Ramban puts it:

> Even though the items are split into Wisdom and Understanding[52] and Knowledge, there is no difference between them since the end is tied to the beginning, and the beginning to the end, and both are included in the middle. That is, all unites like the flame of fire, that is united with various colors that are all the same in one root.[53]

It should be remembered in reading the above quote that the word "beginning" is a reference to Wisdom, "end" to "Understanding," and "middle" to "*Daat*."

The idea of the *Sefirot* being united appears numerous times in the *Zohar* itself. Often it takes the form of an active process. They unite at specific times and also as a result of human action, prayer, or meditation. The well-known section of the *Zohar*, "*KaGavna*," which has become part of the Friday night Sephardic prayers, discusses the

unification of the *Sefirot* on the entry of the Sabbath. There is an
often-quoted kabbalistic saying that "the worship of the lower world
fulfills the needs of that which is higher." This says, in a way, that God
is helped by man. On the surface, such a doctrine seems in stark
contrast to the words of the prophet Isaiah, "Why do I need your
many sacrifices, says the Lord . . . " (Isaiah 1:10). Kabbalah seems to
be saying that while God can certainly do without man, He nevertheless created him for a purpose, which can be advanced by man himself.
Unification of the *Sefirot* through worship advances God's purpose
and thus allows man to *help* God. This, in turn, makes human life more
meaningful.

In his book, *Avodat HaKodesh*, Meir Gabbai tells us to concentrate
during the prayer of *Shmoneh Esrei* on uniting the *Sefirot*. During the
first section, known as "*the shield of Abraham*" and representing Kindness, we are told to think also of the attribute of Isaac, Courage.
During the second part (*Michayeh HaMeitim*), which is the blessing of
Isaac, Courage, we are told to *mix* in the idea of Abraham, Kindness.
This is the active process of unifying God in one's heart, becoming
aware that all stems from a single root.

Rabbi Moshe Botarel states in his commentary that the purpose of
the phrase, "Insert their end in their beginning and their beginning in
their end," is to remind a person looking back to the beginning of this
world, that the beginning of the current world constitutes the end of a
previous world. Likewise, when he looks toward the end of this
civilization, he should also realize it is not merely an end but also a
beginning for the next. Thus, God's rule is not confined to this world,
but is forever and ever.[54] As the *Midrash* says, "God creates worlds and
destroys them."

The Lurian school interprets this *Mishnah* in terms of the structure of
the upper worlds. The Lurians stress that the last *Sefirah* of each higher
world becomes the inner life of the lower world. This concept is
known as "*Atik.*" *Atik* is the name of one of the two *Partzufim*
associated with *Keter*. It is the Hebrew word for "moved," for it is
moved from the higher to the lower world. That is, the *Sefirah Keter* of
the lower world is composed in part by the *Sefirah Malchut* of the upper
world (more exactly, by the seven lower sub-*Sefirot* of *Malchut*, known
as *Atik Yomin*—the moved days[55]).

It has been stressed by Shabbetai Horowitz in *Shefa Tal* that every part of each *Sefirah* is composed of all ten *Sefirot*. Thus, they are all one. That is why Kabbalists talk about *Gevurah* in *Chesed*, *Tiferet* in *Malchut*, and so on. This concept is even found in the *Siddur*, in the ritual of *Sefirat HaOmer*. Forty-nine days are counted from Passover to Shavuot. Each of these seven weeks is associated with a different *Sefirah* (of the lower seven *Sefirot*). Within these weeks, each different weekday is associated with a different one of these seven *Sefirot*. The seven lower *Sefirot* represent God's presence within time, the higher three, God's presence above time. For example, the tenth day (the third day of the second week), is associated with the second (*Gevurah*) of the seven lower *Sefirot* because it is in the second week, and with the third (*Tiferet*) because it is the third day of that week. These associations are commonly printed in prayer books next to each day that is to be counted. Next to the tenth day is "*Tiferet* in *Gevurah*." In a similar manner, when considering all ten *Sefirot*, each is divided into ten sub-*Sefirot*, that is, each contains all the rest.

The phrase in the *Mishnah*, "like a flame bound to a coal," is often quoted by Kabbalists to indicate the unity of the *Sefirot*. They are all rooted in the same source and share the same soul, the Infinite essence. The Raivad points out that a coal is the cause of the flame and can exist without the flame. The flame, however, cannot exist without the coal. So can the spiritual cause exist independently of the result, but not visa versa.[56] Thus, the *Ein Sof* is not dependent on the *Sefirot*, but the *Sefirot* have no existence without the *Ein Sof*.

The *Mishnah* concludes with the strange phrase, "That a single master who has no second, and before one what do you count?" The *Mishnah* seems to be saying that a single master *rules* the *Sefirot*, as stated in *Mishnah* five. In *Mishnah* six, the word "rules" is omitted because it is implied. The single master is the Infinite *Ein Sof*. According to the Ramban, He is called "single" (*yachid*) because everything in the world is equally under His rule. Everything is equal in Him. This is similar to the Yiddish expression, "*Tzu Gut alles is gleich*"—"To God, all things are the same." The Ramban then comments on the phrase "who has no second" as follows: "God has no second, even though the potential for all seconds are from Him." God is the ultimate unity, but the cause for a world that contains nothing that is a true unity. All is a unity in Him, however, since He is the root.

The Vilna Gaon says, "Only that which has a second can be called one. Something without a second cannot truly be called one."[57] Thus, calling God one, as the Torah does, is just a convenience for the ease of the listener. In reality, not even that description is suitable.

The final point made by this *Mishnah* is that "before one what do you count?" There is no number before one. Numbers begin with *Keter*, the first *Sefirah*. The *Ein Sof* is not counted with the *Sefirot*. It has no second, and thus the term *first* does not apply.[58]

THE COVENANT OF SILENCE

Sefer Yetzirah, Chapter 1, Mishnah 8

מ"ח עשר ספירות בלימה בלום פיך מלדבר
ולבך מלהרהר ואם רץ לבך שוב
למקום שלכך נאמר והחיות רצוא ושוב.
ועל דבר זה נכרת ברית :

Ten *Sefirot* of nothing, shut your mouth from talking and your heart from thinking. But if your heart runs, return to the place, for that is the reason it is said, "And the angels [*Chayot*] run and return" [Ezekiel 1:14] and on this matter a covenant was cut.

Mysticism is a dangerous pursuit. When one is dealing with subjects far removed from mundane life, it is easy to lose the way. There are no easily recognizable sign posts. If one becomes involved with practical Kabbalah and practices meditating on various mystic matters, there is a clear danger of his becoming disoriented. The mind is a delicate thing. *Sefer Yetzirah* was fully aware of the danger of esoteric knowledge, but also of its magical allure.

It is often difficult to shut one's mouth from talking. It may be impossible to stop the heart from thinking. Therefore, even though the *Mishnah* instructs us not to talk or think about forbidden esoteric matters, it recognizes the difficulty in stopping this thought process.

It has been said of Yitzchak Luria that the reason he produced so little written material himself was that each new thought provoked within him so many associations that he could not hope to collect all his thoughts together and put them on paper. Kabbalah is that way. It is extremely heavy in symbolism and associations. Each idea can be interpreted in many ways and is related to many other ideas. Thus, the associations seem to "run" by themselves in the mind of the Kabbalist, with his having very little control over them.

There are several notable points in this *Mishnah*. First, the phrase "shut your mouth" in Hebrew is "*Blom Picha.*" The *Sefirot* are called "*Blimah*," "nothing." According to some authorities, *Blimah* has the same root as "*blom*" (shut). They offer this *Mishnah* as proof that the reason they are called *Sefirot Blimah* is because one should practice restraint in talking about them. It is merely coincidental, according to this theory, that the word *Blimah* can be broken into two words, "*Bli Mah*," which means "of nothing."

The *Mishnah* speaks of the thought of the heart and speech of the mouth. Interestingly, the Vilna Gaon explains thought and speech formation as a five-step process as follows:

Talking breaks downs into Will, Idea (*Machashavah*), Thought (*Hirhur*), Sound, and Speech. The *will* is the first desire to speak. The *idea* is the pondering of what to say before the specifics are formed. *Thought* is the formation of the speech in the mind. *Sound* is in the throat, before it enters the mouth. Finally, *speech* is the cutting of the letters. The *will's* place is in the soul, the *idea* is in the brain, *thought* is in the heart, *sound* is in the throat, and *speech* in the mouth. These correspond to the five *Partzufim*.[59]

The element of *will* is, of course, associated with the first *Sefirah*, *Keter*. The *Partzuf* of *Keter* is *Arich Anpin*. Of this first *will*, explains the Gaon, nothing is understood. *Idea* is associated with Wisdom, whose *Partzuf* is *Abba*-Father. While something must be understood to form an idea, the essence of the idea is not clear at this point. The third *Partzuf*, that of *Imma*-mother (associated with the *Sefirah Binah*), is where the speech is formed, though it remains hidden until it reaches the mouth and is actually spoken. *Binah* plays an important role in *Sefer*

Yetzirah, for the main topic in the latter chapters of the book is the Hebrew letters. These letters are formed in *Binah*. Finally, the sound is in the throat, which corresponds to *Zair Anpin* (made of the six extremes), and speech itself is in the Female of *Zair Anpin* (the *Partzuf* of *Malchut*). The Vilna Gaon thus associates the two elements mentioned in this *Mishnah*, Thought and Speech, with *Binah* and *Malchut*. These are "feminine" *Sefirot*. They are often known in *Partzuf* form as "Mother (*Imma*)" and "Daughter (*Barta*)." This is reminiscent of the talmudic statement, "Ten measures of talking descended in the world and women took nine of them."[60]

The *Mishnah* continues, "But if your heart runs, return to the place." What place? Several possibilities have been put forth. It is known that God is often referred to in religious circles as "*HaMakom*" ("the place"). I do not know when this practice began. The earliest explanation of which I am aware is in *Sefer HaBahir*, which states that God is called *HaMakom* because "the world is not the place of God but rather God is the place of the world" (Genesis 1:27). Thus, "return to the place" can mean that we should return to God and not transgress the prohibition against studying the forbidden. This explanation was adopted by Moses Botarel.[61]

Another approach was adopted by Rabbi Moses HaGoleh. He says that we speak of someone filling his father's "place." Here it means reaching his level. Thus, "return to the place" would mean that one should return to the previous level of thought, and not concentrate on what is beyond human capacity.[62]

The Vilna Gaon explains the term *place* by quoting the answer that Moses was given when he asked to see God's honor. He was told, "You will be unable to see my face, for man will not see me and live. And God said, behold, there is a *place* with me, and you will stand on the rock. When my honor passes I will place you in the crack of the rock and will cover you with my hand till I pass" (Exodus 33:20–22). The "place" in this *Mishnah* is a reference to the place where Moses was put. It is a place that limits man's exposure to God. The advice of the *Mishnah* is to limit one's study of God to what can be understood, for even Moses was so limited.[63]

The *Mishnah* tells us that even the angels limit themselves in this manner, as it states in Ezekiel 1:14, "The angels run and return." Maimonides states in his works that angels are "*Skolim Nevdalim*" (bodiless intelligences).[64] There are ten levels of angels, each separated from the others not by anything physical, but only by how much they can grasp intellectually. Man at his best can only reach the level of the lowest angelic group, the *Ishim*. Maimonides claimed that Moses did in fact attain this level of understanding. This *Mishnah* is saying that while the angels attempt to comprehend more, they cannot pass their level. They try to glimpse more but are unable to understand, so they return to their former place. Man, whose intelligence is much less, certainly cannot hope to understand God as He really is.

Not all rabbinic authorities agree with Maimonides' conception of angels. First, angels are described in the Bible as physical beings. In Ezekiel they are pictured as having wings. In Genesis, angels appeared to Abraham in the shape of men. They were created to do physical tasks, to destroy Sodom, to save Lot. However, even according to those who believe that angels have a physical aspect, they are still considered to be above man in understanding, yet unable to comprehend God's essence.[65]

The *Mishnah* concludes, "On this matter a covenant was executed." That is, man has a covenant with God not to concentrate on what is above his understanding. Saadia Gaon takes the term *covenant* (*brit*) quite literally. He implies that the *brit* of circumcision is meant to remind us that we should not go further than we are permitted in spiritual contemplation. It was given to Abraham, according to Saadia, since Abraham is believed to be the author of *Sefer Yetzirah* and the one who first propagated this type of knowledge. It will be remembered that an earlier *Mishnah* said that there are two covenants, that of the tongue and that of the penis. They are similar in that the *brit* is an agreement to limit indulging in one's passions. The passion to think and speak forbidden thoughts must be curbed, as must the sexual passion.[66] Rabbi Eliyahu of Vilna makes a somewhat similar point. He states as follows:

> A covenant is when a person has a beloved from whom he does not want to separate, but who cannot stay with him. He gives the beloved an object that he loves and they are tied together through that object. Thus, the covenant is a promise that through the object he will not separate from the beloved. That is why the phrase is used "to cut a covenant," because he cuts from himself an object that is dear to him and gives it to his beloved. So is it with the rainbow, and the Torah and circumcision. They are all intermediates between God and Israel. All of this is because it is impossible to understand God himself.[67]

It is interesting to note the attitude of Judaism toward *intermediaries*. Maimonides strongly condemns praying to angels or dead people because they are *intermediaries* and man must address God directly. On the other hand, we find that God Himself provides *intermediaries*, such as the "rainbow, Torah, and the covenant of circumcision."[68] They are physical representations of spiritual ideas. Because of man's intellectual limitations, intermediaries are allowed in the cognitive realm. In the realm of emotion, however, man is not so limited, and he himself can pour out his heart directly to God. Therefore, prayer may not be through intermediaries.

The Ramban and Raivad take a different approach to the *Mishnah*'s use of the word *covenant* (*brit*). In Kabbalah, the term *brit* is generally taken as a reference to the *Sefirah* of *Yisod*. *Yisod* is in the middle, between kindness and strictness. It is said that *Yisod* unites the opposites above it. Therefore, it is representative of unity. Through this *Sefirah* we can indirectly think of the ultimate unity, that of the Infinite. While we have no understanding of the Infinite essence in itself, we can have some understanding of its manifestations, which is represented by *Yisod*.[69]

THE FIRST *SEFIRAH*—GOD'S WIND

Sefer Yetzirah, Chapter 1, Mishnah 9

מ"ט עשר ספירות בלימה, אחת רוח אלהים
חיים ברוך ומבורך שמו של חי
העולמים קול ורוח ודבור וזהו רוח הקדש:

Ten *Sefirot* of nothing, One—The spirit of the living God, blessed and blessed is the name of He who lives forever. Sound and wind and speech, this is the holy wind.

The description of the *Sefirot* in *Sefer Yetzirah* is unique. The standard names of the *Sefirot* are not used, and it is often debatable which *Sefirah* is being referenced. As is generally the case when there are several reasonable alternatives, each has its adherents.

This *Mishnah* is exceptionally difficult to translate. The translation depends to a large degree on the commentary chosen to follow. Often, various theories seem equally plausible, yet each would result in a greatly different translation.

About the location of this *Mishnah* in *Sefer Yetzirah*, Ramban says, "Until now we spoke of the number of *Sefirot*, their measure, their aspect, their unity, and their hidden nature. This *Mishnah* now begins to explain what they are."[70] This *Mishnah*, together with the four that follow, describe each of the ten *Sefirot*. Chapter 1 then ends with a final paragraph that summarizes the previous *Mishnayot*.

According to the majority of commentaries, the *Sefirah* that is being described in this *Mishnah* is Wisdom. While it is not the highest *Sefirah*, it is the beginning of creation. Remember, *Keter* is called *Ayin*, (nonbeing), while Wisdom is called *Yesh* (being). The act of creation is bringing being into existence from nonbeing. Thus, creation begins with Wisdom, which is also known as "the beginning," as the first verse of the Torah says, "With the Beginning God created the heavens and the earth."[71]

The *Pree Yitzchak* notes that the term *living God* (*Elohim Chaim*) is generally taken in Kabbalah as a reference to *Binah*. The "spirit" of the living God is thus the *Sefirah* above it, which is its cause and its spirit. This is the *Sefirah* of Wisdom.[72]

Strangely, the Raivad reaches the same conclusion from an opposite hypothesis. He states that the term *living God* refers to *Keter* rather than *Binah*. The *Mishnah*, according to him, is referring to the spirit that is drawn from the living God, that is, to the *Sefirah* below. The *Sefirah* below *Keter* is *Chachmah* (Wisdom).[73]

A completely different approach is taken by the Vilna Gaon. His Kabbalah is based on the Lurian school, which has many higher worlds with full sets of *Sefirot*. The highest is that of *Adam Kadmon*, which represents the first emanations after the *Tzimtzum* (the withdrawal of the Infinite light to create the space for creation). The *Malchut* of this *Adam Kadmon* is known as *Atika Kadisha* and is a complete *Partzuf*. Though this is the lowest *Sefirah* in *Adam Kadmon*, it becomes part of the *Keter* in the world below *Adam Kadmon*. Thus, as the initial aspect of *Keter*, it represents the first *Sefirah*. The Gaon says that this *Atika Kadisha* is what is referred to in this *Mishnah* as *Sefirah* number one.[74]

The next phrase in the *Mishnah* is extremely difficult. The Hebrew is "*Baruch U'Mivorach Shemo.*" In modern Hebrew there is no clear-cut difference between the terms "*Baruch*" and "*Mivorach.*" They both mean *blessed*. However, Kabbalists do see a difference in meaning. This difference is reflected in the *Zohar*, as we shall see later.

In the words of the Ramban, "*Baruch* from the power of High (*Keter*), *Mivorach* from the power of Justice (*Malchut*)."[75] That is, "*Baruch*" means that the *Sefirah* of *Chachmah* (Wisdom) is blessed from the top and "*Mivorach*" means it is also blessed from the bottom.

The Vilna Gaon says something similar, yet different. He says, "'*Baruch*' means through itself, which refers to spiritual flow from the higher levels downward. '*Mivorach*' means through the righteous, which is from the lower levels up."[76] In order to understand the Gaon, it is important to remember that he thinks that this *Mishnah* is speaking about *Atika Kadisha*, an aspect of *Keter*. As *Keter* is the highest *Sefirah*, there is none higher that can bless it. It is thus blessed through itself, for it holds the greatest spirituality (blessing) of the *Sefirot*. However, it is blessed from beneath. Through the righteous, *Malchut* is blessed, and through it, *Atika Kadisha*. This is as the *Zohar* states, "There is no awakening above, without an awakening below." The initial stimulus to arouse heaven's blessing is based on man's deeds below.

There is a famous part of the *Zohar* about this very subject that is recited in Sephardic prayers on Friday nights when one prays without a quorum of ten. Since one may not say the prayer "*Barchu*" without a quorum, this is considered a substitute. It reads as follows:

> Blessed (*Baruch*) is God the blessed (*Mivorach*). This is the source of blessings from the fountain of life and the place from which liquid emerges to water all. Because it is the fountain, according to the secret of the sign of the covenant, it is called *HaMivorach*, for it is the well of the pit. When (the blessing) reaches there, the pit fills, for its waters never cease.[77]

Rabbi Yehuda Leib Ashlag, in his extensive commentary on the *Zohar* known as *The Ladder* (*HaSulam*), states that "*Baruch*" refers to *Binah* (specifically, to its *Yisod*), the "sign of the covenant" refers to the *Yisod* of *Zair Anpin,* and the "pit" is *Malchut*. Thus, while the details in Ashlag's commentary are somewhat different than what the Ramban and Vilna Gaon say in *Sefer Yetzirah*, the same basic idea is present. *Baruch* is from above, *Mivorach* from below.[78]

The *Mishnah* continues by telling us that what is blessed is the name of "*Chai Olamim.*" I translated this phrase "He who lives forever." The rationale is that since the word "*Chai*" means "Life" and "*Olamim*" means "Worlds," together the phrase seems to be saying, "He who lives for the worlds," that is, forever. There are, however, other possibilities.

One theory is that what is meant by "*Chai Olamim*" is *the life of the worlds*. That is, the early *Sefirot* give life to the lower worlds of *Sefirot*. This approach was taken by Ramban, who states, "Since it is from there (*Chachmah*) that blessing and life come, it is called '*Chai Olamim*.' It is life and it contains what is needed to give life to the worlds."[79]

The Vilna Gaon simply states that the phrase "blessed is the name of *Chai Olamim*" means "blessed are all the *Sefirot*." They are blessed through this first *Sefirah* (according to him, *Atika Kadisha*), which provides the nourishment to the entire tree of *Sefirot*.

The *Mishnah* concludes with a phrase rather than a sentence, "Sound and wind and speech, this is the holy wind." The elements that are needed for speech are the plain wind (which is emitted while speaking), the uncut sound, and finally the articulated speech. These elements are often discussed in the *Zohar* and are especially important to *Sefer Yetzirah*, whose main focus is on language and the role of the alphabet in creation. Nonetheless, the connection of the phrase to this *Mishnah* is unclear, and at first it appears to be tacked on for no apparent reason.

Let us begin with the Ramban, whose mystical style always presents a challenge. He states:

> *Sefer Yetzirah* has told us that the first *Sefirah* is called Wind, which is called Sound. Its intermediate, which expands and proceeds, is also called Wind, and the cutting of its parts that separates into letters is called Speech. And even the Sound and the Speech are called Wind as the *Mishnah* explains, "This is the holy wind." *Holy* is the strength of High (*Keter*), which prepares to receive from the Infinite, and from it is the Wind that is called "the holy Wind," and from it come the holy letters and holy language.[80]

It is clear that the Ramban is answering the question of what this phrase is doing in our *Mishnah*. Our *Mishnah* is about the first *Sefirah*, which is called Wind. This phrase is likewise entirely about wind, even though it mentions sound and speech as well, for they too are aspects of wind. The final phrase is, thus, justifiably part of the *Mishnah*.

Speech originates in this first *Sefirah*, since it is Wind. Even the more developed aspects of speech, like sound and articulation, have their source here, though they do not emerge from potential until later. The Ramban continues that the ultimate source is even higher than the *Sefirah* of Wisdom. The source is from *Keter*, which receives it from the Infinite. The word *holy* alludes to the fact that the wind's origin is in *Keter*, which receives it from above. Hebrew is called the Holy Tongue, according to this, because its elements are from the highest sphere.

This certainly lays a strong foundation for the rest of *Sefer Yetzirah*, which is concerned with language. The Holy Tongue is from the Infinite and is thus a divine language rather than a synthetic one. The world could only have been created in this language. The English words "Let there be light" would not have created light, only the Hebrew "*Yehi Or*."

The Raivad, in his commentary to the next *Mishnah*, criticizes those who say that Hebrew is called the Holy Tongue because it has no direct terms for the sexual parts of the body, but rather alludes to them using terms that are not intrinsically sexual. He ends by saying, "We do not want to even answer this argument, but indeed, the truth is clear."[81]

In Kabbalah, the notes with which the Torah is read (commonly known as *Trup* in Yiddish, *Taamim* in Hebrew) are associated in Lurian Kabbalah with the *Sefirah* of *Keter*. This association apparently preceded the Yitzchak Luria, for the Raivad interestingly writes in *Mishnah* 10:

> This is the secret of the notes of the Torah: they enter and exit with the sound of song, like the secret of the high priest entering the inner sanctuary (which represents *Keter*) with golden bells and pomegranates dangling from his garment, so that he will be heard. From this you can learn the secret of the holy spirit (wind) that descends on the prophets through song in order to bring joy, as it is written, "And now bring me a musician" (2 Kings 3:15). This is the spirit that is emanated from *Keter* through the Long Path until it reaches *Tiferet*, which is called Wind, and this is the secret of Prophecy that is emanated from *Tiferet* to *Atarah* (*Malchut*) and this is the secret of "mouth to mouth" (Numbers 12:7).[82]

The important points of the Raivad are that the term *holy* and the concept of Torah notes are connected to the highest *Sefirah* and with the process of prophetic inspiration.

It should be pointed out that "the holy wind" has often been translated as "The Holy Spirit" by Jews and "The Holy Ghost" by Christians. The connection between wind and spirit is obvious, and spirit is often a proper translation, since *Sefer Yetzirah*'s main interest is not the physical world. The word *ghost,* however, in its usual modern meaning, is certainly not what was meant. Nor did the Christian scholars who originally used this term mean it in that sense.

A final thought from the Gaon of Vilna. The three elements of speech—wind, sound, and articulated speech—are the source for the three basic elements that will be discussed later—Wind, Water, and Fire. These are represented by the three Hebrew letters *Aleph, Mem,* and *Shin.* They are known as the "Mother" letters, and they constitute an important topic that will be discussed later. They represent, in fact, the first of the three books with which the world was created. Thus, this *Mishnah* is laying the foundation for future chapters. It is tracing the evolution of the elements of creation.

While all three elements are in the first *Sefirah,* the letters are not articulated in thought until *Binah* and do not proceed from potential into actuality until even later. This all applies to the World of the Emanations. The physical human, it will be recalled, was created in the image of God and is thus thought to undergo a parallel process.

THE SECOND *SEFIRAH*—WIND
FROM WIND

Sefer Yetzirah, Chapter 1, Mishnah 10

מ"י שתים רוח מרוח חקק וחצב בה עשרים
ושתים אותיות יסוד שלש אמות ושבע כפולות
ושתים עשרה פשוטות ורוח אחת מהן :

Two, Wind from Wind. He engraved and hewed in her twenty-two letters of foundation, three mothers, seven doubles, and twelve single ones, and wind is one of them.

The *Sefirah* referred to in this *Mishnah*, according to the majority of commentators, is *Binah*. In the words of the Ramban, "Just as smell is emanated from smell and flame from flame, so is emanated wind from wind."[83] Emanation implies that the result comes into existence without the cause losing anything in the process. You can light a second fire without lessening the original fire. Spirit can inspire spirit without losing itself. The term *wind* in this *Mishnah* is used in the spiritual sense: it implies *spirit.*

According to the Vilna Gaon, this *Mishnah* is referring to *Arich Anpin,* the lower aspect of *Keter,* rather than to *Binah.* The Bible says, "The wind of the Lord hovers on the face of the water" (Genesis 1:2). The Gaon says, "This (second *Sefirah*) is the wind on the face of the water upon which the wind of the Lord hovered."[84] As we will see, the water is the third *Sefirah.* The wind upon the water is the second. The upper wind that rides upon the wind that is on the water is the first. The Gaon's approach has the strength of beginning from the highest *Sefirah* (*Keter*), the one that is usually considered to be first. It seems to present several difficulties, however. First, he is speaking of *Partzufim* rather than plain *Sefirot.* Second, the *Sefirah* of *Keter* is represented twice, since it has two associated *Partzufim.* These difficulties can perhaps be addressed. *Partzufim* are *Sefirot,* but they are reconstructed. Each contains a full set of *Sefirot* within itself, which enables it to tolerate more of the light from above. Counting *Keter* twice does not really represent much of a problem. The first aspect that we counted of *Keter,* that known as *Atik,* is really the *Sefirah* of *Malchut.* In fact, it replaces *Malchut* in the Gaon's count. *Atik* means the *Malchut* of the world above. When *Atik* is counted, the *Malchut* of the lower world is not. Thus, there are still only ten *Sefirot.* Since *Atik* is really from a higher world, it is, of course, counted first.

The *Mishnah* continues that he "engraved and hewed" the twenty-two letters of the alphabet in her. The *Mishnah* says "in her." This implies that this second *Sefirah* is feminine. In Kabbalah, terms of gender are relative. "Masculine" generally means "giving" and "feminine" means "receiving." Thus, a higher *Sefirah* that gives blessing to a lower one is masculine with respect to it, but feminine with respect to *Sefirot* above it.

Of all the *Sefirot,* two are referred to as feminine more than any of the others. *Malchut* is one. It always receives, since it is the lowest *Sefirah.* It is often called *the bride* or *the daughter* for this reason. The other feminine *Sefirah* is *Binah*, the one probably referred to here. It is feminine for several reasons. It is the mother of the seven lower *Sefirot*, the father being Wisdom. It receives the unformed seed from Wisdom. It gives it form during its "pregnancy," in the terminology of the Ari.[85] After birth, it nurses the children, *Zair Anpin* and *Malchut*.

According to this, *Sefer Yetzirah* is here speaking of the formation of the letters in *Binah*. The letters comprise the body of the *Sefirot*. This in many ways parallels pregnancy, where the details of the child are formed. The *Mishnah* uses the phrase, "engraved and hewed." The Gaon says, "*Engraved* means chiseling the letters on a tablet and removing the extra matter. *Hewed* means cutting the letters out of a tablet like you would cut rocks from a mountain."[86] The idea is that sometimes the letters are formed by what is left on the tablet, at other times by what is removed. (The next *Mishnah* expands somewhat on this idea.)

According to the Ramban, as well as the Raivad, who follows the Ramban's approach, the terms *engraved* and *hewed* are two different levels of coarseness. *Engraved* means a fine thin etch, while *hewed* means thicker. In the Ramban's words, "The first wind (Wisdom), which is thin, only has a slight impression. However, that which is graspable (*Binah*) can be spoken of in terms of 'engraving,' and according to its thickness can even be spoken of in terms of 'hewing,' that is, that one hews and splits the parts of the wind. And with what? With its letters."[87] The Ramban seems to be saying that neither term can apply to Wisdom, for that is not graspable at all and can only be said to obtain a "slight impression." However, there are different levels of coarseness in *Binah* itself. "Hewed" applies to the thicker.

The Raivad's comments constitute an explanation of the Ramban. He says:

> The second *Sefirah* is two because it includes the higher *Sefirah* also. It is a thick wind that comes from a thin one, since all that evolves from cause to cause thickens. For instance, the separate spheres are thin and fire is thicker than them, and wind is yet thicker, and water ever more so, and earth is the thickest of all.[88]

He is implying that neither the term *engraved* nor the term *hewed* applies to the *Sefirah* of Wisdom itself. Nonetheless, "engraved" applies to the aspect of Wisdom that is within the *Sefirah* of *Binah*, and this is what the Ramban meant when he spoke of levels of thickness within *Binah*.

The *Mishnah* tells us that the twenty-two letters of foundation are what were engraved and hewed in *Binah*. They are called letters of foundation, according to the Raivad, because "they are the foundation for all that exist."[89] In the Ramban's words, "They are the foundation of the building built from them. Even though the building is comprised of the rolling of letters that sum up to 231 gates [to be discussed in Chapter 2], their root is just these."[90] Another reason for their being called letters of "foundation," according to the Vilna Gaon, is that they all gather in the *Sefirah* of Foundation (*Yisod*). It is here that the three lines of *Sefirot* merge (see Appendix A). It is Foundation that sends their light to *Malchut* and the worlds beneath.

The Ramban explains why there are twenty-two Hebrew letters. He simply states, "Ten for the fingers, ten for the toes, and the two mediators."[91] It will be remembered from *Mishnah* 3 that the tongue and the penis "mediate" between the fingers and the toes, respectively. Remember the theory that Hebrew is the language of reality while the other languages are merely translations. Thus, the twenty-two letters are powers and have various similar natural manifestations. In the world of biology they manifest in the fingers, toes, and so on.

The *Mishnah* continues by telling us that the twenty-two letters contain three mothers, seven doubles, and twelve singles. This was discussed in *Mishnah* 2.

The *Mishnah* ends by telling us that "wind is one of them." Which one? The Vilna Gaon answers that it is the *Aleph*. *Aleph* stands for the Hebrew word *Avir* (air). It represents the highest *Sefirah* and is the source for the other letters.[92] Incidentally, *Aleph* is composed of a slanted *Vav* in the middle, with a *Yud* on top and on the bottom (א). The numeric total of these component letters is 26 (see Appendix B). The Gaon points out that in addition to *Aleph*, there are twenty-six other Hebrew letters, if we include the five duplicate end letters (*sofeyot*). Thus, just as Keter is the source for the other *Sefirot*, so the *Aleph* is the source for the remaining twenty-six letters.

The Ramban comments in his usual mystic style on the phrase, "Wind is one of them." He states, "Like the letter *Shin* of *Tefillin*, which sticks out of the skin but is itself only skin."[93] That is, the letters in the *Sefirah* Wind are made of Wind. They are not different than the *Sefirah* itself. They constitute the body of the *Sefirah*.

The Ramban, in his commentary on the next *Mishnah*, says, "What is called in the first power *paths*, is called in the second *Sefirot*, and in the third *letters.*" By the three powers the Ramban means *Keter, Chachmah,* and *Binah.* Paths, *Sefirot,* and letters are different manifestations of a single basic entity.

The Raivad explains this as follows:

> Those letters are themselves the Paths. The *Mishnah* indeed said "wind is one of them" to tell you that as the *Shin* of *Tefillin* is itself the skin as well as the letter *Shin* and there is no difference between them, so does that Wind itself consist of the letters, and they are themselves also the Holy Wind (Wisdom) that comes from the holy place that is called the high crown (*Keter*), which is the holy of holies."[94]

Note that *Tefillin* (phylacteries) are made such that the letter *Shin* appears on the head phylactery. It is made from the same piece of skin as the remainder of the phylactery. The *Shin* stands for God's name, Shaddai.

THE THIRD *SEFIRAH*—WATER FROM WIND

Sefer Yetzirah, Chapter 1, Mishnah 11

מי"א שלש מים מרוח חקק וחצב בהן תהו
ובהו רפש וטיט חקקן כמין ערוגה
הציבן כמין חומה סככם כמין מעזיבה:

Three, Water from Wind. He engraved and hewed in them *Tohu* and *Bohu*, mud and clay. He engraved them like a type of garden bed. He stood them up like a type of wall. He put them above like a covering.

The wind contains moisture. This moisture is the water that is separated from the wind to form the third *Sefirah.* An often-quoted verse used to show the association of wind and water is from the Book of Psalms, which states, "He will blow his wind and water will flow"

(Psalms 147:18). A related thought is incorporated into the *Shmoneh Esrei* prayers: "He blows the wind and brings the rain."

One of the main points of *Sefer Yetzirah* is that there is a parallelism between the worlds. What exists in the upper realms generally has a correlate in the physical sphere. Amazingly, this is even true in reference to God Himself. He is unique in the heavens, and the nation Israel is unique on earth. This idea has been included in the Sabbath *Minchah* prayers: "You are one, and Your name is one, and who is like Your nation Israel, one nation on the earth." The last *Sefirah*, *Malchut*, is called *Knesset Yisroel* (the Congregation of Israel). Israel is thus considered an aspect of God, as the *Zohar* says, "God and Israel and the Torah are all one." This is emphasized in the often-used term for *Malchut*, *Shechinah*, whose root means "dwells" and implies that "God's presence that dwells on earth."

Most commentators agree that the *Sefirah* being described in this *Mishnah* is *Chesed* (Kindness). The first two, according to these commentators, were *Chachmah* (Wisdom) and *Binah* (Understanding), already described in previous *Mishnayot*. The Vilna Gaon, of course, disagrees. He is consistent with his theory that the two *Partzufim* of *Keter* were the first two items described already. Therefore, the *Sefirah* being described here, in his estimation, is *Chachmah* (Wisdom).

Water in Kabbalah has the attribute of kindness. While the term is usually used in regard to the *Sefirah* of *Chesed* (Kindness), it can be applied to any of the *Sefirot* of the right line (i.e., right side of the heavenly man) or to the entire right line as a group. The term can thus refer to either *Chachmah* or *Chesed*.

The Raivad puts it as follows: "They are the waters of kindness, as it is said, 'And the Wind (spirit) of God hovers on the face of the water' (Genesis 1:2). After He congealed the waters and froze them and strengthened them to the point that they returned to be like sapphire[95] and firmaments, thereafter he hewed in them *Tohu*."[96]

Water is kindness because it gives life; it allows plants and animals to live and grow. The Raivad says that the reason the waters were frozen was to enable them to retain the shapes and letters (which liquid cannot do). This, of course, does not mean that the quality of kindness was lost, but rather that the quality of firmness was added. This was essential for a durable creation.

At this point we come to an especially difficult part of the *Mishnah*. The second verse in the Torah states, "And the earth was *Tohu* and

Bohu and darkness was on the face of the water" (Genesis 1:2). The usual translation for the phrase "*Tohu* and *Bohu*" is chaos. *Chaos* does not, however, sufficiently explain the individual words. Rashi on the Torah states: "*Tohu* means astonishment and desolation, for a person would be astonished and desolate at the emptiness in it (the world). *Bohu* means emptiness and void." Rashi is saying that the root of *Tohu* is the Hebrew word *To'eh*, which means "astonishment." He does not explain the source of the word *Bohu*, but merely uses the translation of *Targum Onkeles*. As we shall see, the *Midrashim* as well as the Kabbalists greatly expand the meanings of these words.

Sefer HaBahir differentiates between *Tohu* and *Bohu* as follows:

> Rabbi Berechia said, what does the verse mean "And the earth was *Tohu* and *Bohu*?" What does it mean "was"? That it already was! What is *Tohu*? Something that confounds man. Then what is *Bohu*? Rather, it was first *Tohu*, but it returned to *Bohu*. And what is *Bohu*? A thing that has substance, for it is written "*Bohu*"—Bo Ho—he is in it.[97]

The *Bahir* seems to be objecting to interpretations like those of *Targum* and Rashi. The problem with these approaches is that they do not differentiate sufficiently between *Tohu* and *Bohu*. According to the *Bahir*, *Bohu* has more substance than *Tohu*, in the same manner that *Binah* is not as "thin" as *Chachmah*. The *Bahir* goes on to say that *Tohu* preceded *Bohu* and that the term *Bohu* implies that "he is in it." This is perhaps the first source of the story of "the death of the kings," which is prominent in the *Zohar* and the writings of the Ari. The Torah in Genesis 36 describes kings of Edom who ruled and died. This is taken in Kabbalah to mean early *Sefirot* (*Olam HaNikudim*), which were unable to stand the strength of the Infinite's light and subsequently broke. The term for the world in which this occurred is known in Lurian Kabbalah as "the World of *Tohu*." This is based on the section of the *Bahir* just quoted. There were first *Sefirot*. Then they broke and became *Tohu*. Then they were returned to *Bohu*, that is, fixed. They were made into *Partzufim* and thus had "substance." What is implied by the word *Bohu* is that "he is in it," that is, the Infinite's light is in them, and they can contain it.

The Ramban explains *Tohu* and *Bohu* as follows: "*Tohu* is the potential for creations that make no impression. *Bohu* is the potential for creations that make an impression."[98] *Chachmah* (Wisdom) was previously described as an unformed mass, the shapes and impressions being formed in *Binah*. *Tohu* is thus being associated by the Ramban with *Chachmah* (Wisdom) and *Bohu* with *Binah* (Understanding).

There are at least four known versions of *Sefer Yetzirah*. In several places they vary slightly. In a different version, *Sefer Yetzirah* describes *Tohu* as a green line and *Bohu* as unknown boulders. Using this variant text, the Raivad says, "*Tohu* is the green line that surrounds the world. This is the line that separates between the upper and lower (world)." He states further:

> From here you should understand that the word *Tohu* used here does not refer to desolation and not to emptiness and not to ruins but rather to thin creations impressed in the unformed mass of Wisdom, that no name or word describes and certainly not speech. Since no name or word applies, therefore they are called with a word of "astonishment" and are called in a negative manner *Tohu*. *Bohu* are unknown stones, from which water flows to the world. . . . They are also hidden, but not as much as the first ones called *Tohu*, since the beings of *Tohu* are hidden both in their own right, and also from the aspect of the observer.[99]

Perhaps the main point of the Raivad is that *Tohu* is a positive entity and is associated with Wisdom. It is called *Tohu* only because nothing can be understood of the thin impressions that begin to form in it. *Bohu* is also hidden, but to a lesser degree. It is associated with *Binah*, and since *Binah* is the source of the water that becomes the *Sefirah* of *Chesed*, *Bohu* is described as stones that contain water.

It should be noted that the *Midrashim* bring many other theories of *Tohu* and *Bohu*. Some don't seem very connected with the story of Genesis at all. For instance, the *Midrash Rabbah* states that *Tohu* refers to the Kingdom of Babylonia and *Bohu* to the Kingdom of Media. While it is sometimes hard to know exactly what the *Midrash* intended, it is clear that most of these explanations are based on the negative aspect of the words *Tohu* and *Bohu*. The Ramban's and Raivad's approach is special in that it takes these terms to connote positive rather than negative concepts.

Regarding the next phrase in the *Mishnah*, "mud and clay," the Ramban says, "The dirtiness of the water is called *Refesh* (mud) and its thickness is called *Tit* (clay) and all of this reaches the Water through

the power of the Wind."[100] *Binah*, which an earlier *Mishnah* called
Wind from Wind, is the source for what we find in the water (that is,
in *Chesed*). The solid earth and the formed letters originated in the
wind and water. The process in the spiritual sphere is similar to the
physical process. The Ramban is not just referring to physical mud and
clay, but to spiritual materials, the matter of the *Sefirot*.

The Gaon of Vilna writes as follows: "At this point *Sefer Yetzirah*
explains the creation of the earth, which was created from water. *Tohu*
and *Bohu* represent *Chachmah* and *Binah*. Mud and clay at the sea
bottom represent the Six Extremes and *Malchut*. Mud is the mire from
which birds of the sky were created. From clay were created the
animals of the land."[101] The Gaon here emphasizes that terms used in
Sefer Yetzirah often refer to both the world of the *Sefirot* and to the
physical world.

The *Mishnah* concludes, "He engraved them like a type of garden
bed. He stood them up like a type of wall. He put them above like a
covering." According to the Ramban, the word *them* refers to "the
mud and clay and the letters." He goes on to explain that the *Mishnah*
describes three different aspects of the letters by comparing them to a
garden bed, a wall, and a covering. He says, "One receives, and one
protects, and one acts like a roof. So are the letters. Some of them
receive. Some are received. And some are upright like a wall." The
Mishnah is thus describing the creation of the letters and their shapes.
One may assume parallel implications to the creation of the other
elements of the spiritual and physical universes.

This *Mishnah* is a bit longer in other versions of *Sefer Yetzirah*. One
version concludes as follows: "He poured on them snow and made
dust, as it is written, 'To the snow he said be thou earth' (Job 37:6)."
The Vilna Gaon sees this as a reference to *Mayim Duchrin* ("Masculine
Water," i.e., semen), that which the male gives to the female. It
represents blessing and abundance. It becomes congealed in the creation process to form a child. It becomes dust, for man is made of dust.
It also forms the letters. The Gaon concludes that the original source
for this *snow* is the inner part of Wisdom (the *Sefirah*'s *marrow*, in the
kabbalistic idiom). He goes on to discuss another type of water, the
lower waters, which are known as *Mayim Nukvin* ("Feminine Water"). Aside from the obvious biological meaning of fluid secreted
during procreation, it also refers to the evaporation of rain from the

earth. The Gaon describes it as "the Wisdom that is on the earth." As
I said before, Kabbalah does not have a single meaning, but rather
many. It is an associative endeavor.

THE FOURTH *SEFIRAH*—FIRE
FROM WATER

Sefer Yetzirah, Chapter 1, Mishnah 12

מי"ב ארבע אש ממים חקק וחצב בה כסא
הכבוד שרפים ואופנים וחיות הקודש
ומלאכי השרת ומשלשתן יסד מעונו שנאמר
עושה מלאכיו רוחות משרתיו אש לוהט :

**Four, Fire from Water, He engraved and hewed
in her the throne of honor, the Seraphim, the
Ofanim, the Holy Animals [angels] and the ministering angels, and from the three of them He
established His abode, as it is said, "He makes
his angels the winds, His ministers flaming fire"
[Psalms 104:4].**

The ability to extract fire from water through magnification of the
sun's rays was understood many years before the invention of lenses
and telescopes. Saadia Gaon, who lived in the tenth century, describes
it as follows:

> Do not be amazed how it is possible to obtain fire from water. Even
> through the small intelligence of man it can be done, the extracting of
> fire from water. How? By bringing a pure glass vessel from the type of
> glass called brik in Laaz, fill it up with water, and put it in the sun in the
> month of *Tamuz* when the sun is strong. Place the chaff of flax around
> the vessel and fire will come from the water in the vessel.[102]

The point Saadia is making is that if man can do this in the physical world, certainly God can do its equivalent in the world of the *Sefirot*. The equivalent to fire in the upper worlds is *Gevurah* (Courage). In the words of the Ramban, "Fire from water means the strength of courage that is drawn from *Chesed* (Kindness), which is compared to fire that is from water, and from the strength of this fire He hewed the throne of honor and the rest of the structure."[103]

Thus, the entire process was as follows, in the words of Saadia: "After He hung the water in the air, He shined radiance from His benevolent and awe-inspiring radiance, and shined in the water, and from the strength of that radiance fire emerged."[104] As usual, most of the commentaries follow the Ramban's theory that the reference here is to the *Sefirah* of *Gevurah* (Courage). The Vilna Gaon, consistent with his approach in previous *Mishnayot*, disagrees and feels the reference is to *Binah*. However, he emphasizes the similarity between *Binah* and *Gevurah*. Much of what applies to one is applicable to the other, and thus the difference in his approach does not result in major conceptual differences. The *Mishnah* says that "He engraved and hewed in her." "Her" is a reference to *fire* (*aish*), which is feminine in Hebrew. *Gevurah* (Courage) is feminine in a way, too, since it is part of the left side—strict law. In this manner it is similar to *Binah*, which likewise is to the left.

Hewed in fire were the following five entities: the throne, Seraphim, *Ofanim*, Holy Animals, and ministering angels. The Vilna Gaon says, "The five items correspond to the letter *Hey* in the Tetragrammaton." That is, it is generally agreed that the first *Hey* in the Tetragrammaton refers to *Binah*. The Gaon holds that this *Mishnah* is about *Binah*. The fact that five items are mentioned strengthens his case.

It is certainly not at all clear to what "the throne of honor" is referring. Among the proposals put forth by the commentators are:

1. *Binah*—It is beneath Wisdom, and therefore a seat to it. Wisdom is called "honor," since it contains the Paths (*Netivot*), and the numerical value of *Netivot* (paths) and *Kavod* (honor) are equal. (See Appendix B.)[105]
2. *Tiferet*—The *Otzar HaShem* states that it is a chair for what is above and is itself called honor. That is, it is a chair since it is the main *Sefirah* of the Six Extremes, upon which *Binah* rests.
3. *Malchut*—It is often referred to as a chair for the upper *Sefirot*.

4. *Briyah*—The world below the World of the Emanations is considered its chair. The Aramaic term "*Cursayah,*" "the chair," is used constantly in the *Zohar* to refer to this lower world, the World of *Briyah*.

5. The four Holy Animals (the angels described in Ezekiel, Chapter 1)—This theory is brought by the Raivad as follows:

> The throne of honor is the four Holy Animals, and they have the face of man, the face of a lion, the face of an ox, and the face of an eagle. Included in them is all that lives, each according to its level. There are ten groups of angels, each one similar to the Animals.[106]

The four Holy Animals are often associated with the World of *Briyah*. This would make option 5 above the same as option 4. According to the Vilna Gaon, the Animals are from the world below *Briyah* (that is, from the World of *Yetzirah*, the third of the *Zohar*'s four worlds of *Atzilut*, *Briyah*, *Yetzirah*, and *Asiyah*). Nevertheless, he admits that their root is the World of *Briyah*, and thus they are indirectly that which carries the divinity, its *throne*. (See the Introduction to this volume for a discussion of the four worlds.)

It seems unlikely that the Raivad meant to imply that *Yetzirah* is the throne, for it is not directly beneath the World of Emanations. Incidentally, the fact that there are ten groups of angels immediately makes them candidates for association with the ten *Sefirot*. Commentators do, in fact, associate the groups with specific *Sefirot*.

The *Mishnah* mentions certain specific angelic groups and not others, perhaps because it wanted exactly five groups. The groups are not mentioned in order of importance. According to tradition, angelic groups differ in their intelligence levels. The Raivad lists them in order of intelligence, whereas the *Mishnah* does not.

The *Mishnah* continues, "From the three of them He established His abode." The three cannot refer to the items just listed, for they are five. The commentators seem to agree that "three" refers to Wind, Water, and Fire, discussed in the previous *Mishnayot*. These three are the basic elements. Earth is a fourth element that is not as elementary as these three. It is formed from the impurities of the water, after it is evaporated by the fire.

The "abode," according to the Gaon, refers to the *Sefirot* above *Zair Anpin*, those that are above time. This fits in well with his theory that

Wind, Fire, and Water refer to the three highest *Sefirot* of *Keter*, *Chachmah*, and *Binah*.

The *Mishnah* concludes with proof from the Bible: "He makes his angels the winds, his ministers flaming fire" (Psalms 104:4). This verse from Psalms mentions winds (plural). *Sefer Yetzirah* also spoke of more than one wind. Remember, *Sefirah* One is Wind and *Sefirah* Two is Wind from Wind. The verse also mentions fire. What it doesn't mention is water. However, the commentators are fast to point out that water is mentioned in the chapter from which this verse comes— "He roofs his heavens with water" (Psalms 104:3). The *Mishnah* chose the verse that had most of the elements, assuming we would find the missing water nearby.

The Gaon stated in a previous *Mishnah* that Wisdom was the water above the firmament. He says here that Fire (*Binah*) represents the sphere of fire beneath the firmament. He continues:

Therefore, *Chesed* (Kindness) is called water for it is from *Chachmah* (Wisdom), and *Gevurah* is called fire, for it is from *Binah*. The firmament between them is the *Sefirah* of *Daat* (Knowledge) which mediates. . . . It is the inside of the seven (lower) *Sefirot* and is their life. It is from fire and water. Where they meet, there the firmament is mixed. Similarly, every pair of elements where they meet requires something between. So it is with the following categories: inanimate, plants, animals, and people. (The mediators are) the corals, the *Yedonim*, and the monkey.[107]

He explains here the closeness of the *Sefirot* of Wisdom and Kindness, and also of another pair, Understanding and Courage. The Gaon then tells us that where they meet is *Daat*, which is a mixture and constitutes the inner life of the lower *Sefirot*.

While merely tangential to our subject, his conclusion is quite interesting. He indicates that the link between inanimate matter and plant life is corals. The link between animals and people are the monkeys. There is also an intermediate between plants and animals. The Gaon says it is the *Yedoni*. In the Bible, we are commanded not to have "an *Ov* or *Yedoni*" (Deuteronomy 18:6). They are used for magical ceremonies, for talking to the dead. No one knows for sure what they are. Rashi says that he believes the *Yedoni* to be the bones of a dead animal that are able to speak when placed under the arm in a magical ceremony.[108] This doesn't quite fit. However, another tradi-

tion exists that a *Yedoni* is a manlike animal that is attached to the earth
with an umbilical cord. This attachment makes him vegetable-like,
and thus a good candidate for the link between animal and vegetable.
It is likely that this is what the Gaon had in mind.

THE SIX EXTREMES AND THE
STRUCTURE OF SPACE

Sefer Yetzirah, Chapter 1, Mishnah 13

מי"ג חמש שלש אותיות מן הפשוטות חתם
רום ברר שלש וקבען בשמו הגדול
יה"ו . וחתם בהם שש קצוות ופנה למעלה
וחתמו ביה"ו . שש חתם תחת ופנה למטה
וחתמו ביו"ה . שבע חתם מזרח ופנה לפניו
וחתמו בהי"ו . שמנה חתם מערב ופנה לאחריו
וחתמו בהו"י . תשע חתם דרום ופנה לימינו
וחתמו בוי"ה . עשר חתם צפון ופנה לשמאלו
וחתמו בוה"י :

He chose three letters from the singles, which
are the secret of the three mothers, *Aleph, Mem,
Shin,* and He put them in His great name, and
He sealed with them the Six Extremes. Five, He
sealed High, and He looked up, and sealed it
with the letters *Yud, Hey, Vav.* Six, He sealed
Bottom, and He looked down, and sealed it with
the letters *Yud, Vav, Hey.* Seven, He sealed East,
and He looked in front of Him and sealed it with
Hey, Yud, Vav. Eight, He sealed West, and He
looked in back of Him and sealed it with *Hey,
Vav, Yud.* Nine, He sealed South, and He looked
to His right and sealed it with *Vav, Yud, Hey.*
Ten, He sealed North, and He looked to His left
and sealed it with *Vav, Hey, Yud.*

The ten *Sefirot* in *Sefer Yetzirah* can be split into two groups. The first four correspond to the four classical elements as follows:

1. Wind—corresponds to earth.
2. Wind from Wind—corresponds to air.
3. Water from Wind—corresponds to water.
4. Fire from Water—corresponds to fire.

Only the first correspondence seems peculiar. There are various ways of associating this first *Sefirah* with earth. The simplest is based on the thinking of the Vilna Gaon, who says that the *Sefirah* of Wind contains an aspect of the preceding world, which is known as *Atik* (i.e., the *Malchut* of the world above). *Malchut* is referred to as "the earth" throughout the *Zohar*, just as *Tiferet* is called "the heavens." Thus, while it is thought of as *Wind* in its role as first *Sefirah* of the current world, it is the earth (*Malchut*) of the previous world.

After discussing the four *elemental Sefirot*, *Sefer Yetzirah* must now address the second group, that known as the Six Extremes. The Extremes complete the tally of *Sefirot* (to ten). There is a dispute as to which *Sefirot* comprise the Extremes. Many commentators, following the theory of the Ramban, feel the *Sefirot* of the Extremes are: *Keter*, *Malchut*, *Tiferet*, *Yisod*, *Netzach*, and *Hod*. These are not, however, the *Sefirot* that are generally referred to as the Six Extremes in the *Zohar* and in later Kabbalah. It is only because the elements of Wind from Wind, Water, and Fire are strongly associated in Kabbalah with *Binah*, *Chesed*, and *Gevurah*, that these commentators felt forced to conclude that the first form of wind referred to Wisdom, the *Sefirah* directly above these three. As a consequence, there was no room for *Keter* in the group, and so the commentators concluded that it had to be one of the extremes.

The Vilna Gaon, on the other hand, says the extremes are the usual ones found in the *Zohar*: *Chesed*, *Gevurah*, *Tiferet*, *Netzach*, *Hod*, and *Yisod*. According to him, the first two *Sefirot* in *Sefer Yetzirah* are *Atik* and *Arich Anpin*, the two aspects of *Keter*. *Atik*, of course, is the *Malchut* of the world above, and so *Malchut* (earth) is included in the ten *Sefirot* and completes the four elements.

The current *Mishnah* tells us that of the twelve single letters, three were chosen to seal the Extremes. These three letters were *Yud*, *Hey*, and *Vav*, the letters of which the Tetragrammaton is composed. They are known as the *Chotmot* ("Seals"). The Raivad says that the term "*Chotmot*" has two meanings: (1) completion; (2) knot. The *Sefirot* are "the completion of all existence," according to him, in their aspect of spheres that surround all. However, in their relationship to each other, the *Sefirot* of the Extremes are knotted together, and the bond is the three letters *Yud, Hey, Vav*.[109] Therefore, the *Mishnah* tells us that the Extremes were sealed, that is, bound together with the *spiritual glue* of these three letters.

Rabbi Moshe HaGoleh ties this to the talmudic statement that God is named *Shaddai* because "*SheOmar LeOlamo Dai*" ("He said to His world, enough"). That is, He told the world to stop expanding. The process of limiting the world is what the *Mishnah* means by the sealing of the extremes (i.e., the directions).[110]

The *three mothers* referred to by the *Mishnah* are the letters *Aleph, Mem,* and *Shin.* These are letters from the Hebrew words, *Avir, Mayim,* and *Aish* (air, water, and fire). These letters are also known as Rings. In contrast, the letters of the Tetragrammaton—*Yud, Hey,* and *Vav*—are called the Seals.[111] In a signet *ring*, the *seal* is part and parcel of the ring. It is created from the body of the ring. So are the Seals in this *Mishnah* (*Yud, Hey, Vav*) created from the very essence of the Rings (*Aleph, Mem, Shin*).

The Rings are the basic Elements, the Mothers, each representing one of the three columns of *Sefirot* in the "Heavenly Man." *Aleph,* standing for *Avir* (air), is the middle column, *Rachamim.* *Mem,* a letter of *Mayim* (water), represents the right side, Kindness. *Shin,* a letter from *Aish* (fire), is associated with the left side, Strict Law. In the world of the *Sefirot* these are the basic three elements. There is a fourth, also, earth, associated with *Malchut,* but it is derived from the first three and thus is not as elemental.

All creation stems from these three elements (called "*Emesh,*" which is how it would be pronounced if one formed a word using the first letters of the three elements—*Aleph, Mem, Shin*). The letters *Yud, Hey,* and *Vav* are a result of *Emesh,* for they contain the attributes of these "mother" letters.

The *Pree Yitzchak* tells us that the letters of *Emesh*—*Aleph, Mem,* and *Shin*—are in the first three *Sefirot.* The second group of letters, known as the seven double letters or *Beged Kafarta* (Bet, Gimel, Dalet, Kaf, Peh, Resh, Tav) belong to the seven lower *Sefirot.* Finally, the twelve single remaining letters are all associated with the *Sefirah* of *Tiferet*. Included in this group are the letters of the Tetragrammaton.[112]

We already know that the first three *Sefirot* are the cause for the rest of the *Sefirot*. In a similar way, the letters of *Emesh* are the cause for the rest of the letters. The first three *Sefirot* are known as being "in thought." The later ones are "in action." The same can be said of *Emesh* and the remaining letters. *Emesh* is in thought, and the rest are in action. We know God from His "actions," so the name we know Him by (the Tetragrammaton) is composed of letters from the "action" group. We have no knowledge of God as He really is, however, so there is no name referring to this aspect.

The Kabbalist Shlomo Alkabits, in his famous poem "*Lecha Dodi*," says, "That which is *in action* in the *end* is *in thought* in the *beginning*." This refers to the lower *Sefirot*, which were formed in the first three *Sefirot* and later emerged. So is it with people: our actions are first formed in thought (or should be) and only afterward are actually carried out.

The rabbis tell us that God first created the world with the attribute of strict law. He saw that the world could not continue to exist by strict law, so He gave it a partner, the attribute of mercy. This partnership is stressed by the letters in God's name: *Yud* is kindness and *Hey* is strict law. These attributes are derived from the antithesis of the elements of *Emesh*—Water and Fire. However, the *Yud* is not derived from the *Mem* (*Mayim*—water) alone, nor the *Hey* from the *Shin*. Each of the letters—*Yud*, *Hey*, *Vav*—are composites from all three letters of *Emesh*.

The Ramban says, "First He sealed in *Yud*, through the power of the letters *Emesh*. After He sealed in *Yud* the strength of the three, He returned and established each letter of them in a letter of the Name known as His Great Name."[113] The Ramban is saying that *Yud* alone was first given properties of all three letters of *Emesh*. It must be pointed out that when the letter *Yud* is spelled out in full (like the letter *b* would be spelled out in English *bee*), it is spelled *Yud* (י), *Vav* (ו), *Dalet* (ד). A *Hey* (ה) is composed of a *Dalet* (ד) with a small *Vav* (ו) under it. Thus, the elements of the other letters in God's name (*Hey* and *Vav*) were originally present in *Yud*. Since *Hey* refers to the left line, *Vav* to the middle, and *Yud* to the right line of *Sefirot*, and *Yud* contains the other letters, therefore *Yud* even by itself includes all three attributes of

Emesh. Of course, the *Yud* (Wisdom) eventually emanated the others as separate *Sefirot*, but this could only be because they were originally contained in the *Yud*.

Six arrangements of the letters of God's name (Tetragrammaton) are possible. Each combination was used to seal one of the directions (Extremes). They are as follows:

1. *Yud, Hey, Vav*
2. *Yud, Vav, Hey*
3. *Hey, Yud, Vav*
4. *Hey, Vav, Yud*
5. *Vav, Yud, Hey*
6. *Vav, Hey, Yud*

The Vilna Gaon explains that the first two arrangements begin with *Yud*, which is associated with the right side (Kindness). Therefore, they refer to *Chesed* and *Netzach*, the right arm and leg. The two that begin with *Hey* refer to the *Sefirot* of the left, *Gevurah* and *Hod*. The middle *Sefirot*, *Tiferet* and *Yisod*, are associated with the last two combinations.[114]

This approach cannot work for the Ramban, who says the first combination of *Yud, Hey, Vav* was used to seal *Keter*. *Keter* is in the middle column of *Sefirot* and should have been sealed with a combination beginning with *Vav* (the letter of the middle), according to the paragraph above. It works out well only for the Vilna Gaon, who says the first combination sealed *Chesed*. It all hinges on what the term "High" refers to in the *Mishnah*, *Keter* or *Chesed*.

The Ramban does not clarify his position very much, but is content to comment in his terse manner: "'He looked up' means to the high level, which is the upper side of the Six Extremes, and sealed it with *Yud, Hey, Vav*, that is, with *Chachmah*, *Tevunah*, and *Daat*. These letters are associated with the power of *Emesh* and they are called rings."[115] Just like the letters of *Emesh* represent the attributes of the three lines of *Sefirot*—Kindness, Mercy, and Strict Law—so do the letters *Yud, Hey,* and *Vav*. That the Ramban uses the term "*Tevunah*" rather than *Binah* and *Daat* instead of *Keter* is not problematic, since *Tevunah* and *Binah* are closely related, as are *Daat* and *Keter*. A little peculiar is the fact that he seems to be calling *Yud, Hey, Vav*, the rings, while most of the commentators clearly say the letters of *Emesh* are the rings. Perhaps the word "they" refers back to *Emesh* and not to *Yud, Hey, Vav.*

The Vilna Gaon explains *Emesh* and *Yud, Hey, Vav* as follows: "In the three first *Sefirot* the letters of *Emesh* (*Aleph, Mem, Shin*) are plain, each one is alone, but in the Six Extremes, each is composed of all three of *Emesh*'s letters, and are only different in how they are ordered (the different combinations above)."[116] It was previously explained that *Sefer Yetzirah* was meant to be interpreted on various levels. In this spirit, the Gaon concludes by saying the Six Extremes represent the following:

> In man, the hands, the feet, the body and the genital. They are the Spirit of man.[117] In the world, they are the Six Extremes of the world, that contain air, as was previously explained. In the year, they are the six moving celestial bodies, excluding Saturn (which is associated with the Sabbath, *Malchut*). In the worlds, the Extremes are the World of *Yetzirah*, which is Mattatron, the six orders of *Mishnah*.[118]

While much of the Gaon's statement is fairly clear, the end is somewhat difficult. The reason he associates the Six Extremes with the World of *Yetzirah* (the third of the *Zohar*'s four worlds—*Atzilut, Briyah, Yetzirah*, and *Asiyah*) is because *Keter* is associated with *Adam Kadmon, Chachmah* with *Atzilut*, and *Binah* with *Briyah*, so the next *Sefirot* should naturally be associated with the next world. Thus, the Extremes get *Yetzirah* and *Malchut* gets *Asiyah*.

Also interesting is the Gaon's mention of Mattatron and the six orders of *Mishnah*. The six orders comprise sixty-three volumes of Jewish law composed from 100 B.C.E. to 200 C.E. (the use of the term *Mishnah* in *Sefer Yetzirah* was borrowed from these six orders). The Extremes run the world. They are represented by the letters that have both strong and weak forms, because they change from one to the other in reacting to the world (i.e., they determine whether kindness or strictness should apply). Mattatron is known as the Prince of the World. He carries out the rulings of the *Sefirot*. He is thus associated with the World of *Yetzirah*.

The orders of *Mishnah* emphasize different aspects of Jewish law, just like the Six Extremes emphasize different attributes. Each order of the *Mishnah* can be associated with an Extreme. *Mishnah* represents law, and the Extremes represent administering the world justly. This is true for the Six Extremes in all the worlds, but especially in the World of *Yetzirah*. The World of *Yetzirah* is the third world of the four, just like *Vav* is the third letter of the Tetragrammaton. *Vav* has the numerical value six, and represents the Six Extremes in God's name. Just as the letters of the Tetragrammaton are associated with *Sefirot*, on a higher level they are associated with whole worlds. The third world, *Yetzirah*, associated with *Vav*, is thus the Six Extremes of the Worlds.

SUMMARY OF THE EMANATIONS

Sefer Yetzirah, Chapter 1, Mishnah 14

מי״ך אלו עשר ספירות בלימה אחת רוח
אלהים חיים ורוח מרוח ומים מרוח
ואש ממים ורום מעלה ותחת מזרח ומערב
וצפון ודרום :

These are the ten *Sefirot* of nothing: One, the Wind (Spirit) of the living God, and Wind from Wind, Water from Wind, Fire from Water, the High heights, Bottom, East, West, North, and South.

This *Mishnah* provides a summary of the ten *Sefirot*. The commentators try to explain why the repetition was needed. The Ramban says, "The reason he (the author) returned to explain this *Mishnah* was to make known that the Six Extremes are the main part of the building."[119] The Ramban goes on to explain that this building was built through the strength of the four letters of God's name (Tetragrammaton). These are the elements of creation. The Ramban does not make explicit why he thinks this *Mishnah* stresses the extremes. He then proceeds to tells us, "These letters are but the seals with which the extremes were sealed and through them the twenty-two letters spread in all things, from three to four and from four to five and so forth to ten. Anything that is in the first power, it should not be necessary to explain, spreads from there to ten."[120] All twenty-two Hebrew letters, not just the letters of the Tetragrammaton, are in the *Sefirot*. The letters of God's name are special because they are the seals. They tie the *Sefirot* together. They are the inner water that is uniform in all the *Sefirot*; only its appearance differs as it is viewed through the different vessels of the *Sefirot*. The seals are always from the same three letters.

Because the first three *Sefirot* contain the basic letters, *Emesh*, the Ramban begins describing "the spreading" with *three*, saying, "They spread from three to four." He ends that "anything that is in the first power, it should not be necessary to explain, spreads from there to ten." The first power is *Keter*. What it contains is eventually externalized in the development of the lower *Sefirot*. A similar process is true of the development of the letters. *Otzar HaShem* puts it this way: "The letters are an impression in the Elevated Crown (*Keter*), a potential in the second (*Sefirah*), and in actuality in the third. From there they spread from three to four and from four to five until ten."[121]

The Raivad, in a very strangely worded statement, says that the reason that this *Mishnah* was included was "to let it be known that just as all the *Sefirah* essences are found in the depth of thought, so are they also found in the essence of the *Sefirot*."[122] While this statement is more than a little cryptic, the message, nevertheless, comes through. All that is hidden in the first three *Sefirot*, the *Sefirot* of thought, eventually comes from potential into action in the lower *Sefirot*. Each of the lower *Sefirot* contains, in some manner, all the rest.

Finally, the Vilna Gaon gives a different reason entirely for this apparently redundant *Mishnah*. Until this point, says the Gaon, *Sefer Yetzirah* was discussing the ten *Sefirot* of *Zair Anpin*. This *Mishnah* is not a repetition, for it is not talking about the same *Sefirot*. It is instead discussing the *Sefirot* of the *Female* of *Zair Anpin*. It teaches that she, too, has a similar set of ten *Sefirot*.[123]

2

The Alphabet
of Creation

THE THREE LETTER GROUPS

Sefer Yetzirah, Chapter 2, Mishnah 1

פ"ב מ"א עשרים ושתים אותיות יסוד
שלש אמות שבע כפולות
ושתים עשרה פשוטות . שלש אמות אמ"ש
יסודן כף זכות וכף חובה ולשון חק מכריע
בינתים :

Twenty-two letters of foundation, three mothers, seven doubles, and twelve singles. Three mothers, *Emesh* [*Aleph, Mem, Shin*], their foundation is the Palm of Merit and the Palm of Guilt, and the Tongue of Decree mediates between.

From this chapter on, *Sefer Yetzirah* is mostly about the letters—the powers with which the world was created. The first part of this *Mishnah* already appeared in Chapter 1. It is repeated here because it addresses the three letter groups—*Emesh*, doubles, and singles. These groups will be the main topic in the chapters that follow.

Chapter 2 of *Sefer Yetzirah* deals with the twenty-two letters of the *Aleph Bet* as a unit. After this *Mishnah*, no mention is made of the three groups for the rest of the chapter. This *Mishnah*, while technically a part of the second chapter, is really an introduction to the rest of the book. It lays out the plan for the book, which is to first discuss the letters in general, then to devote a chapter to each of the three groups. The *Mishnah* does go into some detail about the first group, *Emesh*, since it considers it the source for all of the letters.

The following list summarizes the structure of *Sefer Yetzirah*:

Chapter 1 —Concentrates on the *Sefirot*
Chapter 2 —Discusses the alphabet as a whole
Chapter 3—Deals exclusively with the first group of letters, *Emesh*
Chapter 4—Deals with the second letter group, the seven doubles
Chapter 5—Is concerned mainly with the twelve singles
Chapter 6 —Is about that which is derived from the letters, rather than the letters themselves, and about the powers, known as the *fathers*, that emerge from *Emesh*

The first part of the current *Mishnah* was explained in Chapter 1, *Mishnah* 2, where the wording first appeared. The *Mishnah* continues, "The three mothers, *Emesh*, their foundation is the Palm of Merit and the Palm of Guilt." It will be remembered that *Emesh—Aleph, Mem, Shin*—stand for the elements *Avir, Mayim, Aish* (air, water, and fire). Air mediates between water (merit) and fire (guilt). In the words of the Gaon from Vilna: "*Emesh* are the three (elements)—water, wind, and fire—and they are the three books (mentioned in Chapter 1, *Mishnah* 1) that dress the arms and tongue."[1]

Dressing in Kabbalah has special meaning. A garment is less important than the wearer. The wearer is the purpose the garment exists. That which is further out is less important than that which is central. Garments, though less important than the person they dress, are, nonetheless, closer to the wearer than the building in which he stands. The body in turn dresses the soul, which is more central yet. That which is dressed is always more important.

The arms and tongue in the quote above refer to the arms and tongue of the "heavenly man." They correspond to the *Sefirot* of *Chesed, Gevurah*, and *Daat*. The inner light of these *Sefirot* are dressed by the letters of *Emesh*. The letters are the material of which the vessels of the *Sefirot* are made.

The Gaon believed that the three books are comprised of the two tablets and the oral recitation of the ten commandments, that is, a tablet for each *arm*, and the recitation by the *tongue*.

Otzar HaShem states that the phrase "their foundation" could refer to either the foundation of *Emesh* itself, or to that of which *Emesh* is the foundation. He concludes that the *Mishnah* means the latter, because the foundation of *Emesh* itself is not the Palms of Merit and Guilt, but rather the *Sefirah* of *Keter*, which is the source of all the twenty-two letters.[2]

This is in accord with the Ramban, who writes in his usual cryptic manner: "*'Their foundation,'* since the only thing prior is something hidden, therefore, it mentions 'foundation' just to indicate the power that is derived from them, that they are based in that power, that through that power man realizes that they have power to found."[3]

The source prior to *Emesh* is hidden. The letters of *Emesh* are associated with the *Sefirot* of *Chachmah*, *Binah*, and *Daat*. The *Sefirah* before these is *Keter*, which, due to its closeness to the Infinite *Ein Sof*, is hidden. By hidden is meant that nothing of it is understood. Therefore, *Emesh* is seen as the foundation for that which is below, specifically, the scale of justice.

The Raivad explains how *Emesh* is the source for all the letters:

In truth, even the doubles and the singles exist from the mothers (*Emesh*). Similar to this is the way in which the wise physicians refer to the organs of man according to the elements, to the point that they called the brain with the name "the white moisture," and the spleen "the black." The liver they called "the blood," and the bile in the liver they called "the green." These relate to fire, earth, wind, and water. I do not believe that any man to whom God gave sense would think that the brain is merely the moisture alone or the bile from green alone, or the liver from blood only, or the spleen from black alone. Rather, each is composed of all of them, and so is it with all the organs of man, and so with the essence of the double letters and the singles, which were established through *Emesh*. Indeed, those that are called the singles are plain only in relation to that which is combined from them, or because they have no substitution (they do not have two forms, like the doubles).[4]

By "the Palm of Merit and the Palm of Guilt," the *Mishnah* means the two hands of the scale of justice. The right palm, of course, is associated with merit, the left with guilt. The tongue, or bar in the middle of the scale, mediates and decides the case.

I translated the words "*lashon chok*" as "the tongue of decree." The word "*chok*" often means a law or judgment. The Vilna Gaon says it comes from the verse, "He fed me my fitting portion of bread" (Proverbs 30:8). That is, "*chok*" means just the right amount, no more and no less. That is what justice is supposed to be.

Many of the commentators explain the scale as referring to *Sefirot*. The *Otzar HaShem* differs, however, and states:

> We already explained the Mothers as referring to the *Sefirot* themselves, and the Elements as that which emerge from them. Therefore, the foundation is that which are (in turn) produced from them. They are the Palm of Merit, which means the heavenly hosts that stand on the right and find merit, and the Palm of Guilt, the heavenly hosts that stand on the left and find guilt. They hold the side of *Chesed* (Kindness) and Fear (*Gevurah*) and are called merit and guilt.[5]

Although he says that hands of the scale mean the two groups of angels, he nevertheless associates each group with a *Sefirah*. These are the same *Sefirot* that the Ramban feels apply. The Ramban simply says, "Merit is *Chesed*, Guilt is *Gevurah*."[6] However, he appears to be speaking of the *Sefirot* themselves and does not mention angels.

Incidentally, the *Pree Yitzchak* states that the letters of *Emesh* are in the first three *Sefirot*. The Ramban, however, states that *Binah* is the mediator between *Chesed* and *Gevurah*. This is strange, because *Binah* is on the left side. However, because of its elevated position (above the seven lower *Sefirot*), it is considered Mercy nonetheless. It is the mother of the lower *Sefirot*, and thus has mercy for her children (*Rachamei HaEim*).

The Raivad makes the following interesting comment when discussing the scales of justice in our *Mishnah*:

> Just like we are commanded to worship our creator with the 613 commandments, so are each of the ten *Sefirot* commanded to worship the Creator of all and to elevate the King forever and ever. That is why we say in our blessings, "Blessed be He who sanctified us with his commandments," for the commandments were given from the world to the world. This is also the secret from where we know that God puts

on *Tefillin*, and the secret why the talmudic rabbis said, "How do we know God prays, because it is written 'I will make them rejoice in the house of *my* prayer'(Isaiah 56:7)." . . . Angels are also subject to punishment and reward. The angels who came to destroy Sodom were subject to [a punishment which consisted of] a postponement for 138 years, because they revealed the secret of the Lord and said, "We are destroying" (Genesis 19:13). They were pushed out of their place from then until the time of the ladder of Jacob our father, where it is written, "Behold the angels of God go up and down on it" (Genesis 28:12). Investigate the time between these events and you will find it to be 138 years.[7]

Some of the interesting points the Raivad is making are:

1. The *Sefirot* have commandments. As *Sefer Yetzirah* says in Chapter 1, "They bow before His throne."
2. The scales apply to the angels as well as to people.
3. The angels are open to punishment.
4. There is a parallelism between worlds. The commandments were given from one world to the other, but apply in all. Thus, not only do mortals lay *Tefillin*, but the concept even applies to God and the *Sefirot*. So can be explained the various other earthly-type deeds attributed by the sages to God. A parallel action (though certainly not exactly the same) takes place in the higher worlds as on earth.

The Raivad's remarks about angels being morally responsible for their actions is universally accepted by the rabbis. Maimonides says that angels are merely noncorporal intelligences who do not have free choice. It is widely accepted in Judaism that man is superior to the angels because of this. Without free choice, there can be no moral responsibility. Nevertheless, there are stories of fallen angels even in Judaism. For instance, we are told that "The Sons of God saw the daughters of man were good, and took wives from whoever they chose" (Genesis 6:2). The Torah then speaks of the *"nefilim,"* which literally means "the fallen." In his *Targum*, Yonatan ben Uziel states that these angels were "Shimchazoay and Uziel, who fell from the heavens."[8] It sounds as if they were punished.

The term *palm* (*kaf*), referring to a side of a scale, is not unusual in Hebrew. It appears in the *Mishnah* in *Ethics of the Fathers*, where it states that if Rabbi Elazar ben Arach was on one palm of the scale, and many other rabbis on the other, he would outweigh them in wisdom.[9] It also appears in the Torah in an interesting context. God told Moses that he may not see His face, and that when He passed by, He would cover Moses with His palm (Exodus 33:22). This is the same palm referred to in this *Mishnah*, that of the *Heavenly Man*.[10]

The *Mishnah* uses the term "Tongue of Decree." It not only refers to the tongue of the scale, but to the tongue of the mouth as well. In the first chapter the tongue was described as one of the two mediators. The *Pree Yitzchak* puts it this way: "The tongue of the mouth is the mediator between the palate and the throat, which are the secret of *Chachmah* (Wisdom) and *Binah* (Understanding), and *Daat* (Knowledge), which mediates between them.[11]

Some versions of *Sefer Yetzirah* conclude this *Mishnah* as follows: The three mothers, *Emesh*: *Mem* is quiet; *Shin* whistles; *Aleph* is *Avir* (Air), which mediates between them. The Vilna Gaon comments:

> *Mem* is from the lips and does not involve movement of the tongue and the voice, and so its pronunciation is with particular ease, without sound. Similarly, the attribute of kindness tolerates all, and remains silent, and so is water that rests in its place. The *Shin* is from the tongue in the teeth, and it whistles more than the other letters, and so does the sound and so does the attribute of Strict Law, which screams, and so the fire that does not rest a minute and burns everything. *Aleph* is air and wind, when the throat is open with wind alone, without the tongue, and this is related to the wind and also to the attribute of *Rachamim* (Mercy).[12]

In the above manner the Gaon associates the letters with the attributes and *Sefirot*. There is a natural, rather than an arbitrary, connection. From the quiet and easy sound of *Mem*, it is natural that it should be associated with kindness. The *Sefirah* of Kindness (*Chesed*) is often associated in kabbalistic writings with water, in particular, with water at rest. Fire, on the other hand, burns, cannot rest, crackles, and is thus appropriately associated with Strict Law. *Shin*, which makes a hissing sound like fire, is the likely letter to represent this. *Aleph* is all air. It is not harsh, nor is it as soothing as the hum of the *Mem*. It is *Rachamim*, in the middle.

GOD'S USE OF THE LETTERS

Sefer Yetzirah, Chapter 2, Mishnah 2

מ"ב עשרים ושתים אותיות חקקן חצבן
שקלן והמירן צרפן וצר בהם נפש כל
כל היצור ונפש כל העתיד לצור :

Twenty-two letters, He engraved them, hewed them, weighed them, interchanged them, combined them, and formed with them the soul of all that was created and the soul of all that will be created in the future.

This *Mishnah* begins to describe the creation of the letters. They were first engraved. *Sefer Yetzirah* already described this engraving in Chapter 1, *Mishnah* 11, stating, "They were engraved like a garden bed." The Ramban indicates that every letter was first engraved in *Binah*. Then the letters were hewed, that is, separated from each other. This is similar to the Ramban's earlier statement that *engraved* indicates a finer action, *hewed* a grosser.[13]

God weighed the letters. This is sometimes described, says the Ramban, as Him *weighing* the parts of the Wind. *Binah*, where the letters were first formed, has been described in an earlier *Mishnah* as a form of wind. The Ramban refers to a verse in Job to prove that God weighed the wind: "To give the wind a weight and water He fixed with a measure"(Job 28:25). As for interchanging them, we have already seen this described in the sealing of the Six Extremes in Chapter 1, *Mishnah* 13, of *Sefer Yetzirah*. The order of the letters was altered, which resulted in the different "seals." Finally, He combined them, attaching letter to letter to form the 231 gates.

The Raivad says that all the letters were engraved in each of the elements of *Emesh*—air, wind, and fire. To prove this he brings biblical verses that speak of engraving (*chakikah*) in reference to each. Then he discusses the "weighing" of the letters as follows:

After the letters came into being, He arranged them according to measure and amount. (He decided) which was fit to be the head of the

248 organs and 365 blood vessels, which would be fixed, and which would be mobile, for the letters have the wind of life, for the Torah (and its letters) is a tree of life for those who cling to them, and they are from the Spirit of the Living God.[14]

The Raivad is saying that the letters are literally alive. They are the life of the body and are associated with all the organs and vessels and give them life. There is a widely known theory in Judaism that the total amount of body parts—248 organs plus 365 blood vessels—equals 613, the same number as the amount of commandments in the Torah. The Torah is composed of the letters, which are alive, and thus it is a living Torah. So is the body. But just as the order of the letters is important in the Torah, so is the correct association of letters with organs important in people. The act of God associating the letters is what the *Mishnah* calls His "weighing the letters."

The *Mishnah* continues, telling us that God "formed with them the soul of all that was created." The Vilna Gaon comments, "With them everything was created, as it is said (Genesis 1:1), "with the 'Beginning,'" which refers to the Torah, the world was created. Likewise, it is written, 'All of them you created with Wisdom' (Psalms 104:24), which has the twenty-two letters."[15]

The *Midrashim* say that the term *Beginning* (*reishit*) refers to the Torah because of the verse in Proverbs, "God established me the *beginning (reishit)* of his way" (Proverbs 8:22). The speaker in this verse is the Torah, or what is basically the same, Wisdom, since the Torah is wisdom. Therefore, the twenty-two letters that compose the Torah and began to come into existence in the *Sefirah* of Wisdom, were the cause of the creation.

The *Mishnah* ends by telling us that not only what was created in the past was done through the *Aleph Bet*, but also "the soul of all that will be created in the future." The Gaon comments, "Everything was created in the six days of creation, as it is written in Ecclesiastes, 'There is nothing new under the sun' (Ecclesiastes 1:9). Only, God made them pass from potential to actuality [afterward]."[16]

The Gaon does not emphasize the fact that the *Mishnah* seems to be speaking about souls only. The Gaon speaks of "everything." This is because he had a slightly different version of *Sefer Yetzirah*. The text of the *Mishnah* in his version does not mention souls, but merely states, "God created with them (the letters) all the creation and all that will be

created in the future." This differs from the version of commentators
such as the Ramban and the *Pree Yitzchak*. The Ramban states, "He
created with them [the letters] the image of the soul of all that was
created, the spirits and higher souls that are in the world."[17] *Pree
Yitzchak* explains the end of the *Mishnah* as follows: "[The *Mishnah*
means] all the souls in this world and the souls that will be renewed in
the world to come."[18] The letters are living and are involved especially in the creation of life. This does not mean they have no other
role, for *Sefer Yetzirah* clearly indicates that they are involved in the
creation of the "world" and the "year" as well as the soul.

The term for *soul* used in this *Mishnah* is *"nefesh,"* a term that
generally refers in Kabbalah to the lowest of the five levels of soul (see
Appendix F). This is the part that all living beings have, without which
life could not exist. The Ramban clearly implies that we should not
understand the *Mishnah*'s reference to *nefesh* in this narrow context,
but that the *Mishnah* means the higher parts of the soul as well.

Another explanation is that the *Mishnah* is speaking of the broadest
group of entities with souls. Thus, anything possessing a soul, be it
even the lowest level of soul, is meant to be included. Exactly what
objects have souls, of course, is a matter of debate. For instance,
Maimonides has said that all the stars and planets, excluding the earth,
have souls, and so when the Psalmist says "The heavens tell God's
glory," he takes the verse quite literally.

THE LOCATION OF THE LETTERS

Sefer Yetzirah, Chapter 2, Mishnah 3

מ"ג עשרים ושתים אותיות יסוד חקוקות
בקול חצובות ברוח קבועות בפה
בחמשה מקומות אחה"ע בומ"ף גיכ"ק
דטלנ"ת זסשר"ץ :

**Twenty-two letters of foundation are engraved
in sound, hewn in wind, fixed in the mouth in
five places:**

(1) *Aleph, Chet, Hey, Ayin*
(2) *Bet, Vav, Mem, Peh*
(3) *Gimel, Yud, Kaf, Kuf*
(4) *Dalet, Tet, Lamed, Nun, Tav*
(5) *Zayin, Samech, Shin, Resh, Tzadi.*

The Raivad states, "The twenty-two letters are the basis for every utterance and action of the soul."[19] While it is clear that *Sefer Yetzirah* considers them the foundation for the entire spatial and temporal worlds as well, they have special meaning in reference to man's soul. This *Mishnah* concentrates on the operation of the letters of the *Aleph Bet*, specifically in man. *Pree Yitzchak* reminds us, however, that "they are the foundation of all the worlds."[20]

The letters manifest differently in speech than in writing. We have said previously that there are three letter groups, *Emesh*, the doubles, and the singles. In speech, however, the letters divide into five pronunciation groups. The letters of each group are articulated differently. One group of sounds is formed mainly by the lips, one by the palate, one by the teeth, one by the tongue, and one by the throat. In kabbalistic terminology, the sounds are formed using different *vessels*.

All the letters are first "engraved in sound and hewn in the wind." Rabbi Eliyahu of Vilna claims, however, that "there is a mistake in the text. It should read 'engraved in wind and hewn in sound.'"[21] To understand this, one must understand the difference between sound and wind. Wind is the plain air, upon which the letters are eventually impressed. It alone makes no sound, except when it blows against something else. The wind howls because it blows through the trees or a building or even against the earth. Sound, on the other hand, is caused by wind rubbing. Rabbi Eliyahu is saying that if wind is plainer than sound, it should be listed first in the *Mishnah*. It should be associated with *engraving*, a less coarse form of letter formation than *hewing*. Nevertheless, not all the commentators agree. Most of them stick to the regular version of the text. The *Pree Yitzchak* comments:

The letters are engraved in sound, which is the secret of *Binah*, which is at times called by the term "throat" from which the sound emanates.

Binah is called the great sound, the sound from which the coupling of Wisdom does not halt, as it states in the *Zohar* (*Parshat VaEtchanan*, page 261, side 1): "The first *Hey* in God's name is the great sound that does not stop, whose fountains do not stop for eternity. . . ." Hewn in wind refers to *Zair Anpin*. "Fixed in the mouth" refers to *Malchut*, which is the secret of the mouth, the word of God.[22]

Thus, according to the *Pree Yitzchak*, the order in the *Mishnah* is correct. Sound refers to the high *Sefirah* of *Binah*, wind to the lower *Zair Anpin*, and speech (mouth) to the last *Sefirah*, *Malchut*.

The language of the Ramban is difficult. He states, "*Sound* means the thinnest of the middle wind, and the letter is engraved in it."[23] He seems to be indicating that sound is one of the forms the wind can take. It is the form that eventually carries the letters. The Raivad, likewise, uses the Ramban's term *middle wind*, and, in a possible attempt to explain the Ramban, states:

Know that the wind pipe fills with wind drawn from the lungs. The wind that clings to the side of the rings of the wind pipe and the wind that beats on the rings and is drawn from ring to ring, ascending the rings and descending the vertebrae and ascending the rings (again), is that which makes the sound in the mouth of the heavenly man and (the earthly) man (as well). The *middle wind*, that which is not pulled by the rings, is called *wind*, and the wind that is sent to the mouth and splits and is cut to five organs which are the throat, tongue, palate, teeth, and lips, is called *speech*.[24]

According to the above, the term *middle wind*, in the Raivad's opinion, means the wind from the middle of the throat. While *sound* is made by the wind at the sides, the letters are impressed into the wind in the middle. It is this wind that is distributed to the five places of the mouth to form the five groups of letters.

Even though we appear to be analyzing human speech, we are really tracing the heavenly forces, the *lights* of God. If sound is from *Binah* and wind from *Zair Anpin*, the way to effect events based on these powers might depend on a knowledge of anatomy (both heavenly and earthly). Knowledge of the structure of heavenly speech, in theory, has practical as well as theoretical implications.

While legends abound as to miracles performed using *Sefer Yetzirah*, the book itself is not at all a manual of practical Kabbalah. It gives us information without giving us any practical uses. It implies that knowledge of God is a sufficient goal for studying Kabbalah.

The letter groups, says the *Mishnah*, are fixed in five places of the mouth. These groups are commonly known in Hebrew as *Chamishah Motzaot HaPeh* (the five utterances of the mouth). The first one (*Aleph, Chet, Hey, Ayin*) are the guttural letters, those that are formed in the throat. Current pronunciation treats both *Aleph* and *Ayin* as silent letters. Among many of the Sephardic Jews, however, *Ayin* is not completely silent. I do not know how *Aleph* was originally pronounced, but it is possible that it, too, was not totally silent either. The second group (*Bet, Vav, Mem, Peh*) are pronounced using the lips. The third are of the palate (*Gimel, Yud, Kaf, Kuf*), and the fourth (*Dalet, Tet, Lamed, Nun, Tav*) are the letters formed by the tongue. Finally, *Zayin, Samech, Shin, Resh,* and *Tzadi* are the letters that are formed through the teeth. It is a bit odd that *Resh* is in this group, for it seems more guttural than toothy. Perhaps its pronunciation originally was somewhat different than today. It is included in the group of double letters, *Beged Kafarta*, although in modern usage it has but one pronunciation.

The Ramban concludes his remarks on this *Mishnah*: "The *sound, wind* and *speech*, in which the letters are engraved, hewn, and fixed, are called *the holy wind (spirit)*."[25] That is, all three are aspects of this holy wind. It is holy, for its original source is the highest *Sefirah*. They represent God's influence and inspiration. They are the elements of both creation and prophesy. Consequently, prophesy is a form of creation, and conversely, the universe is but a prophetic dream.

The Vilna Gaon remarks, "*The five places of the mouth* is represented by the *Hey* in God's name. Also, the root of the letters are from the wind of God (*Binah*), which is [the first] *Hey*."[26]

Hey has a numerical value of five (see Appendix B). The Tetragrammaton has two *Heys*. The first is usually said to represent *Binah*. The Gaon says it is represented by a *Hey* because it is the source of the five letter groups. The mouth itself is generally associated in Kabbalah with *Malchut*. *Malchut* is feminine, and according to the Talmud, women talk nine times more than men. The second *Hey* therefore represents *Malchut*, and the pronunciation groups are called "the *five* utterances of the *mouth*."

THE GATES OF LETTERS IN THE
HEAVENLY SPHERE

Sefer Yetzirah, Chapter 2, Mishnah 4

מ"ד עשרים ושתים אותיות יסוד קבועות
בגלגל ברל"א שערים וחוזר הגלגל פנים
ואחור וזהו סימן לדבר אין בטובה למעלה
מענג ואין ברעה למטה מנגע:

**Twenty-two letters of foundation are fixed in
the sphere in 231 gates. The sphere goes forward
and backward. The following is a sign for this
thing—nothing is greater in goodness than pleasure [*Oneg* in Hebrew—*Ayin, Nun, Gimel*] and
nothing is lower in badness than plague [*Nega* in
Hebrew—*Nun, Gimel, Ayin*].**

This and the next *Mishnah* are about the 231 gates that the letters form
when combined. These gates play an important role in *Sefer Yetzirah*.
This *Mishnah* stresses that through the combining of letters, all combinations of sounds and words are possible. Also, by the transposition
of letters, opposite meanings may result.

The simplest way of understanding why there are 231 gates is as
follows: There are twenty-two letters in the *Aleph Bet*. If you combine
each letter with each other letter you have 22 × 21 letter pairs, for a
total of 462. For instance, you can combine *Aleph* with each of the
other twenty-one letters to form *Aleph Bet, Aleph Gimel, Aleph Dalet*,
and so on. The same procedure can be done with *Bet* to form *Bet Aleph,
Bet Gimel, Bet Dalet*, and so on. Continue this for all twenty-two
letters, and the result is 462 pairs of letters.

The 462 are redundant, however, since it is half duplication. That is,
it has both *Aleph Bet* and *Bet Aleph*. These are the same letters in reverse
order. The unique combinations are only 231, and these are called the
gates.

The *Mishnah* tells us that "the sphere goes forward and backward."
It has the combinations in both orders. The commentators point out

that the numerical value for the Hebrew word *Netiv* (Path) is 462, for
it is the paths that become the body of the *Sefirot*, and these are
composed of the 462 letter combinations. Not all commentaries agree,
however, that only two letters form a gate, nor do they agree on how
the alphabets are to be combined.

The *Otzar HaShem* explains some of the terms in the *Mishnah*. He
says they are called "gates" because the letters that belong in each
group remain separate from the other letters and do not mix. It is as if
they have their own separate residence, their own gate. A second
reason, he says, is that the word for "gate" in Hebrew is *"shaar,"*
which also means measure, as in the verse "They found in that year a
hundred measures (*Shaarim*)" (Genesis 26:12). Each pair of letters
receives from above only according to the measure that it is able to
hold. The *Mishnah* calls them "gates" in order to stress this idea.[27]

Sefer Yetzirah tells us that the letters are fixed in the *Galgal* (sphere).
The Kabbalists speak of the "sphere of the letters" as well as the
"sphere of the *Sefirot*." Both are composed of letters. Neither implies a
physical sphere, but, rather, they act in a "spherical manner." The
Otzar HaShem explains that the Hebrew word for sphere, *Galgal*, has
the same root as the verb "to turn." "*Galgal* is a term for things that
turn, whether they are alive, like the sky, as I have previously explained, or inanimate, like wheels of silver and gold."[28] The sky is
often referred to as *"Galgal HaRake'ach*—the sphere of the sky" and
appears to rotate. The sky is alive, according to Maimonides and
others, since the Psalms tell us, "The heavens tell God's glory"
(Psalms 19:2). The reference to wheels of silver and gold is taken from
the Book of Esther, chapter 1, which describes the party of Achash-
verosh. It says the decorations were elaborate and included *Glilei
Kesef*—wheels of silver. The word used here for wheels—*"Glilei"*—is
similar to the term *Galgal* used in the *Mishnah*.

Strangely, the *Otzar HaShem* does identify the sphere of this *Mishnah* with a physical sphere. Perhaps he means that the letters, which
certainly apply to the nonphysical worlds of the *Sefirot* above, also
manifest physically below. In any case, he states the following:

> Here [in *Sefer Yetzirah*] *Galgal* (sphere) is a term for the sphere of the
> constellations, which has many stars that are like letters, forward and
> backward, and this is the meaning of "from them" and "toward them."
> "From them" means the front, "toward them" the back. Whenever the

sphere is descending, it performs actions opposite to those when it is ascending. According to the opinion of the author of *Sefer Yetzirah*, all this is dependent upon the letters: according to the reversal of the letters, so will the effects be seen in the lower world.[29]

I believe the *Otzar HaShem* means to say that the letters in the physical world manifest in the form of the stars in the sky. Of course, they also have higher, nonphysical manifestations. Of the 462 letter combinations mentioned above, 231 are duplicates but in reverse order. They are known as the "back," while the 231 in straight order are called the front. The front combinations are used in building and creating. The back ones are for destruction. The letters identified with the stars in the sky must also have a way of distinguishing front from back. Light coming from them, the *Otzar HaShem* is saying, is considered positive, the front. Light going toward them is the opposite. Thus, even in the physical world, the concept of front and back letter combinations exists.

The Kabbalists often jump from explanations on a totally spiritual or conceptual plain to physical models. The problem with physical models is that it is often difficult to know exactly to what the allegory refers. This is especially true in Lurian Kabbalah, where the cosmology is massive, but its translation to meaningful spiritual terms is generally not explicitly made. Even when the Kabbalist does, in fact, mean something on a physical level, he also means to imply a parallel occurrence in the higher, nonphysical worlds. The Raivad's explanation of this *Mishnah* is of that nature, and his intent is not readily apparent. His remarks are interesting, nonetheless.

The twenty-two letters of foundation are fixed in the sphere of the *Sefirot*. Each letter is further inside than the other, until its center. The *Mishnah* says that there are actual letters protruding that are created by digging around, until, as a result, the actual letter stands out. The digging out of the sides around the body of the letters is what was referred to earlier [in the *Mishnah*], "He engraved them like a garden bed." This is because, like the plower in a furrow plows and digs on one side until the other side next to it rises [as a result], so was it with the digging around the letters, until the body of the letters came into being as an automatic result. Afterward, He took the letters and set them like a frame, one after the other, like a wall that is arranged stone after stone. So were the stones of the letters that were hewn from the body of the

sphere put one next to the other, until He surrounded the frame of the
sky with them like a wall. This is the secret of what is meant by saying
they are fixed in the sphere. A previous *Mishnah* said, "He covered them
like a roof." This means He covered the Paths of letters, for the Paths
from which the letters were dug, those Paths transverse the thickness of
the sphere, which is a distance of a 500-year walk, as we learned in the
Midrash Bereishit Rabbah and in the Talmud, Chapter *Ain Dorshin*. He
covered that path as with a roof. Thus, the number of alphabets are 231
that are fixed and protrude from the sphere.[30]

The Raivad appears to be jumping between the spiritual and the
physical realms. He begins by speaking of "the sphere of the *Sefirot*."
The *Sefirot* are spiritual entities. Later he mentions the "frame of the
sky" and the "thickness of the sphere." His terminology becomes
physical.

The Raivad expects the reader to understand that the various worlds
exist in parallel, and what is said of one applies to the others. Thus, the
width of the physical sphere (a 500-year walk) has a spiritual parallel.
He uses the terminology of the most convenient world to describe
what applies to all of them. The difficulty is that the parallel in the
other worlds is not always apparent. In this case, it is not at all apparent
what the "500-year walk" corresponds to in the spiritual realm.

The *Mishnah* continues, "The sphere goes forward and backward."
We already indicated that forward is creation and backward is destruction. The Raivad describes it as follows:

The sphere returns and revolves but the letters are fixed and do not
move from their place—those letters that He erected like a wall and
fixed in the sphere. The sphere returns from the side of kindness to its
creation, and back, from the side of strict law [*din*] and courage [*gevurah*]
to break and destroy. All mention of *face* is from the side of mercy, and
mention of *back* is from the side of law, from beneath. This is what the
Talmud says: "God coupled the attribute of mercy with the attribute of
law and created the world." Know that the order of letters from the
front side is opposite that of the side of *law* called the *back*. If you find
forward the letters *Aleph Lamed*, you will find on the side of strict law,
called *back, Lamed Aleph*, etc. From this you should understand that
some letters are fixed and are in the sphere, and some letters return and
roll and they are in the air of the spheres of the *Sefirot* (the insides), and
there is an order for creation and an opposite order for destruction.[31]

Thus, changes take place by two methods. One is the revolving of the entire sphere, which affects which fixed letters are dominant. The other is the rearranging of nonattached letters, which are in the air of the sphere.

The *Mishnah* ends, "The following is a sign for this thing—nothing is greater in goodness than pleasure [*Oneg* in Hebrew—*Ayin, Nun, Gimel*] and nothing is lower in badness than plague [*Nega* in Hebrew—*Nun, Gimel, Ayin*]." That is, we said the order of the letters decided whether they represent kindness or strict law, back or front. The *Mishnah* is here giving us an example, which is a way to remember this rule. There is a Hebrew word, *Oneg*, spelled *Ayin, Nun, Gimel*. It means pleasure. The same letters, rearranged, spell *Nega*, plague. Thus, two opposite results are obtained from the same letters. The first is the forward arrangement, that of the *face*, while the second is of the *back*.

We conclude this *Mishnah* with a thought from Rabbi Eliyahu of Vilna. He states that the forward combinations, those of the *face*, get increasingly smaller, while the reverse is true of the combinations of the *back*. Thus, going in the forward direction, the first combination is with *Aleph* and all the twenty-one letters after it. The second combination is *Bet* and all the twenty letters after it. This continues until we reach the last letter, which has no letters after it. Going backward, the opposite is true. The first combination is only the *Tav*, the last letter. The second is *Shin Tav*. This continues until the last combination that has the full twenty-two letters. The Gaon says that this is the secret of the "squaring" of the name, as well as "whispers" (or echoes). Let me explain.

Kabbalists are very fond of using the numerical values of letters, especially the letters of God's names. This can be done in many ways, but one of the ways is known as "squaring" (*rebuah*). For example, suppose a name is spelled ABCD and suppose A had the value 1, B 2, C 3, and D 4. The plain value of the word ABCD would be ten. Squaring would work like this: A + AB + ABC + ABCD = 20. The letter combinations grow. This is what happens with the letters of the *back*, which are associated with destruction. The *back* (*achorayim*) of the holy name is thus considered inferior to the *front*. Remember, God told Moses he could only see His *back*, not His *front*.

The opposite is true of *echoes*. They diminish. First it sounds like "Hello," then "lo," then "o." This is what happens with the letter combinations of the *front*. They become smaller. Thus the Gaon says,

"All the whispers diminish, like *Shebariri, bariri, riri, iri, ri.* So it is with all the whispers, since whispers rule the *back* and not the *face*, and when the face is mentioned they disappear."[32]

That is, while the original whisper *rules the back*, the diminishing syllables of the echo represents *"mention of the face."* This mention makes the whisper further disappear, since it cannot tolerate the *face*. It is like dark disappearing before light.

COMBINATIONS AND PERMUTATIONS OF LETTERS

Sefer Yetzirah, Chapter 2, Mishnah 5

מ"ה כיצד שקלן והמירן אל"ף עם כלם וכלם
עם אל"ף , בי"ת עם כלם וכלם עם בי"ת
וחוזרת חלילה נמצא כל היצור וכל הדבור
יוצא בשם אחד :

How did He weigh them and switch them? *Aleph* **with all of them and all of them with** *Aleph*, *Bet* **with all of them and all of them with** *Bet*, **and it returns back. Thus, it turns out that all creation and all speech emerge from one name.**

God weighed the letters as a doctor weighs the ingredients of a medicine. They were combined in exact measure. In some cases, a doctor may substitute one herb for another, if both have similar properties. In a similar way the letters were sometimes switched with each other.[33]

They were switched for another reason as well. It was necessary that they read backward as well as forward. This is because they must accomplish not just creation but also destruction. The world is based on what the medieval Jewish philosophers called "*Havayah VeHef-seid*," birth and decay. Both are needed for the world to exist. Thus, just like a house, the *sphere of letters* has two sets of gates, front and back. They are formed by the same letters, but in reverse order.

This is similar to what Kohelet tells us: "This to the level of this God created" (Ecclesiastes 7:14). The *Zohar* comments that *evil* was created with a structure similar to that of *good*. Whatever exists on the side of holiness (God) has a counterpart on the side of uncleanness (Satan). There are ten *Sefirot* of *Kedushah* (Holiness) and also ten of *Tumah* (Defilement).

Not that the back gate is evil in itself. Nor is decay. Decay is necessary for life. However, as a by-product, pain and suffering may arise. Thus, evil may, in a sense, derive its "nourishment" from it. The same is said of the *Sefirah* of *Gevurah*. There is no evil in the *Sefirot* of Holiness. Yet *Gevurah*, which represents Strict Law, is said to be the indirect cause of evil. The back gates, like *Gevurah*, are associated with Strict Law (*Din*).

While the *Mishnah* explains the construction of the 231 gates, it is light in detail. That is left for the commentators. It merely says, "*Aleph* with all of them [the letters] and all of them with *Aleph*." That is, each letter gets combined with all the others and vice versa. The process yields us the two sets of gates.

The first question we must address is what each gate holds. Some Kabbalists say that each holds a two-letter pair. Others say that each of the twenty-two letters yield twenty-one full alphabets. Together, these total 462, that is, 231 alphabets for the front gates, 231 for the back. In this configuration, each letter not only contributes to the 462 alphabets on the larger scale, but in addition, its own permutations are composed of 462 letter pairs. Of course, whether the gates consist of letter pairs or whole alphabets, there are numerous different ways in which they may be formed.

The first method is put forth by the early Kabbalist Shabbetai Donnolo, in his book *Chachmoni*. He states, "The gates are two-letter words." He provides the illustration found in Appendix G. Although he divides the gates into two groups of 231, one is not a mirror image of the other. Each group is composed of combinations from both the back and front. The total of 462 combinations contain all the forward and reverse letter pairs.

A different approach is taken by the Ramban and the Raivad. The Ramban says, "How did He weigh them and switch them? He did one against the other. The first was twenty-two letters, the second eleven, and so the rest. When He skips a letter from the right, He skips correspondingly from the left. How did He switch them? The letters are in their proper order to build, out of order to destroy."[34] The Ramban is saying that the first alphabet is full, the second contains every other letter (for a total of eleven letters), the third skips two letters, the fourth three, and so forth. This process takes place both in the back and front gates.

While it would seem that the Ramban did not think all the alphabets had full sets of twenty-two letters, the Raivad and *Otzar HaShem* disagree. As they usually follow the lead of the Ramban, it is possible that they do not think they are in conflict with him, but interpret him differently than I have. In any case, the Raivad explains the structure of the gates at length. Here is a portion:

> The first alphabet begins with *Aleph* in its usual order. Thus we have *Aleph* with *Bet*, and the rest of the letters with them. Then, skip one, and *Aleph* will come with *Gimel*, and eleven letters, each skipping one, will come with them. Then, begin with *Aleph* and skip two letters, and all the rest [of the letters will come] with them. Then skip three, then four, . . . then twenty, and what will remain is *Aleph Lamed* in the middle, in the combination of "*Aleph* with all of them." [This completes the combinations of *Aleph*.] Now, throw the *Aleph* to the back of the alphabet and follow the same procedure of skipping as you did with *Aleph*. You will be left with *Bet Mem* in the middle, with ten alphabets above and ten below. Then follow this procedure with *Gimel*, then *Dalet*, etc. through *Kaf* (the eleventh letter). This ends the forward combinations.[35]

The process is then resumed until the end of the alphabet, which forms the back gate.

There are several oddities in this excerpt. He says that the second alphabet is formed by skipping a letter throughout the entire alphabet. This would result in eleven letters total. Afterward, he seems to be saying, however, that there are eleven letters *in addition* to the *Aleph* and *Gimel*. Even if we assume that he meant eleven letters total, it still is very strange, for when discussing the other alphabets, he says, "The rest of the letters will come along," that is, the alphabet will have a complete twenty-two letters. In fact, later he says explicitly, "All the alphabets above and below the middle are of twenty-two letters, therefore they total 231, for 11 times 20 is 220, plus the eleven middle ones equals 231, and this is for *building*, and the same is true for *destroying*."[36] He appears to be trying not to contradict the Ramban, but as a result he is not consistent. I am not sure how he would explain himself.

Now let us look at the *Otzar HaShem*, whose method is similar to that of the Raivad. He is quite clear, however. He, too, has twenty-two sets of 462 letter pairs. One set is associated with each letter. The 462 letter pairs (924 letters) comprise forty-two alphabets (twenty-one straight, twenty-one with reversals). Each alphabet has a full set of twenty-two letters. Thus we have 42 × 22 = 924 separate letters. The set for *Aleph* is formed as follows:

1. The first alphabet is based on the normal order.
2. The second is the same, but the first letter pair is reversed (*Bet Aleph*).
3. The third starts with *Aleph*, but skips a letter and goes to *Gimel*. It then continues to the end, but then attaches the missing letter *Bet* at the end.
4. The fourth reverses the first pair to be *Gimel Aleph*, then supplies the missing *Bet*, and continues from *Dalet* to the end.
5. Then two letters are skipped, and the same procedure is followed; then three, and so on, until the end.
6. All of the above are just the combinations of *Aleph*. The combinations of *Bet* are similar, but the first alphabet begins with *Bet* and goes through to the end and then attaches the missing *Aleph*. This continues through all the letters. (See Appendix H.)

The *Mishnah* says, "It returns back," that is, each letter pair appears backward as well as forward. The Vilna Gaon says that actually only the first two letters of each alphabet comprise the gate. However, the other letters are still present. In modern computer terms, the gate is what is called the *key* or *index* field. The entire record has many additional fields, however.

The *Mishnah* concludes that the result of all this is that "all creation and all speech emerges from one name." The *Pree Yitzchak* states:

The *Mishnah* means that everything that has a form, even though there are no words to describe it, in addition to all the items that have words

to describe them, were formed in the letters of the 231 gates that turn in
the name *Yud, Hey, Vav, Hey* [Tetragrammaton] and the Tetragrammaton is in them. It is known that the upper garment is woven from the
231 front gates. The 231 back gates are also woven from the four letters
of the Tetragrammaton, and that is what is meant by "emerge from one
name."[37]

To understand this, you should be aware of the following concept,
in the words of the Vilna Gaon: "The thirty-two Paths are the ten
Sefirot [which are the secret of God's name] and the twenty-two
letters. The ten *Sefirot* that are God's name are the insides of the letters,
and are [also considered to be] the dots [vowels]. They are the life of
the letters."[38]

Thus, the alphabets are fueled by the name of God, which is their
inner life. Since any word can be formed by the letters, and the life of
all the letters is the one name of God (the Tetragrammaton), creation
and speech are the result of the one name of God. The *Mishnah*
mentions two classes of things that the letters produce—all creation
(*Yetzur*) and all speech. By *Yetzur* is meant that which has shape
(*Tetzurah*). By speech is meant that which is articulated, that is, that
which has clearly defined shape. Perhaps the intent is to exclude
unformed Wisdom, which precedes shape. Wisdom (*Chachmah*), in a
sense, precedes the letters themselves, which were formed after it, in
Understanding (*Binah*).

ESSENCE FROM CHAOS AND BEING
FROM NOTHINGNESS

Sefer Yetzirah, Chapter 2, Mishnah 6

מ"ן יצר מתהו ממש ועשה אינו ישנו וחצב
עמודים גדולים מאויר שאינו נתפש וזה
סימן צופה וממיר עושה כל היצור ואת כל
הדברים שם אחד וסימן לדבר עשרים ושתים
(מניינים) [חפצים] בגוף אחד:

> He formed *substance* from *Tohu*, and made *absence* into *being*, and He hewed great pillars from ungraspable air. This is the sign—He *observes* and *switches*. He makes all that is created and all things one name. A sign for this is *twenty-two objects in one body*.

He dressed primal unformed matter with a shape. This is the form of creation known as *Yetzirah*, and hence the name of the book. A more primitive form of creation, *Briyah*, is too abstract to be grasped, and is, therefore, not discussed very much. It involves the creation of the original amorphous matter (*heyuli*) from that which is so beyond comprehension that it is called nonbeing. The term *nonbeing* is often used in Kabbalah not to refer to something that truly lacks existence, but rather to that which is merely beyond human grasp. For instance, the *Sefirah* of *Keter* is often called *Ayin*, *nonbeing*. This *Sefirah* is associated with the very first creative process, which is known as *atzilut*, emanation.

While the word *atzilut* (emanation) properly refers to the *Sefirah* of *Keter*, it is also used in a more generic sense. The process of creating the entire Ten *Sefirot* in the World of Emanations is referred to as *atzilut* (emanation). This is because in the next lower world, the process used to create the Ten *Sefirot* was *Briyah*, below that *Yetzirah*, and finally *Asiyah*.

Exactly how the creation process differs in the four worlds is not terribly clear. All four terms (*atzilut*, *briyah*, *yetzirah*, and *asiyah*) certainly indicate an active, creative process. The commentaries do not go into much detail as to how these processes differ. It is clear, though, that *atzilut* is a finer, more spiritual method of creation than *briyah*, and *briyah* is in a like manner finer than *yetzirah*, while *asiyah* is the lowest method and directly results in the physical world.

While the term *atzilut* is generally recognized as having its own special meaning (emanation), the other three terms (*briyah*, *yetzirah*, and *asiyah*) are synonyms in Hebrew. They all are verbs associated with *creating*. Kabbalists believe, however, that no two words in the Holy Tongue are truly synonymous. Thus, different terms for creation must refer to somewhat different processes.

The four terms for creation—*atzilut*, *briyah*, *yetzirah*, and *asiyah*—are used in at least three distinct ways:

1. To refer to the various creation processes
2. To refer to the spiritual level of the contents of each of the four worlds
3. To refer to the relationships of the worlds to each other.

The *Zohar* associates the *Sefirah* of *Chachmah* with the highest world (Emanations—*Atzilot*), *Binah* with *Briyah*, *Zair Anpin* with *Yetzirah*, and *Malchut* with *Asiyah*. This is not to gainsay that each world has a full set of *Sefirot*. Rather, it means that the same relationship exists between the worlds as between the *Sefirot*. This is what is meant by the well-known phrase in the *Zohar*, "*Binah* nests in the throne (*Briyah*)."

Even though the *Yetzirah* process takes place in the *Sefirah* of *Binah*, it is not *Binah* but *Zair Anpin* that is associated with *Yetzirah*. This is because *Binah* just performed the act of creation that we call *Yetzirah*, but *Zair Anpin* was *produced* by it. In a similar manner, *Binah* itself is associated with *Briyah* and *Chachmah* with *Atzilut*.

This is confusing, because all the *Sefirot* of the World of Emanations were produced by emanation, the *Sefirot* of the World of *Briyah* were produced by the *Briyah* process, and so on. Within each world, however, there were relative differences. Thus, in the World of Emanations, the creation of *Zair Anpin* in relationship to that of *Binah* was like the relationship of *Yetzirah* to *Briyah*. Nevertheless, the overall method of creation of each of the worlds applies to all of the worlds' *Sefirot*.

The *Mishnah* begins, "He formed substance from *Tohu*." *Tohu* is an unusual word. It appears in the second verse of the Torah, "And the earth was *Tohu* and *Bohu*" (Genesis 1:2). *Tohu* has been at times associated with *Chachmah* and at times with *Binah*. The Raivad stated in Chapter 1 that *Tohu* refers to "the high Wisdom."[39] The *Otzar HaShem* likewise stated, "*Tohu* refers to the second *Sefirah*, *Bohu* to the third."[40] Even the Vilna Gaon and the *Pree Yitzchak*, who here clearly state that *Tohu* means *Binah*, seem to associate it more with *Chachmah* in Chapter 1, *Mishnah* 11. Everything in Kabbalah must be understood in context. The same words have very different meanings when the contexts are different.

The Hebrew word for *wonder* is *toheh*, which has the same root as *Tohu*. Based upon this, the *Pree Yitzchak* says as follows:

"He formed substance from *Tohu*, and made absence into *being*." This means from *Binah*, which is called *Tohu*, for man cannot study the first three *Sefirot*, as it is written, "Send away the mother bird [the first three *Sefirot*] but the children [the seven lower *Sefirot*]) *take for yourselves*" (Deuteronomy 22:7). That is, send it away from your thoughts and do not contemplate it. Therefore, man wonders (*toheh*, the same root as *Tohu*) about it because he cannot grasp anything at that level. From it was formed the shape of substance, of *Bohu* (*Bo Hu* means substance, as expounded in *Sefer HaBahir*). That is, the shape of the Six Extremes of *Zair Anpin*, which are associated with *Yetzirah*.[41]

According to the above excerpt, we are speaking of the creation of *Zair Anpin*, which is associated with the World of *Yetzirah*. It is this that is considered actual being, of which some understanding is possible. The first three *Sefirot* are those of the head, of thought, rather than concrete action and being.

The Vilna Gaon tells us that the phrase in the *Mishnah* that says that God "made absence into being" is not just a repetition of the previous phrase, "He formed substance from *Tohu*." The latter phrase speaks of forming—*Yetzirah*—and thus refers to *Zair Anpin*'s creation. The first phrase, however, speaks of "making," which is a clear reference to *Malchut*, which is associated with the World of *Asiyah* (Making).

The *Mishnah* continues, "He hewed great pillars from ungraspable air." The Ramban comments, "He hewed pillars—these are elevated items that all the world stands upon and is supported by. They are called 'great' because they are from the power of 'greatness' (*Chesed*), which constitutes the inside of sound, wind, and speech."[42]

By "world" the Ramban means *Zair Anpin*. The term *great* refers to the *Sefirah* of *Chesed* (Kindness), which is also often called *Gedulah* (Greatness). Speech is associated with *Malchut*, the female aspect, whose inner spirit comes from the *Partzuf* above her, *Zair Anpin*, whose first *Sefirah* is *Chesed* (greatness). See discussion of *Zair Anpin* in the Introduction.

The Raivad explains that the pillars are the seven lower *Sefirot*, as the biblical verse says, "He hewed their pillars seven" (Proverbs 9:1). Most of the commentaries agree. However, Moses Botarel says, "In the second *Sefirah* there are great pillars, that is, there are three pillars."[43] He goes on to identify them with the three letter groups— *Emesh*, *Beged Kafarta*, and the twelve singles.

The *Mishnah* says the pillars were created from air that cannot be grasped. Moses Botarel took this to mean the second *Sefirah*, *Chachmah*. Not all commentators agree.

The *Pree Yitzchak* says that the air that cannot be grasped is *"Daat,* which spreads inside *Zair Anpin."*[44] *Daat* is the inner being, the life, of *Zair Anpin,* and of *Malchut* as well, and thus it is the substance of which the seven pillars are made.

The Raivad is somewhat more obscure in his remarks. He says: "Air that cannot be grasped refers to the Spirit of God (*Binah*) that lives (*Chachmah*). They have 620 pillars of light, and each is a pillar and foundation for the world."[45] The 620 refers to what is called in Kabbalah *"Tarach Amudei Or"*—620 pillars of light. The numerical value of *Keter* is 620 (*Kaf* is 20, *Tav* is 400, and *Resh* is 200). The *abundance* that it passes to the lower worlds is sometimes referred to by this phrase. It is this light from *Keter* that ultimately forms the pillars of this world. The Raivad is saying that *Chachmah* and *Binah* have these pillars in the sense that they are the direct recipients of it. Thus we have at least three opinions about the pillars mentioned in the *Mishnah*— that there are 3 or 7 or 620.

The *Mishnah* continues, "This is the sign—He observes and switches." "He observes," says the Ramban, means that God looks "from beginning to end, [and determines] which is fit to be the first and which the end."[46] That is, the order of the alphabet is not random. There is a reason why *Aleph* is first and *Bet* second, and so on. While *Sefer Yetzirah* does not go into detail, there are *Midrashim* that do give reasons for the order of the letters. The Ramban continues, "'And switches' means that which was the first is switched to become the last and that which was the last is switched to become the first, in order to equalize, the high, the low, and the medium."[47] The order of letters in the back gates are opposite to those of the front. While the order of the letters is according to "worthiness," God also put a mechanism in the world that impels toward equality. This is a repeated theme in the Bible. God raises the humble and humbles the haughty. This mechanism is part of nature, in the sense that it was implanted in the process of creation.

The *Mishnah* continues that God "makes all the created and all things one name." One name is a reference to the name of God. The term *makes* means in the lower world, since the World of *Asiyah* (Making) is the lowest of the four worlds. There is a unity in everything, for they are all of one name. The name of God is the inner part of the gates of letters and unifies all creation. Nothing is independent. There is only one dominion, that of God.

The Ramban comments, "'He makes all the created'—in this way

He completes the natural, formed, and sentient creations. 'One name'—The power of the natural comes but from the sentient, and the power of the sentient is only from the intelligent and all is one root."[48] He speaks of completion because the word *Asah* (made) is used, meaning the last and lowest world. The *Sefirot* are composed of three groups: the highest three are call the intelligent ones (*Sichliyim*), the middle ones the sentient *Sefirot* (*Murgashim*), and the rest the natural ones (*Teviyim*). The word *natural* here refers to life-sustaining functions, *sentient* means feelings, and *intelligence* means thought. Although the lower forms of life were created first, the power to sustain them comes from the top. This is what the Kabbalists mean when they tell us there is an inverse relationship between the vessels and the lights of the *Sefirot*. One is created top down, one bottom up. The order of receipt of heavenly *abundance* is opposite the order of creation of the outer shells.

The Raivad comments, "The Adornment (a synonym for *Malchut*) is the name of God, *Tiferet*. She is the '*one name*' [mentioned in the *Mishnah*]. She does every action and new deed by means of these letters."[49] The Raivad is saying that *Malchut* is the *name* of *Tiferet*. A name describes the subject. *Malchut* is the embodiment of that which produced her and, in that sense, its name. In addition to the Raivad, the Ramban and most other commentators also associate the *Mishnah's* phrase—"one name"—with *Malchut*.

The *Mishnah* concludes, "A sign for this is twenty-two objects in one body." The sign is for the purpose of showing, according to the Ramban, that "the One is the foundation for the many and that there is naught outside the One." Interestingly, the *Otzar HaShem* states that there is an alternate version of the text that reads not "twenty-two objects in one body" but "twenty-two objects and [are] one body." That is, there is just one body, and the twenty-two objects are part of it. They are not independent. The objects are the ten fingers, ten toes, the tongue and the *brit*, as were mentioned in the *Mishnah* in Chapter 1. The letters are part of a unity, and not twenty-two separate powers.

An interesting theory of the Vilna Gaon ties Hebrew grammar to this model of the *Sefirot*. The *Sefirot* are symbolized by the fingers, which are five on each hand. The Gaon states:

> These twenty-two letters are the *Sefirot*, their vessels. The vowel dots are the insides of the *Sefirot*, since the vowels to the letters are like the soul to the body. As the *Zohar* explains, there are ten vowels (dots), five

long vowels (*Tenuot Gedolot*) and five short vowels (*Tenuot Ketanot*). This
is the "five against five" that was stated in the first chapter (*Mishnah* 3).
Therefore, a *dagesh* [dot to signify harsh pronunciation] or a *sheva* comes
after them, for they are from [the *Sefirah*] *Gevurah* [harsh law]. In
addition, there are five types of *sheva* [also associated with *Gevurah*]—
sheva na, *sheva nach*, and three *chatafim*, and these are also associated with
the five *Gevurot*, but these are not softened [sweetened] though the first
group [of short vowels] are. These [two groups] represent tough and
soft *law*. Therefore, one should not drag out pronouncing the short
vowels, and especially the *sheva's*.[50]

Thus we have it—grammar according to Kabbalah! Kabbalah interprets everything in the world in terms of its own model. To extend the
pronunciation of harsh letters brings harshness into the world. Proper
pronunciation has ramification beyond itself. All is connected.

3

The Mother Letters—
Aleph, Mem, Shin

THE SCALE OF DIVINE JUSTICE

Sefer Yetzirah, **Chapter 3, Mishnah 1**

פ"ג מ"א שלש אמות אמ"ש יסודן כף
חובה וכף זכות ולשון חק
מכריע בינתים :

The three mothers, *Emesh* **[***Aleph, Mem, Shin***],
their foundation is the Palm of Merit and the
Palm of Guilt, and the Tongue of Decree mediates between.**

This *Mishnah* is an exact copy of part of the first *Mishnah* of Chapter 2.
However, there is a difference between the intent of that chapter and
this one. Therefore, while the words are the same, this *Mishnah* is not
merely a duplicate of the same idea.

In the words of the Raivad:

> In the first chapter, paths, letters, and *Sefirot* were mentioned. In the
> second chapter, mothers, letters, and their transpositions were dis-
> cussed. [*Sefer Yetzirah*] did not want to mention their value [in affecting
> the lower world] since in those two previous chapters it spoke of the
> elevated *Keter* and *Chachmah* and *Binah*. For that reason it hid their
> value as far as their relationship to the world, year, and soul. However,
> in this chapter, which alludes to the Kindness (*Chesed*) of God, [*Sefer
> Yetzirah*] began to speak of their value in relation to the world, year, and

soul. It says that just as the upper world contains a source for *Emesh* from which spreads the *Emesh* of that world, so too there is in the world of Kindness an *Emesh* that is the foundation of the Palm of Merit and the Palm of Guilt, and the Tongue of Decree that mediates between them. They (*Emesh*) are the essence of the books and are the three books that are opened on Rosh HaShanna, one for the purely righteous who are on the Palm of Merit, one for the evil who are on the Palm of Guilt, and one for the mediocre who are on the Tongue of Decree that mediates between.[1]

The *Mishnah* in Chapter 2 was speaking of the *Emesh* of the upper worlds, the first three *Sefirot*. They are not in action, but in thought only. Therefore, the ramifications of *Emesh* in the world, year, and soul was not discussed. The rest of *Sefer Yetzirah* is not speaking about the highest level of *Sefirot*. It is discussing the World of Kindness. Remember, the *Sefirah* of *Chesed* (Kindness), is below *Binah* and is the first of the *Sefirot* that comprise *Zair Anpin*, who is also known as the "World." This is the world that begins with kindness. Incidentally, the *Sefirot* of *Zair Anpin* are associated with the days of the week and are thus the connection with the concept of "year." Of course, *Zair Anpin* is in the shape of man, and thus the term *soul* is likewise appropriate. Therefore, when *Sefer Yetzirah* speaks of world, year, and soul, it is to be taken on two levels: the world of the lower *Sefirot* as well as the actual physical world. For instance, the constellations of the Zodiac are in the physical world but also are identified with the twelve diagonals of the *Sefirah* of *Tiferet*. While the discussion might be in physical terms, it must be understood that the intent is not only in the physical sphere.

The Raivad continues with a very interesting theory:

Go and learn that the shape of the soul is composed of the holy letters in the order that they're written in the commandments; if a person does them he will literally live because of them. This is because they will add to him life and peace, to his soul in the upper worlds. From there life and kindness will reach the physical man, and every organ of the soul will be strengthened with the power of the spirit of the living God. If a person transgresses the commandments, then the order of letters will be changed in his soul and will be written according to the transgression that he committed, as the verse says, "Their sin will be upon their bones" (Ezekiel 32:27). So it is in the Palm of Guilt, and God, the master of kindness and mercy, leaves him. That organ, if the soul is dependent upon it, immediately dies or is cut off. If it is an organ upon which the soul is not dependent, then the organ is sick or deteriorates, in accord with the verse, "I will appoint confusion upon thee, consumption and fever" (Leviticus 26:16). This is not in agreement with the doctors who claim that one of his fluids is too great, since nature does not act upon those who seek the Lord, but rather God will provide life to them, and if they do not desist [from transgression] the bitterness of death.[2]

By sinning, the order of the letters is changed, and this automatically affects man, as the soul itself is composed of the letters, and the body's life is the soul. The Raivad also suggests that those who reject God are abandoned to the laws of nature, while the seekers of God are directly controlled by Him, bypassing nature. Every organ is connected with a commandment. There are 613 commandments and 613 body parts (organs and blood vessels). Transgressing a commandment affects the corresponding body part.

A final remark comes from Saadia Gaon. In discussing the "Tongue of Decree," he states that the Hebrew word for tongue, *Lashon*, comes from the root *Lash*, to knead. The tongue kneads and mixes. It does this to both food and words in the lower sphere. It acts upon merit and guilt in the upper. Therefore, the tongue [of the scale] produces the decree, for it mediates between the two palms of the scale of justice.[3]

EMERGENCE OF FIRE, WATER, AND THE SEXES

Sefer Yetzirah, Chapter 3, Mishnah 2

מ"ב שלש אמות אמש סוד גדול מופלא
ומכוסה וחתום בשש טבעות וממנו
יוצאים אש ומים מתחלקים זכר ונקבה:
שלש אמות אמ"ש יסודן ומהן נולדו אבות
שמהם נברא הכל:

The three mothers, *Emesh*, a great and exalted secret, hidden and sealed in six rings from which emerge fire and water, which split into male and female. The three mothers, *Emesh*, are their foundation, from them were born the fathers and from them everything.

Each word in Kabbalah has meaning. According to the Ramban, *Emesh* is called by the *Mishnah* a "great" secret, in order to emphasize that the *Mishnah* is speaking here of the ramifications of *Emesh* at the level of the *Sefirah* known as Greatness (*Gedulah*). Greatness is an alternate name for the fourth *Sefirah*, more commonly called Kindness (*Chesed*). In the first two chapters we discussed *Emesh*'s nature at a very lofty level, that of the first three *Sefirot*. Here we will discuss its manifestations in more concrete terms at a somewhat lower level, that of the *Sefirah* of Greatness (*Chesed*).

As a way of hinting that the source of *Emesh* is from above, the *Mishnah* uses the term *exalted* (*Mufla*). This term is always taken in Kabbalah as a reference to something that is beyond grasp. A word with the same root as *Mufla* was used at the very beginning of the book to describe the thirty-two paths. They were called "wondrous"—*pliyot*. This is because the *Mishnah* was alluding to their source, *Keter*, which is the highest of the *Sefirot* and beyond understanding.

The Raivad gives the following reason why *Emesh* is called "a secret" by the *Mishnah*: "When we investigate how two opposites like fire and water emanated from a single, plain, undifferentiated source, it turns out that intellect falls short of comprehending the cause for such a thing. Therefore, the *Mishnah* called it a secret, which means something hidden."[4]

The Ramban states, "'A great secret' means it stems from the power of [the *Sefirah*] Greatness, 'exalted' means it is from the power of *Binah* that ascends to the High Crown (*Keter*)."[5] That is, *Emesh* has its origins in the first three *Sefirot*. *Binah*, the lowest of these three, is the "Mother" of the lower worlds and the source of their continued nourishment and renewal. Therefore, *Binah* is described as rising to the level of *Keter* for the sake of the lower worlds. In a sense, it is impregnated with *Emesh* by its spouse, *Chachmah* (Wisdom). *Chachmah* is to the right, *Binah* the left, and thus the union, like all kabbalistic unions, is through a mediator, in this case *Keter*, which is in the middle. The Talmud tells us that there are three partners in man's creation, the two parents and God, who is the ultimate source and silent partner. *Keter* here plays a similar role. *Binah* is sometimes described as both giving birth to the lower worlds and nursing them. This analogy is used extensively in Lurian Kabbalah, but it is clearly based on statements from the *Zohar* that use this imagery.

The Ramban goes on to explain what the *Mishnah* means by "sealed in six rings." He states as follows, "The six extremes are the six seals. [He sealed them] with the three letters of God's name [*Yud Hey Vav*) that contain the letters of *Emesh*. . . . These three letters of *Emesh* and the three of God's name are called six rings, and all is sealed with them, as a person who seals (letters) with a signet ring."[6]

This statement of the Ramban is somewhat problematic, as it differs from what was said previously. We explained earlier that *Sefer Yetzirah* defines the "seals" as the six permutations of the three unique letters of the Tetragrammaton. Here, the Ramban seems to be saying something different, namely, that the seals are the combination of the three letters of *Emesh* plus the three of the Tetragrammaton. To further complicate matters, it will be remembered that the *Otzar HaShem* in Chapter 1, *Mishnah* 13, stated that the rings and seals are separate entities. The seals are the letters of God's name, and the rings are the letters of *Emesh*. The former, he concludes, are thus greater than the latter.

There appears to be a real difference among the commentators in their understanding of this *Mishnah*. *Sefer Yetzirah* does not make clear exactly what the relationship is between *Emesh* and *Yud Hey Vav*. It seems to me they represent similar ideas on different levels. *Emesh* represents these concepts in the highest three *Sefirot*, *Yud Hey Vav* in the Six Extremes.

The *Mishnah* continues, "From which emerge fire and water, which split into male and female." That is, these elements result directly from *Emesh*. The Raivad points out that only in the lower worlds can we really speak of male and female, not at the level of *Emesh*. At that level, male and female exist only in potential.[7] However, *Emesh* is their source.

The Vilna Gaon, whose commentary is perhaps the clearest and most systematic, explains it as follows:

We have already said that the source of the three Mothers (*Emesh*) is the first *Sefirah*. They are incorporated in the first *Sefirah* in a very hidden way. Afterward, the Mothers are divided among the first three *Sefirot* (each gets a letter). Thereafter, they are dispersed to each of the Six

Extremes, all three to each, according to the six permutations. Foundation (the last of the Six Extremes) contains them all; thus it is called *Chai*—"life"—since all together they total eighteen letters, the numerical value of *Chai* (life). All these aspects at this point are still extremely tenuous, and they are similar here to a slight engraving. All this is in the subdivisions of the first *Sefirah* only.[8]

The last line of the Gaon comes as a shock. It means that the references to the various *Sefirot* in the Gaon's statement were actually meant to refer to the subdivisions of *Keter*. Here in *Keter* the manifestation of *Emesh* is somewhat different than in the lower *Sefirot*. In *Keter* it is very thin, only a slight engraving.

Thus, according to the Gaon, the first part of the *Mishnah* refers to the intra-*Keter* subdivisions, while the end refers to the *Sefirot* on the larger level, namely that of the entire World of Emanations. The Gaon's text of the *Mishnah* was somewhat different than the standard one presented above. It concludes, "Air, water, and fire emerged from them [*Emesh*], and from these were born the fathers and from the fathers the offspring." Thus, the Gaon states that the phrase "from which emerge air, fire, and water" refers to the first three of the ten *Sefirot* (of the World of Emanations). "Fathers" refer to the second triad—*Chesed*, *Gevurah*, and *Tiferet*. "Offspring" refers to the lower *Sefirot*. This is on the level of *Sefirot*.

Sefer Yetzirah is to be understood on many levels, however. The Gaon goes on to explain that each of these aspects of *Emesh* affects not only the structure of the world of *Sefirot*, but also has its parallel in the anatomy of man's physical body. It has parallels in the spatial universe as well. In addition, it is integrated into the structure of time.

THE MOTHER LETTERS AND THEIR MANIFESTATION IN THE UNIVERSE

Sefer Yetzirah, Chapter 3, Mishnah 3

מ"ג שלש אמות אמ"ש בעולם אויר מים אש
שמים נבראו תחלה מאש וארץ נבראת
ממים והאויר מכריע בין האש ובין המים:

The three mothers *Emesh* in the world are Air, Water, and Fire. The heavens were first created from Fire, the land was created from Water, and the Air mediates between the Fire and the Water.

The Ramban explains the creation of the land as follows: "From the impurity in the water snow was created, and the snow turned to be land, as the verse states, 'To the snow He will say, be thou land' (Job 37:6)."[9] According to this, the land evolved from water, and although Aristotle considered earth to be one of the four basic elements, in Kabbalah it is considered a derivative, not as elemental as the other three. Thus it is not part of *Emesh*. The idea that snow is an intermediate stage in the formation of land is not as far-fetched as it first might seem. Modern science believes that snowflakes form about dust particles. Thus they contain the basis of the earth.

The Ramban also differentiates between "Wind" and "Air." In Hebrew, the word *Ruach* means both "wind" and "spirit," and so when the Ramban states that *air* was created from the *wind*, he implies from *spirit*, that is, physical air emerged from the nonphysical spirit, at a lower level. All that is below has roots above.

There are various statements in rabbinic literature to the effect that the heavens were made not from fire alone, but rather from water and fire mixed. The Raivad brings several of these statements from the *Midrash Bereishit Rabbah* and *Sefer HaBahir* and tries to resolve the contradiction. He states that the *Mishnah* in *Sefer Yetzirah* is referring to a higher heaven. The rabbinic statements that speak of both water and fire as the cause of the heavens, however, refer to a different lower heaven. The biblical statement, "Let there be a firmament in the midst of the water" (Genesis 1:6), is referring to the firmament of fire that is mentioned here in *Sefer Yetzirah*.[10] There are lower heavens, in addition, however, that are called the "heavens of *Tiferet*," and these are of water and fire. Water and fire refer to the right and left side, Kindness and Strict Law. The lower heavens are mixed with Kindness, which the lower creation needs to exist. If God were to deal with the lower worlds in a strict, harsh fashion, they could not pass the test of strict judgment and would be doomed.

The Raivad is also troubled by a fundamental difficulty. He states, "The *Mishnah* is somewhat difficult since the letters of *Emesh* are the foundation for the heavens, earth, and wind, and they are themselves among those letters that are engraved in the sphere, since they are from the twenty-two letters of the alphabet. The engraving in the sphere must be after the creation of the [sphere] of heavens, which is the recipient of the engraving."[11] In other words, he is asking how *Emesh* can be part of the creation of the heavens, when their very existence consists of their being engraved in the heavens. This is similar to the question, "What came first, the chicken or the egg?"

The Raivad attempts to resolve this question as follows:

> The first heavens, which received the engravings, are themselves the shape and the cause for *Emesh*. From them came into being all the other skies, land, and water, and all their hosts. Understand this! This secret was hinted at when the *Mishnah* mentioned the six rings from which emerged fire, wind, and water. Understand this, the third *Mishnah* of this chapter.[12]

The Raivad obviously considers this a very important point. At the earliest and highest levels, the elements of *Emesh* are different than in the lower worlds. At the high levels, *Emesh* is formed by the heavens themselves, or as the Raivad puts it, the heavens are the shape of *Emesh*. As *Emesh* descends into the lower worlds, however, their manifestations *thicken* and eventually even become physical, until the physical elements of air, water, and fire result.

MANIFESTATIONS OF THE THREE
MOTHER LETTERS IN TIME
AND THE SOUL

Sefer Yetzirah, Chapter 3, Mishnah 4

מ"ד שלש אמות אמ"ש בשנה אש ומים
ורוח חום נברא מאש קור ממים
ורויה מרוח מכריע בינתים . שלש אמות
אמ"ש בנפש אש ומים ורוח ראש נברא מאש
ובטן נברא ממים וגויה נברא מרוח מכריע
בינתים :

> **The three mothers *Emesh*: in the year they are
> Fire, Water, and Wind [as follows]: Heat was
> created from Fire, Cold from Water, and Satu-
> ration from Wind, which mediates between. The
> three mothers *Emesh*: in the soul they are Fire,
> Water, and Wind [as follows]: The Head was
> created from Fire, the Stomach was created
> from Water, and the Body was created from
> Wind, which mediates between.**

The previous *Mishnah* discussed the manifestations of *Emesh* in the physical universe at large. As already explained, *Sefer Yetzirah* is interested not only in this level of existence, but in at least two other levels as well: time, often referred to as the level of "the year," and the soul. This *Mishnah* discusses the remaining two levels.

Time is composed of seasons. The summer is characterized by heat, the winter by cold, and spring and fall by moderate temperatures. These are seen as the result of the powers of *Emesh* as they manifest in time. The same basic powers that created the physical elements of air, water, and fire in the world of matter are those that create the seasons in time. These are the powers that the three Hebrew letters, *Aleph*, *Mem*, and *Shin*, connote, and these powers combine in the words of the holy tongue to constitute the essence of the objects to which they refer.

Incidentally, the word *saturation* (*Riviyah* in Hebrew) that the *Mishnah* uses is very unusual. Most commentators ignore its literal meaning and understand it as meaning "moderate temperature." The *Otzar HaShem* states the word has the same root as that found in the biblical verse, "You will be like a *saturated* garden [*Gan Ravei*]" (Isaiah 58:11). Perhaps the word is used to imply that the *moderate* state has some special value, something more than just the mixture of the extremes. As was mentioned before, in the resolution of antitheses something is lost, but something else is also gained.

Sefer Yetzirah uses the word *soul* in a peculiar manner. As used in the *Mishnah*, it seems to be referring to the physical body of man rather than his spiritual essence. There are several possible ways of understanding this. Each physical part of man has a spiritual parallel. The soul fills the body, and when the soul is incomplete, the corresponding bodily part withers. In medieval times it was not uncommon to view physical disabilities as resulting from spiritual deficiencies. Isaac Luria himself is said to have held such a theory.

Thus, when the *Mishnah* speaks of the *head* and *body* in its discussion of *Emesh*'s manifestations in the *soul*, it might very well mean more that just the physical body parts. By *head* it might mean "the life of the head," that is, the head's soul. The head, in Kabbalah, is in fact associated with a different soul (*neshamah*) than the heart (*ruach*) or the liver (*nefesh*) (see Appendix F). I do not mean to say that *head* docs not refer to the physical head at all, but that it refers to the corresponding spiritual *soul* as well.

While the correspondence of the seasons to wind, water, and fire is easy to understand, the relation of *Emesh* to Head, Stomach, and Body is less clear. *Sefer Yetzirah* is keenly aware that cool heads are hard to come by, which it explains by the fact that their root is fire. The connection of the body to air is certainly not apparent. In view of this, the Ramban states that the word *body* is really a reference to the penis and is related to air, since the air pressure expels the semen. His explanation is doubly difficult. First, the accuracy of his physiology is suspect. Secondly, air is said to mediate, and if the penis is air's bodily manifestation, it should be located between the head and the stomach! Perhaps for these reasons, the *Pree Yitzchak* and other commentators feel that the term *body* is meant literally and does not refer to the penis. The *body* does contain the lungs, and this is likely what associates it with air.

The relationship of *stomach* and *water* is also difficult to understand. Perhaps the connection lies in the fact that the digestive process extracts the water from foods.

Incidentally, according to the Vilna Gaon, each of the parts of the body contain all three elements (air, water, and fire), even though one dominates. Thus, he states that the brain in the head is itself water, and on the brain is an airlike membrane (air), and surrounding these is a brilliant shining light (fire). These he likens to the description of God in the first chapter of Ezekiel. God is pictured on a throne that is surrounded by shining light. The Gaon describes the throne as being of air. Also, in the beginning of Genesis, the *spirit* of God, and presumably His *throne*, are described as hovering over the *water*.[13]

The Ramban comments on the *Mishnah* as follows:

The year contains cold, heat, and saturation, which are three. It also contains the seven days of the week of creation as well as the twelve months of the year. These represent the three letter groups, *Emesh*, the seven double letters, and the twelve singles. The *Mishnah* explains to you that the power is extended from the letters to the world and from the world to the year and from the year to the soul. In a similar fashion, the wise investigators say that the light of wisdom is emanated on the spheres, and from the spheres to the stars, and from the stars to man.[14]

The movement of *Emesh* through the worlds is from the higher to the lower levels. It is analogous to the descent of wisdom. Man gets it last and is thus not as wise as the angels in the heavens and the higher creation.

The Ramban continues by telling us that the *soul* referred to in the *Mishnah*

> *is the body*, since when light is renewed in the Zodiac, and when vegetation is renewed in the year, likewise will be renewed the *offspring* of the *soul*. Animal life born in one year differs from that of a different year. Therefore, the Rabbis (*Tana'im*) said that it is forbidden to tithe [one animal in ten to the priest] from animals that are born in one year to satisfy the tithe requirements of the next year.[15]

MALE AND FEMALE ASPECTS OF THE MOTHER LETTERS IN SPACE, TIME, AND THE SOUL

Sefer Yetzirah, Chapter 3, Mishnah 5

מ"ה שלש אמות אמ"ש חקקן וחצבן וצרפן
וחתם בהן שלש אמות בעולם ושלש
אמות בשנה ושלש אמות בנפש זכר ונקבה:

The three mothers, *Emesh*—He engraved them and hewed them, combined them and sealed with them the three mothers in the world, the three mothers in the year, and the three mothers in the soul, male and female.

The Ramban comments: "Here the *Mishnah* once again explains their engraving, hewing, and combining in order to let us know that they are all present in the world, and all in the year, and all in the soul, both in the form of *one without the others* as well as *with the others*."[16] That is, all combinations are possible. Elements combine but also may remain uncombined. The Ramban is explaining whence comes the diversity in the world.

This *Mishnah* is both a summation of the previous *Mishnayot* of this chapter as well as an introduction to the last three *Mishnayot*. There are six permutations of the three letters of *Emesh*, two beginning with *Aleph*, two with *Mem*, and two with *Shin*. Each of the remaining *Mishnayot* discusses the combinations beginning with a specific leading letter. Since there are two combinations for each leading letter, one is said to refer to the male and one to the female. The breakdown into male and female is not reserved just for animal life. The Raivad puts it this way:

> Just as there exist male and female on the level of the soul, so is the secret of male and female present in the year, to the degree that the astrologers attributed to six of the constellations of the Zodiac the male aspect, and to the other six the female. The male constellations are: Aries, Taurus, Leo, Libra, Sagittarius, and Aquarius. The female are: Gemini, Cancer, Virgo, Scorpio, Capricorn, and Pisces. What is meant by female is that through the power of the female are born the females in all four categories:
>
> 1. Inanimate
> 2. Vegetable
> 3. Living
> 4. Speaking (man).

In parallel to this we find that six of the twelve permutations of the Tetragrammaton are male and six female. Similarly, some of the seven moving stars (Mercury, Venus, Mars, Jupiter, Saturn, Sun, Moon) are male, some female. So is it with the year and time; some portions point to and create males, some females. So are the winds, some male, some female. The males will switch to females and the females to males according to the value of the four quarters that they revolve in and according to the day and the night. From this you will understand that all these powers are influenced by the stars and the constellations and the day and the night and the quarters from the names of the permutation of the Tetragrammaton, as well as the name of forty-two letters, as I previously hinted.[17]

While this quote of the Raivad is somewhat obscure, certain of the ideas expressed here are abundantly clear. First, all of nature, even inanimate matter, contains male and female elements. The four letters of the Tetragrammaton have twelve unique combinations, which parallel the Zodiac of the physical universe. Each combination dominates a sector of time, as the constellations of the Zodiac are thought to do. The combinations beginning with the Hebrew letter *Hey* are female, just as the *Hey* is associated with the female gender in Hebrew grammar. This feminine attribute of the combinations beginning with *Hey* has a feminine influence on the portion of time with which it is associated. Male and female are not absolute terms, and one gender may acquire aspects of the other as a result of different influences.

The Raivad's last line needs comment. The Bible uses various terms to refer to God. The Kabbalists have greatly expanded the list. One popular name is known as "the Name of Forty-Two" because it contains forty-two letters. The Torah tells us that the Jews camped and traveled forty-two times between leaving Egypt and entering Israel. This reflects an attribute of God, which is hinted at by this name. While it is unclear exactly what this attribute is, some have claimed that it is mercy, since forty-two trips in forty years is not overly burdensome. This association of the name with mercy is probably why Nechunia ben HaKaneh, the traditional author of *Sefer HaBahir*, composed a famous prayer based on this Name of Forty-Two. This prayer has found its way into the prayer book and is recited in regular Friday services. It is called *Ana BeKoach* and has exactly forty-two words, each beginning with a letter of this name. This might help explain the Raivad's comment. *Ana BeKoach* is arranged in seven lines and can thus be assigned to the seven days of the week. According to this scheme, each section of the name would influence a representative portion of time.

Incidentally, the words that compose this name are said to have meaning in themselves. Some are regular Hebrew words. For instance, the third and fourth words are "*Kra Satan*," which means "destroy Satan" and represent God's attribute of destroying evil. Others do not conform to plain Hebrew very well, but all have been ascribed meaning. Thus, each section of time differs from all others.

THE ACTION AND PERMUTATIONS OF
THE LETTER *ALEPH*

Sefer Yetzirah, Chapter 3, Mishnah 6

מ"ן המליך אות אל"ף ברוח וקשר לו כתר
וצרפן זה עם זה וחתם בהן אויר
בעולם ורויה בשנה וגויה בנפש זכר באמ"ש
ונקבה באש"ם :

**He made the letter *Aleph* King of the Wind, and
He tied a crown to it, and He combined them
[the letters] each with each. He sealed with them
Air in the World, Saturation in the Year, and
Body in the Soul, Male with [the letters ordered]
Aleph Mem Shin, Female with [the letters or-
dered] *Aleph Shin Mem*.**

Saadia Gaon explains the *Mishnah*'s phraseology that *Aleph* was made
King as simply meaning that the letters of *Emesh* were ordered so that
Aleph was first. This happens in two of the six permutations of the
letters of *Emesh*.[18]

The phrase "He tied a crown to it" is not just another way of saying
that it was put first. *Crown* is a special key word in Kabbalah and means
the first *Sefirah* of *Keter*. The *Mishnah* is telling us here that *Aleph* was
tied to its original source and emanator, the *Sefirah* of *Keter*, and is a
link in the chain and in no way independent. The powers of the letters
are the power of the Infinite as it descends through the worlds.

The *Mishnah* continues to explain that the combinations of *Emesh*
that begin with the *Aleph* are the cause of the Air, the moderate seasons
(Saturation), and the Body (between the head and the stomach).
Remember, of the triad *Emesh*, *Shin*, and *Mem* (representing Fire and
Water) are the extremes, and *Aleph* is the mediator. Thus, all that is
derived from *Aleph*—Air, Saturation, and Body—must have the trait
of mediator.

The *Mishnah* does not actually say that the combination of *Emesh*
"caused" the Air but rather "sealed" the Air. Sealing is the last step.
The original cause of everything is, of course, the Infinite. However,

Air did not take its ultimate form as "air" until the light of the Infinite was transformed by its descent into lower worlds. The creation of air was sealed—completed—by the combinations of *Emesh* beginning with *Aleph*. The same is true of the other continuums, time and soul.

The two combinations of *Emesh* that begin with *Aleph* are *Aleph Mem Shin* and *Aleph Shin Mem*. The first is masculine, the second feminine. This is true for the different levels *Sefer Yetzirah* discusses—world, year, and soul. It is this aspect that seems to catch the interest of the commentators. The Ramban sets forth several interesting theories:

> There is in the female a place that contains the shape of *Aleph Mem Shin* and the shape of *Aleph Shin Mem*. When the drop (semen) is heated with *Aleph Mem Shin*, the child is male, but when it is heated with *Aleph Shin Mem*, it is female. When it falls in both of them it is androgynous. Sometimes the child has the organs of both male and female (*Tumtum*) when there is a second intercourse. When the offspring is twins, if they are both male the drop splits into two in *Aleph Mem Shin*. If female, it splits in *Aleph Shin Mem*. It one is male and the other female, it splits into both *Aleph Mem Shin* and *Aleph Shin Mem*. Even though the (early) rabbis have said if the woman gives the seed first the offspring will be male, that is only because the later power that comes from the man cancels the first.[19]

This is interesting from not only a theological, but from a historical and scientific perspective as well. The Ramban seems to think that there is an actual place in the woman that is shaped by *Aleph Shin Mem* and is female, and another shaped by *Aleph Mem Shin* and is male. If the semen falls into the male spot, and is there incubated, the result will be a boy. This does not fit well with modern biology. The Ramban also speaks of the "drop" splitting. Modern science speaks about the cell splitting, rather than the drop. Nevertheless, here the Ramban was not far from science. Remember, he lived in the thirteenth century.

The last part of the Ramban's words deserve comment. The talmudic theory that the Ramban quotes seems to imply that the female (rather than the male) is the cause for male offspring. The Ramban says this is not what the rabbis meant. The reason a male is born when the woman "gives the seed" first is not because her seed is dominant, but rather because the man's, which comes later, will overpower it.

The *Mishnah* states that the letter combination with the *Mem* before the *Shin* is male and the *Shin* before the *Mem* female. The Vilna Gaon explains it this way: "The rule is that the female contains the strict laws and she is hotter than the man, as is known. Therefore, [in the female], fire is dominant over the water and the air."[20]

Thus, of the two combinations beginning with *Aleph*, the one composed of *Aleph Shin Mem* is feminine. This is because the *Shin* precedes the *Mem*, that is, Fire precedes Water and Heat precedes Cold. In the next *Mishnah* we find the same pattern. It is the ordering of the letters that determines what gender is dominant.

THE ACTION AND PERMUTATIONS OF THE LETTER *MEM*

Sefer Yetzirah, Chapter 3, Mishnah 7

מ"ז המליך אות מ"ם במים וקשר לו כתר
וצרפן זה עם זה וחתם בהן ארץ בעולם
וקור בשנה ובטן בנפש זכר ונקבה זכר במא"ש
ונקבה במש"א :

He made the letter *Mem* King of the Water, and He tied a crown to it, and He combined them [the letters] each with each. He sealed with them Earth in the World, Cold in the Year, and Stomach in the Soul, Male and Female—Male with [the letters ordered] *Mem Aleph Shin*, Female with [the letters ordered] *Mem Shin Aleph*.

This *Mishnah* is in the exact format of the previous one, except here it is the letter *Mem* that comes first. *Mem*, you will remember, represents *Mayim*, water, and is associated with the right side of the Heavenly Man, that of Kindness. Water in nature is usually cold, and *cold* itself is seen as emerging from water. Earth, we already explained, is thought to be derived indirectly from water. The water becomes snow and the snow earth, as it is stated in Job, "To the snow He said, be thou land"

(Job 37:6). Finally, the stomach extracts liquids and nutrients from food. It is thus considered to be a product of water's influence and is associated with the combination of *Emesh* where *Mem* is first.

When *Mem* is the first letter of *Emesh*, gender is determined by the position of the *Shin*. When the *Shin* is the second letter, the feminine dominates, since *Shin* (*AiSH*) represents fire, and females are said to be hotter than males. Thus, *Mem Shin Aleph* is female and *Mem Aleph Shin* is male. This is true not only for people and animals, but also on the level of the *year* and the *world*.

The Ramban comments on the mishnaic phrase, "Earth in the World": "There is masculine earth, which in Hebrew is called *Afar*, and there is feminine earth, known as *Adamah*."[21] It is not accidental that the Hebrew words for earth have both masculine and feminine form.

In the same vein the Ramban proceeds to explain the *Mishnah*'s phrase, "Cold in the year": "There are male fruit and female, which come because of the cold. Likewise, in the soul there is the fruit of the womb, the offspring that is through the body of Man, that give birth to male and female."[22]

Masculine and feminine traits are not always apparent, yet they are always present. In people these aspects are distinct (most of the time, anyway). In fruit, they are less clear, yet biologists often do classify trees and plants as male and female. The strength of the Ramban's assertion is that even in nonliving earth these categories exist. The Vilna Gaon explains that some countries are prone to produce gallant warriors, and some weaklings.[23] The former might be known as masculine lands. On all levels, there exist aspects that may be considered male or female.

THE ACTION AND PERMUTATIONS OF
THE LETTER *SHIN*

Sefer Yetzirah, Chapter 3, Mishnah 8

מ"ח המליך אות שי"ן באש וקשר לו כתר
וצרפן זה עם זה וחתם בהן שמים בעולם
וחום בשנה וראש בנפש זכר ונקבה:

He made the letter *Shin* King of the Fire, and He tied a crown to it, and He combined them [the letters] each with each. He sealed with them the Heavens in the World, Heat in the Year, and the Head in the Soul, Male and Female.

This *Mishnah* ends Chapter 3. Some versions of *Sefer Yetzirah* have a final line in which the *Mishnah* tells us which letter combination (beginning with *Shin*) is masculine and which is feminine. This would follow the pattern that we found in the previous two *Mishnayot*. Thus, this line should probably be included. I believe that the reason it is omitted in our version is because of confusion as to the correct order the letter combinations should have. Let me explain. We said previously that heat is associated with the feminine. In the previous *Mishnayot*, *Shin* was not *king*, that is, it was not the first letter. When *Shin* was the second rather than the third letter, the combination was said to be feminine, since *Shin*, which represents fire and heat, preceded the remaining nonfeminine letter. In the current *Mishnah*, however, *Shin* rules. It is first in both the masculine and the feminine. It would seem logical, then, that where *Mem* (associated with *cold* water) is the second letter, the combination would be male. The text of the Ari, in fact, does have it in this logical order. Nevertheless, most other texts contain the reverse. Perhaps, due to the uncertainty as to which combination is male, the standard version omits this line altogether.

Chaim Vital's *Etz Chaim* is the primary source for Lurian Kabbalah. In the Gate of Tenta he provides an overview as follows:

Behold, the letters are the powers of emanation from the essence of the *Sefirot*. They are the secret of the words and combinations found in *Sefer Yetzirah*. The matter is like this: None of the powers will operate except through their return to and attachment with their source. Then they will receive a great and strong abundance, which will allow them to do their actions with strength. That is what is meant by He made a certain letter King, for He isolated it and tied it to its root and then He extracted a single action from it. Ten of the twenty-two Hebrew letters, *Emesh* and *Beged Kafarta* (*Aleph, Mem, Shin, Bet, Gimel, Dalet, Kaf, Peh, Resh, Tav*) represent the secret of the ten *Sefirot* according to their order from the top to the bottom. The other twelve single letters are the twelve diagonals (to be discussed later). The secret of *Emesh* and *Vav Yud Hey* (the three unique letters of the Tetragrammaton) are the first three *Sefirot*. The reason *Aleph* is first in *Emesh* is that even though all things are combined from fire, water, and wind, the main root of all is through the wind (spirit), which is the letter *Aleph*. Therefore, in the Male, *Vav Yud Hey*—wind, water, and fire. For the wind is first of all, for it is *Aleph* (Air) and corresponds to the *Vav* in the Tetragrammaton. Afterward is *Mem*, which is Kindness, and afterward fire—Strict Law. Thus we have *Emesh*. The female is opposite, from bottom to top—*Aleph Shin Mem*—corresponding to *Vav Hey Yud* in the Tetragrammaton. When He made *Mem* King and put it first, the male was *Mem Aleph Shin*. That is, the *Aleph* before the *Shin*. Corresponding in God's name is *Yud Vav Hey*. The female was *Mem Shin Aleph*, corresponding to *Yud Hey Vav* in God's name. When He made *Shin* King, the male was *Shin Mem Aleph*, corresponding to *Hey Yud Vav*. However, since the basis of the *Shin* is Strict Law (*Din*), He put *Mem* before the *Aleph* since water is pure mercy in relation to the wind, which is mixed. Therefore, He put *Mem* before *Aleph* (for the male) but for the female [the order was] *Shin Aleph Mem*, corresponding to *Hey Vav Yud* of the name.[24]

The somewhat obscure relationship of *Emesh* to *Yud Hey Vav* was already mentioned. *Yud Hey Vav* are part of the twelve single-letter group. In that context they are not special. However, their function as part of God's name is special. This function parallels the very special letters *Emesh*. However, we usually think of *Emesh* in more physical terms, representing physical elements. Their parallel in the higher spheres is *Vav Yud Hey*. Thus, when used in this context, they represent the same relationships as *Emesh*, and are not different powers; rather, they are the same, on a higher level. Sometimes we use the letters of *Emesh* themselves to refer to the higher level. Here Chaim Vital speaks of them as if they are the same as *Emesh*.

The correspondence of the letters to the *Sefirot* has been mentioned briefly before. Ten letters correspond exactly. These are the first two letter groups. *Emesh* was the main topic of this chapter. *Beged Kafarta* will be the main topic of the next. The twelve remaining letters are all thought to belong to the *Sefirah* of *Tiferet*, the main *Sefirah* of the Six Extremes. They are the source for the Tribes of Israel, the constellations of the Zodiac, and other such manifestations. The fifth chapter discusses them.

This concludes the first three chapters of *Sefer Yetzirah*. The wonderful commentary of the Ramban does not continue after this chapter. Whether it ever existed is uncertain. If it did exist, however, the other Kabbalists probably did not have access to it, as evidenced by the fact that they did not quote from it. The Ramban is a prime source for many of their remarks on the first three chapters of *Sefer Yetzirah*.

4

The Seven
Double Letters—
Beged Kafarta

THE LETTERS' DUAL NATURE—
KINDNESS AND HARSHNESS

Sefer Yetzirah, Chapter 4, Mishnah 1

פ"ד מ"א שבע כפולות בג"ד כפר"ת
(מתנהגות בשתי לשונות), יסודן
חיים ושלום וחכמה ועושר חן וזרע וממשלה,
ומתנהגות בשתי לשונות ב"ב נ"ג ד"ד כ"כ
פ"פ ר"ר ת"ת תבנית רך וקשה תבנית גבור
וחלש כפולות שהן תמורות . תמורת חיים
מות תמורת שלום רע תמורת חכמה אולת
תמורת עושר עוני תמורת חן כיעור תמורת
זרע שממה תמורת ממשלה עבדות :

The seven doubles are *Bet, Gimel, Dalet, Kaf, Peh, Resh, Tav* [*Beged Kafarta*]. Their basis is Life, Peace, Wisdom, Wealth, Beauty, Seed, and Rule. They take on two forms [as follows]: *Vet Bet* [soft and hard]; *Gimel Gimel* [soft and hard]; *Dalet Dalet* [soft and hard]; *Chaf Kaf* [soft and hard]; *Feh Peh* [soft and hard]; *Resh Resh* [soft and hard]; *Saf* and *Tav* [soft and hard]. Their structure is soft and hard, courageous and weak, doubles that are replacements. The replacement of Life is Death,

the replacement of Peace is Evil, the replacement of Wisdom is Foolishness, the replacement of Wealth is Poverty, the replacement of Beauty is Ugliness, the replacement of Seed is Desolation, and the replacement of Rule is Slavery.

The special significance of the numbers *three* and *seven* seems to be nearly universal. For instance, in magical ceremonies, doing things three times is the rule rather than the exception. Three seems to have an important, although somewhat elusive, meaning. Seven also is a very special number in magic, in dice, and in the religious ceremonies of vastly different groups. Hindu marriages, for instance, often have seven revolutions strangely similar to the seven circles many Jewish brides make around their husbands. The week contains seven days in almost every culture. While it is easy to understand why the use of a thirty-day month is widespread, there is no observable astronomical phenomenon that occurs in seven days. Thus, the widespread use of the seven-day week, which corresponds to nothing observable in nature, seems strange.

I believe the unique quality of these numbers is due to three factors:

1. They add up to ten.
2. They are prime numbers.
3. They are different from each other.

If ten is broken into two numbers whose sum is ten, five pairs are possible: 1 and 9, 2 and 8, 3 and 7, 4 and 6, and 5 and 5. Each pair except (3 and 7) and (5 and 5) have elements that can be divided by a number other than themselves or one. For instance, 9 can be expressed as 3×3 and thus is not prime. The pair 5 and 5 is redundant and does not produce two separate numbers. Thus 3 and 7 are special.

Among the issues with which *Sefer Yetzirah* is concerned is how the *many* items of which the world is composed could emerge from the absolute *oneness* that we call God. Also it ponders how the *many* could continue to exist when the ultimate truth is the One Unity (God). The above analysis of numbers is an attempt to resolve these questions.

One and ten are very similar. As pointed out previously, the digits of ten sum to one. In the Jewish tradition, an often-used method of figuring numerical values of letters is *Prat Katan*. It counts 20 and 200 both as 2, 30 and 300 both as three, and so on. The zeroes are disregarded.

The ten *Sefirot* are thus, in the final analysis, one. Their vessels separate them, but the true essence that represents their divinity is all one. There are ten *Sefirot* because ultimately they are One. Ten stresses this connection, for in *Prat Katan* it equals one.

In the creation of the universe, what needed to be stressed was not the *one*, however, but the *many*. God did not want the world to return to the One, for then there would be no world. At first all that existed was the One. The emanation of the *Sefirot* created ten that were really one. To establish a world that would continue to exist, and not return to the One, the ten (*Sefirot*) split into the most unbreakable, irreducible, unique pair. As shown above, this pair could only be 3 and 7. Thus, these numbers are special because of their uniqueness. Not all cultures that consider three and seven special know why consciously. But somehow their specialness is felt, and the pair is accorded appropriate status.

In the previous chapter we dealt with the three, that is, with *Emesh*. In this chapter, the subject is the seven. It has been pointed out that together they represent the ten *Sefirot*. This, in a sense, is everything. The Vilna Gaon points out that the first letter of *Emesh* is *Aleph* and the last letter of *Beged Kafarta* is *Tav*. These are the first and last letters of the Alphabet. Thus, all is encompassed.[1] There is a Christian saying that God is the Alpha and Omega. Perhaps the Jewish version is that He is the *Aleph* to the *Tav*.

The difficulty in translating *Sefer Yetzirah* is that it is rooted in Hebrew grammar. While I will try not to get overly involved in grammatical technicalities, some grammar is unavoidable. Those familiar with Hebrew are aware that six of the seven letters mentioned in the *Mishnah* constitute the well-known letter group, *Beged Kefet*. This group contains the only letters that can have an emphasized form at the beginning of a word. In Hebrew, the term *to emphasize* is *LeHaDgish*, which has the same root as the word *dot* (*dagesh*). Therefore, letters that are emphasized are written with dots. The other letters, explains Rabbi Eliezer of Garmiza, either do not take dots at all, or have them only as a result of their proximity to certain other letters and vowels. They are not dotted independently in their own right.[2]

The Kabbalists, not surprisingly, saw in these two forms of letters, plain and dotted, an analogy to kindness and harshness. That is, they saw the representation of God's justice in these letters. Therefore, these letters are associated with the lower seven *Sefirot*. It is these that are within time and are God's vehicle to control the world. The first three *Sefirot* are above time; they are only the root of the lower *Sefirot*. They are, therefore, represented by the letters of *Emesh* (*Aleph, Mem, Shin*), letters that do not receive a *dagesh kal* (dot at the beginning of a word).

There is some question as to whether the *Resh* has a right to be included in the seven letters of *Beged Kafarta*, because it is rare to see a dotted *Resh*. The commentaries usually quote the verse from 1 Samuel 1:6, which has the word "*HaRima*" with a dot in the *Resh*. I know of at least one other example of a dotted *Resh*. It is not that the *Resh* does not fit at all. It sometimes does take a dot, and is thus included as one of the seven letters representing the lower *Sefirot*.

The weak form of these seven letters are naturally associated with Kindness. The dotted form represents Strength, *Gevurah*, Strict Law. Actually, the Vilna Gaon points out that the breakdown is somewhat finer. There are two types of dots, one strong and one lighter. Each is law, one harsher and one lighter. The *Sefirah* of Courage (*Gevurah*), is known as the Attribute of Hard Law. *Malchut* is the Attribute of Easy Law. They have their grammatical correlates in these two types of dots.

The seven letters, *Beged Kafarta*, without a dot represent seven positive assets. They are: Life, Peace, Wisdom, Wealth, Beauty, Seed, and Rule. Each is associated with a *Sefirah*. Likewise, the *Sefirot* can change from kindness to harshness. The same letters, with a dot, represent: Death, Evil, Foolishness, Poverty, Ugliness, Desolation, and Slavery. Each letter represents a *Sefirah*, and each pair of attributes is associated with a *Sefirah*.

The *Pree Yitzchak* explains the associations as follows:

> These seven attributes that work in the world come from the seven *Sefirot*, which are the structure of the world. They are *Chesed, Gevurah, Tiferet, Netzach, Hod, Yisod,* and *Malchut*. "Wisdom" comes from the direction of *Chesed* (Kindness), for the Talmud states, "He who wants to become wise should turn south when praying."[3]

The Torah tells us that the *Menorah* was in the south side of the Tabernacle. It represents wisdom. The *Pree Yitzchak* continues: "Wealth comes from the side of Courage, as the Talmud says that one who wishes to become rich should turn north while praying."[4]

This is based on the biblical verse, "From the north will come the gold" (Job 37:22). Also note that in the Temple the Table with the special twelve breads was in the north. The table represented wealth. Seed is from *Tiferet* (Glory), as the verse says, "The glory of children are their parents" (Proverbs 17:6). Likewise the *Pree Yitzchak* tells us that Life is from *Netzach*, Rule is from *Hod*, Peace is from *Yisod*, and Beauty is from *Malchut*. Interesting. Regarding *Yisod* and *Peace*, he explains that *Yisod* is intermediate between *Malchut*, the female *Sefirah*, and her husband *Zair Anpin*, consisting of the six prior ones. It is through *Yisod* that they are united. It is the peacemaker between man and his wife, *Zair Anpin* and *Malchut*.[5]

A word about *Temurot* (replacements). This is a tainted term in Kabbalah. *Replacements* are thought of negatively. This stems from the Torah's statement concerning an animal once it is pledged for a sacrifice: "Do not switch it or *replace* it, good for bad or bad for good" (Leviticus 27:10). In any case, the *Temurot* of our *Mishnah* are all the exact opposite of the positive terms and need little explanation.

The list of life, peace, wisdom, wealth, beauty, seed, and rule covers all of man's basic needs. It does not include happiness, however. This will emerge naturally, as a result of these seven, unless, of course, God wills otherwise.

THE SIGNIFICANCE OF SEVEN

Sefer Yetzirah, Chapter 4, Mishnah 2

מ"ב שבע כפולות בנ"ד כפר"ת שבע ולא
שש שבע ולא שמונה בחון בהן וחקור
מהן (וצור וחשוב) והעמד דבר על בוריו
והשב יוצר על מכונו:

The seven doubles, *Beged Kafarta*, are seven and not six, seven and not eight; contemplate them, and study of them, and establish the matter clearly, and seat the Creator on His place.

This *Mishnah* is a duplicate of the fourth *Mishnah* of Chapter 1, except that the number being discussed is seven rather than ten. We explained there that if there were any other number of *Sefirot*, God's unity would not have been emphasized. Ten is in a sense the same as one, but on the level of the double digits. It may be said that ten is the one of the double digits.

The present *Mishnah* speaks of the uniqueness of seven. While the specialness of seven is not the same as that of one, the concepts are related. All physical objects have three dimensions. Three dimensions imply six sides, namely north, south, east, west, top, and bottom. But physical objects have a seventh area as well. This is the middle, known to Kabbalists as "the *place* that carries all the other dimensions." This place is special, in the same sense that the Sabbath is special. It represents "place" in the physical world analogous to God being the "place" of the spiritual. As the rabbis have said, "The world is not the place of God, but rather God is the *place* of the world."[6] Matter rests in space as the Sabbath rests in the week. It is God's presence in the world. Thus, to say there are only six sides is to deny God.

Just as the *Mishnah* felt it had to speak out against the temptation to include only six letters, representing six *Sefirot*, in *Beged Kafarta*, so does it find it necessary to speak against the addition of an eighth letter. The eighth letter could only represent the aspect of God outside of space and time. However, there is no spatial plane in nature that conforms to this model. In addition, it would disrupt the time–space parallelism, each having seven main elements (the days of the week for time and six planes plus the center for space). The eighth aspect cannot be grouped with the lower seven. It is not of the physical world. In kabbalistic terminology, the eighth aspect cannot rule within time and space, for it contains only the attribute of Kindness but not of Strict Law. It, thus, cannot judge. The letters of *Beged Kafarta* represent specifically the attributes that change to and from harshness. It represents divine judgment and law. Nonjudgmental aspects cannot be included in this grouping.

The Vilna Gaon puts it this way: "Do not think that *Binah* is also included, even though strict laws spring from her, for *Binah* is in herself pure mercy. Likewise, 'seven and not six,' for do not exclude *Malchut* from them."[7] That is, there are grounds to think that *Binah* belongs, even though it is above time. *Binah* is the direct cause of the lower seven *Sefirot*, and thus "strict laws spring from her." Nevertheless, since *Binah*, in itself, has no strictness, it cannot be included. Likewise, there is reason to think *Malchut* may be excluded. *Malchut* is like the moon, which has no intrinsic light of her own, but only shines due to the light of the sun. It is like the Sabbath, passive. On the Sabbath the Jewish court (*din*) does not convene. Nevertheless, crimes committed on the Sabbath are not excused. The Sabbath is not an unimportant day, and *Malchut* is not a second-class *Sefirah*. The elevation of *Malchut* at the end of days is, in fact, one of the central themes of Kabbalah. *Malchut*, therefore, is not to be excluded from this group of letters (*Sefirot*).

THE LETTERS AND THE NATURE OF SPACE

Sefer Yetzirah, Chapter 4, Mishnah 3

מ"ג שבע כפולות בג"ד כפר"ת כנגד ז'
קצוות מהם ו' קצוות מעלה ומטה מזרח
ומערב צפון ודרום והיכל הקדש מכוון באמצע
והוא נושא את כולן :

The seven doubles, *Beged Kafarta*, represent the seven extremes. From these are top and bottom, east, west, north, and south. The Holy Palace is located in the middle and carries the others.

The connection of the physical world with the spiritual is not coincidental, but rather that of cause and effect. The properties of physical space parallel those of the letters of the Holy Tongue because the structure of the entire creation is based on these. We have seen in the previous chapter that the first group of these letters is the cause of the three "elements" that compose the matter of the universe (as well as higher spiritual "matter"). The second group of these powers, the seven letters of *Beged Kafarta*, are the powers responsible for the properties of physical space.

All physical bodies exist in space. They have a top side, a bottom, and sides that face east, west, north, and south. These are the "extremes" of the object, the parts furthest from the center. The center of the object is no less important. It, in a sense, is the most crucial, for without it no object could be defined. In this sense, "it carries the others."

This *Mishnah* is an appeal to view the world as more than physical. When considering objects, we always think of them as existing in physical space, between the six directions (up, down, east, west, north, and south). We often neglect to think of their middle. This seventh aspect represents God in the physical universe. As the *Bahir* says, "God is the 'Place' of the world." His place is in the center and enables the existence of all else. In the words of the *Mishnah*, He "carries the other dimensions."

An astute reader might object. The Six Extremes in Kabbalah represent the six *Sefirot* of *Zair Anpin*, which are *higher* than the seventh *Sefirah*, *Malchut*. In a sense, this is correct. However, the part of the divine sphere that interacts with man is *Malchut* (the *Shechinah*). It represents God in the lower spheres. It is *this* that is being emphasized, at least on the simplest level of interpretation.

The Vilna Gaon speaks of a higher level. He quotes *Tikunei HaZohar*, which states, "The Chair—there is the *Shechinah*, and a man is sitting on it, this refers to the Six Extremes."[8] The Gaon concludes that it is this "chair" that the *Mishnah* refers to when it says, "The Holy Palace is located in the middle and carries the others."[9]

The reference above to a *chair* is from the prophet Ezekiel. It states, "Above the firmament on their head is like the aspect of sapphire stone, the likeness of a *chair*, and on the likeness of the chair is an image, like the aspect of a man, on it from above" (Ezekiel 1:26). The "chair" is the seventh dimension of our *Mishnah*, the "Holy Palace" that carries the others. The others are represented by the man on the chair. The Kabbalists would call him *Zair Anpin*, the six *Sefirot* above the *Shechinah* (*Malchut*). In this model the chair is lower than the others, that is, it *carries* the higher aspects of God.

How can the seventh be both higher and lower than the other six? We have the same situation with the Sabbath. It is the "choicest of days,"[10] yet it is represented by the last *Sefirah*. It is considered female, whereas the others are male; it is likened to the moon, whereas the six earlier days are compared to the sun.

The fact is that there are two Sabbaths associated with each week,

one before and one after. The eternity that preceded the very first
week, the week of creation, was a Sabbath. This Sabbath is above all
the *Sefirot* and is greater than the rest. The Sabbath afterward is lower
in a sense. However, the object of creation is to elevate it above the
other six, to make it a crown on the head of the other six, which are its
husband, the "man" on the chair.

This elevation of the *Shechinah* (also known as Sabbath and *Malchut*)
is what we refer to when we speak of the days of the messiah, when
instead of working, man will learn Torah. Not working makes the
messianic era like the Sabbath, Sabbath the Crown, the highest. Thus,
Sabbath is sometimes spoken of as the least important, sometimes as
the most important.[11]

The Raivad comments on this *Mishnah* as follows:

> Every physical body and all that exists cannot escape having these Six
> Extremes. However, the middle of them all is the Holy Palace, which
> represents and is ordered like all that is in heaven. Our Rabbis said, "*A
> place for you to reside you made, O Lord* (Exodus 15:17), the Holy Temple
> on earth is set parallel to the Holy Temple above." Our Rabbis have also
> said, "In the Temple in Heaven the High Priest is the angel Michael, and
> he sacrifices the souls of the righteous. Understand this as the secret
> meaning of the verse "A person who will sacrifice *from you* a sacrifice to
> God" (Leviticus 1:2)—literally '*from you.*' "[12]

The Raivad is quoting two of the more mystical statements of the
talmudic rabbis. Based on a verse in Exodus they conclude that there
are two Temples, one on earth and one in heaven. Expanding this
principle, Kabbalists believe that the one on earth parallels the one
above. The middle of matter represents the centrality of God. Just as
He is central in heaven, so is He on earth. In addition to the actual
Temple, *all* matter contains a temple for God. Matter's actual essence
is, in effect, a Temple. In the Temple on earth animals are sacrificed.
The Temple above, while similar to the one on earth, is nonetheless of
a higher nature. So are its sacrifices. By sacrifices, however, it is not
meant the destruction of souls. On the contrary, the root of the
Hebrew word sacrifice, *korban*, means to bring close. The souls of the
righteous are not destroyed; rather they are brought close to God.

There is not unanimity in the assumption that the "palace" to which
the *Mishnah* is referring is *Malchut*. In a divergent opinion, the *Otzar
HaShem* says:

The Holy Palace is the Middle of the extremes. Since every combined body must have the aforementioned Six Extremes and a middle, in the *Sefirah* world the middle of all of them and their palace is the third one, which is *Tiferet*. As to the year, it is dependent on the sphere, whose center is the earth. As to animals, the center is the heart. As to the different climates, the center is the Land of Israel. In Israel, the center is the Holy Temple, which is set opposite the Holy Temple in heaven.[13]

A final quote from the *Pree Yitzchak* explains the *Mishnah* in the context of Lurian Kabbalah:

Malchut, the female of *Zair Anpin*—she is the palace of *Zair Anpin* and his home, as our rabbis said that biblical references to a man's "home" (*Bayit*) means his wife. The word *Heichal*, Palace, has the same numerical value as the word *Adonai*, the name of God that refers to *Malchut* . . . She is in the middle (of the seven) because the position of *Malchut* is from two-thirds of *Tiferet* (down).[14]

In the above quote, the *Pree Yitzchak* first offers several proofs that the Holy Palace does, in fact, refer to *Malchut*. Then he explains why the *Mishnah* says that it is "in the middle." In Lurian Kabbalah, the positions of the various *Partzufim* are discussed. *Malchut* is not as tall as her husband, *Zair Anpin*, but comes up to two-thirds of the *Sefirah* of *Tiferet* that composes him. *Tiferet*, you will recall, is the third of the lower seven *Sefirot*. This is approximately their middle. Thus, the *Mishnah* supports the Lurian structure of the *Sefirot*.

MANIFESTATION OF THE DOUBLE
LETTERS IN SPACE, TIME, AND THE SOUL

Sefer Yetzirah, Chapter 4, Mishnah 4

מ״ד שבע כפולות בג״ד כפר״ת חקקן חצבן
צרפן וצר בהם כוכבים בעולם וימים
בשנה ושערים בנפש ומהן חקק שבעה
רקיעים ושבע אדמות ושבע שבתות לפיכך
חבב שביעי תחת כל השמים:

> **The seven doubles, *Beged Kafarta*, He engraved them and hewed them, combined them and fashioned with them the stars in the World, the days in the Year, and the gates in the Soul. From them He engraved the seven firmaments, the seven continents, and the seven Sabbaths. Therefore, He loved the seventh the most [of all] under the entire heavens.**

The *Mishnah* is describing the creation and use of the seven double letters, *Beged Kafarta*. The description of their creation is similar to the description of the creation of letters in earlier chapters. The *Mishnah* says that they were engraved, then hewed, then combined, and so on. The Raivad explains as follows: "They were engraved in [the *Sefirah*] *Chachmah*, hewed in *Binah*, weighed in *Chesed*, combined in *Gevurah*, and interchanged through *Tiferet*."[15] There are no concepts here that we have not seen before. The most notable item in the Raivad's statement is that his text appears to diverge from the standard one, which lacks the terms *weighed* and *interchanged*. Later in *Sefer Yetzirah*, the differences between versions become more significant.

The *Mishnah* informs us that with the seven letters of *Beged Kafarta*, God created various other important groups of sevens. The groups mentioned in our *Mishnah* are as follows:

1. The stars in the world
2. The days in the year
3. The gates in the Soul
4. The seven firmaments
5. The seven continents
6. The seven Sabbaths.

Several additional groups of sevens have special significance as well. They are:

7. The seven attributes and their opposites that were mentioned in the first *Mishnah* of this chapter
8. The seven names of God that compose "The Name of Forty-Two." As you may have guessed, each name has six letters, for a total of forty-two letters.

The *Otzar HaShem* quotes a work by Rabbi Eliezer HaGadol, who lists many other significant groups of seven. Not all sevens are created equal or have the same significance. Before examining the interconnections between the above groups, I will try to clarify their meaning.

1. The stars in the world—This refers to what the ancients called "moving stars." The moving stars, with the exception of the Sun, were not stars at all. They consisted of the visible planets Mercury, Venus, Mars, Jupiter, and Saturn, as well as the Sun and the Moon. The Sun has apparent motion around the earth, so it is included.

2. The days in the year—What is meant is the seven days of the weeks that compose the year. The seven-day week is by no means considered arbitrary. God established the week and it is part of the natural order.

3. The gates in the Soul—What is meant is the holes in the skull. The seven holes are for the two eyes, two ears, two nostrils, and the mouth. These in a way are the gates to the soul, for they are the portals that allow man access to sight, sound, taste, smell, and possibly more.

4. The seven firmaments—The tractate *Chagigah* of the Babylonian Talmud speaks of the various heavens. There are seven names associated with heaven. Each is said to represent a distinct firmament.

5. The seven continents—Actually the wording is "the seven lands" (*Aratzot*). Exactly what was intended is hard to say.

6. The seven Sabbaths—The Torah commands that every seventh year should be treated somewhat like the Sabbath. No farming may be done. The Torah calls it "the Sabbath of the Land" (Leviticus 25:6). After *seven* of these groups of *seven* years is a Jubilee year. Thus both the forty-ninth and the fiftieth years are set aside as special. The "seven Sabbaths" of the *Mishnah* do not refer to days but rather to years. They are the seven groups of seven years of each fifty-year period. Incidentally, there is a similar situation in relation to days. The Bible commands us to count seven weeks between Passover and Shavuot. The fiftieth day, paralleling the Jubilee year, is the holiday of Shavuot. In the words of the Scripture, "Count unto yourselves, from the morrow of the Sabbath, from the

day you bring the Omer, seven full Sabbaths they should be. Till the morrow of the seventh Sabbath count fifty days and bring a new meal offering unto God" (Leviticus 23:15).

7. The seven attributes and their opposites—This was already discussed in the first *Mishnah* of this chapter.

8. The seven names of God that compose "The Name of Forty-Two." This name is considered a key name in the creation, mainly because it emphasizes seven (there are seven sub-names), the number of days in the week of creation. It also emphasizes six (six letters per name), the number of active days.

Some of the commentaries put the details of the groups of sevens into table form. The table on the following page is translated from the *Otzar HaShem*.

The order of the groups is important, at least according to the Raivad. The earlier groups influence the later. Raivad states, somewhat obscurely: "The moving stars receive from them [the names], and from them the power and the 'usage' enters into the seven days, and from them the seven Gates receive [the power] in man."[16] He is clearly describing a one-directional passage of influence among the groups. The characteristics of each of the week's days come from the powers that we call by the names of God. The attributes of the senses are tied in with the same forces that molded the days. Specific senses correspond with certain names and days. I do not know if the other commentators would agree that the influence is only one-way. This certainly is not explicit in *Sefer Yetzirah* itself.

The Vilna Gaon quotes the *Zohar* in connection with the soul's Gates: "In the *Zohar* it says, '*He looks through the windows* (Song of Songs 2:9)—these are the holes of the eyes, ears, nose, and mouth into which the senses enter and exit from the brain.'"[17]

The *Zohar* is quoting from the Song of Songs, which describes God's romance with Israel. Israel, who is pictured as the maiden Shulamit, says her beloved, God, peeks in through the windows. According to the *Zohar*, the windows in question are the windows of the soul. Thus, the portals of the soul enable contact between God and man and connect with the brain, the higher soul of man.

The correspondence among the elements of the different groups of seven, which is the basis for the table on page 134, is given in detail in

	1	2	3	4	5	6	7
Names	AbgYtz אבג יתץ	KraStn קרע שטן	NgdYcs נגד יכש	BtrZtg בטר צתג	CkvTna חקב טנע	YglPzk יגל פזק	SkuZyt שקו צית
Stars	Saturn	Jupiter	Mars	Sun	Venus	Mercury	Moon
Days	Sunday	Monday	Tuesday	Wednesday	Thursday	Friday	Saturday
Gates	Right Eye	Left Eye	Right Ear	Left Ear	Right Nostril	Left Nostril	Mouth
Attribute	Life	Peace	Wisdom	Grace	Wealth	Seed	Rule
Skies	Vilon	Rakiya	Shechakim	Zevul	Ma'on	Mechon	Aravot
Lands	Eretz	Adamah	Arkah	Charavah	Yabashah	Tavel	Cheled

the following *Mishnayot*. It is not random, but meaningful, for example, that the right eye, Saturn, and Sunday are related. Unfortunately, there seem to be important differences in the versions of this part of *Sefer Yetzirah*. The list in our version contradicts that of the Vilna Gaon. It also is not in accord with the correspondences found in *Etz Chaim*, the central work of Lurian Kabbalah.[18] The *Pree Yitzchak* states that it appears that *Sefer Yetzirah* would best be understood in accordance with the words of Chaim Vital in *Etz Chaim*.[19] This is not surprising, for *Pree Yitzchak* was, after all, a Lurian Kabbalist.

THE LETTER *BET*'S RELATION TO SATURN, SUNDAY, AND THE RIGHT EYE

Sefer Yetzirah, Chapter 4, Mishnah 5

מ"ה כיצד המליך אות ב' בחיים וקשר לו
כתר וצר בו שבתי בעולם ויום ראשון
בשנה ועין ימין בנפש:

How? He made the letter *Bet* king of Life, and tied a crown to it, and formed with it Saturn in the universe, Sunday in the year, and the right eye in the soul.

Text used by the Vilna Gaon

He made *Bet* King of Wisdom, and tied a crown to it. He combined them [the letters] with each other and formed with them the moon in the universe, Sunday in the year, and the right eye in the soul, male and female.

At this point, *Sefer Yetzirah* proceeds to describe what was created with each letter. The first word of the *Mishnah*—"How?"—is asking how the letters are connected with the various creations. The rest of

Chapter 4 is basically an answer to this question. This *Mishnah*, as well the six that follow, explain the creation that resulted from specific permutations of the letters *Beged Kafarta*. Each associates an item in the world, an element of time, and a part of the body with one of the seven attributes mentioned in *Mishnah 1*.

These associations do not seem to have logical connections. That the right eye is grouped with Saturn is not something that one would expect. Nor is it clear what it means to be in the same grouping. However, the implication is clear that there is an interconnection. One would suspect, for example, that the *Mishnah* is suggesting that what happens in the sky to Saturn has more significance for the right eye than for the other parts of man. It is not difficult to imagine how such connections might be used by astrologers. A cure for an infection of the right eye might be thought more effective on Sunday, for example.

The *Mishnah* tells us that when the seven letters of *Beged Kafarta* are ordered so that the *Bet* is first, the result is the combination of forces that were used in the creation of certain items. The combination of powers resulting from *Bet* being placed first is what God used to create Saturn, Sunday, and the right eye. What the *Mishnah* means by saying that a letter was made king is that it was positioned first. The positions of the remaining six letters for each permutation are not supplied, but it appears that they would be arranged differently for each category of creation.

The term *tying a crown* has been taken by most commentaries to refer to the connection of the letters with *Keter*, the crown of the *Sefirot*. It is meant to stress that no creation is independent of the levels that precede it. It is through *Keter* that all exists. After all, *Keter* represents God's will.

The *Mishnah* states that *Bet* was made king of Life. There is some ambiguity in the Hebrew. An alternative translation is that God made *Bet* king *with* Life. In either case, the meaning is not altogether clear. Perhaps, the intent is that *Bet* is associated with the attribute of life, and it was the predominance of this force that gave the associated creations their unique characteristics.

"Life," of course, refers to the first of the seven attributes mentioned in *Mishnah 1* of this chapter. This differs from the version of the Vilna Gaon, which has Wisdom as the first attribute. In his version of the current *Mishnah*, it states that *Bet* was made the "king of Wisdom" rather than of "life." His text also differs as to the "star" associated with *Bet*. The standard version (the one used above) states "Saturn," whereas the Gaon's text substitutes "the moon." The Gaon brings convincing support for his text from the *Zohar*. We will discuss this later.

Most of the commentaries have surprisingly little to say about the rest of this chapter. The main exception is the Raivad, who goes into detail as to the functions of these seven letters (*Beged Kafarta*) and their associated planets. Although much of his comments are astrological in nature, they also contain theological and philosophical speculation and are extremely interesting. The following are some of his comments on the current *Mishnah*:

> What the *Mishnah* is trying to say is that God elevated the letter *Bet* to be the head, through the power of the high Crown (*Keter*). He invested the *Bet* with the power of Wisdom (*Chachmah*) and formed with it the planet Saturn that is beneath the name *Abg Ytz* [the first of the seven subnames that form the name of forty-two]. It is this name that gave Saturn Wisdom, despite the fact that Saturn is the star of destruction. It is through the secret of the *Shemitot* (seven-year cycles) that it contains the power of Wisdom. The reason it is in charge of destruction is as follows: since it is not interested in the affairs of the body, it therefore destroys them and does not look at them or their adornments, but rather at the plain intelligences [angels] and at divine understanding and knowledge of the sevens. From it [Saturn] is the power to restrain the evil spirits that destroy the organs of the body. . . . You might ask, "If Saturn is in charge of Wisdom, how can it be that it produces those who lack sense?" The answer is, "[It produces] those who lack sense as to this world, but have extra prophetic power." This is as the rabbis said in the Talmud, Tractate *Bava Batra*, "From the day the Holy Temple was destroyed, prophecy was given to fools and infants"[20]

The Raivad states that God's name is above Saturn and gives it its attributes. Clearly, he is asserting that the stars are not supreme but act through higher control. Saturn is associated with destruction, but only physical. The physical interferes with spiritual and intellectual growth, as one must be free from physical labor to be able to study. Therefore, the Raivad states, Saturn is also associated with Wisdom. Even fools born under its influence are not true fools. While they are foolish in worldly affairs, they are gifted with prophetic power.

Continuing along this line of thought, the Raivad put forth a theory as to the suffering of the Jews in this world. He claims their planet of influence is Saturn. He says, "Since Saturn is appointed over wisdom and knowledge, it is over the Jews. Therefore, they are constantly in trouble in this world."[21]

Sefer Yetzirah is not a book of astrology. It never suggests uses for the connections it contains. It is also not a book of superstition. Nevertheless, some of the commentators have based astrological systems upon it. The most noted is that of Shabbetai Donnolo, a famous doctor who is quoted by Rashi in the Talmud. In Donnolo's commentary on *Sefer Yetzirah*, he states that he met the greatest of the Arabian astrologers, who taught him his entire system of astrology. It is related at length in his commentary, and it should be of great interest to those studying the history of astrology. The commentary of the Raivad is also full of astrology. While he is certainly steeped in the religious tradition, he incorporates many ideas, based on beliefs and superstitions common in his time, that lack any theological basis.

The Vilna Gaon also makes several interesting remarks on this *Mishnah*. He says as follows:

> The six remaining letters are 720 combinations, as mentioned at the end of this chapter [see *Mishnah* 12]. Three hundred and sixty are "forward" combinations, 360 "backward." They represent the 360 degrees of the sphere that each planet, as well as the sun, travel each day. (The 360 backward combinations represent their returning backward from west to east. Thus, the sky is composed of the Six Extremes, and in them are the 720 combinations, 360 and 360. The earth, which is the Holy Palace, completes their number to seven.)[22]

Several parts of the above quote need comment.

1. The degrees of the sphere—While breaking a circle into 360 degrees was certainly prevalent in the eighteenth century when the Gaon lived, it is unclear whether this convention existed when *Sefer Yetzirah* was first composed. It is, thus, doubtful whether this allusion was intended by *Sefer Yetzirah*'s author.
2. The sun's movement—The Gaon lived after Copernicus and must have been aware of the heliocentric model of the solar system. I do not know whether he accepted this model.

Perhaps his comments should be understood as merely referring to the sun's "apparent" motion.

3. Retrograde motion—The statement about the planets returning from west to east is quite strange. It is in parentheses
   in the text of the Vilna Gaon, and I am uncertain whether he
   himself actually wrote it. I do not know where this idea
   originated. Incidentally, the planets do show retrograde motion. Every once in a while they appear to be traveling backward. This was explained by a device called epicycles in the
   Ptolmeic model of the universe. However, this motion is not
   repeated on a daily basis, as is *the return of the stars from west to
   east* in the quote above.

4. The centrality of the earth—It is strange that the Gaon seems
   to be suggesting that the seventh "star" is the earth. He seems
   to be saying that it is not part of the permutations since it is in
   the middle and does not revolve. This whole line of thought
   does not seem correct. The seven "stars" of the *Mishnah* are
   named explicitly in this and the following *Mishnayot*. This list
   excludes the earth. This sentence is in parentheses in the text,
   and probably does not belong. I suspect the Gaon is not its
   author.

We mentioned earlier that the Gaon's text states that the "star"
associated with the letter *Bet* is not Saturn, but rather is the moon. He
says as follows:

> The moon in the physical world represents Kindness; therefore it is
> white, since white is Kindness. This [the *Mishnah*] is in the same order as
> their creation, as is stated in the *Tikunei HaZohar*,[23] "White is associated
> with the moon, red with Mars, yellow-green with the Sun, black with
> Saturn, and blue with Jupiter. These are the colors of *Chesed* (Kindness),
> *Gevurah* (Courage), *Tiferet* (Beauty), *Yisod* (Foundation), and *Malchut*
> (Kingdom). *Netzach* (Eternity) and *Hod* (Beauty) are associated with
> Venus and Mercury.[24]

The Gaon is following the usual order found in the *Zohar*. The first
of the seven lower *Sefirot* is *Chesed* (Kindness). Associating it with the
moon is sensible, as it is white. White generally symbolizes kindness in
Kabbalah. The second of the seven lower *Sefirot* is *Gevurah*. The *Zohar*

associates it with Mars, which is red. Red, of course, is associated with blood, war, harshness. Thus, *Gevurah*, representing Strict Law, is the obvious candidate to be associated with this planet. In the symbolism of the *Zohar*, the Sun consistently represents *Tiferet*, the third *Sefirah* of the lower seven. The third day of the week is naturally associated.

The rest of the Gaon's remarks are in the same vein. They are in accord with the established symbolism of the *Zohar*. The Gaon's text seems to fit better than that of the standard version, although one cannot be sure what was in the original *Sefer Yetzirah*.

GIMEL'S RELATION TO JUPITER, MONDAY, AND THE LEFT EYE

Sefer Yetzirah, Chapter 4, Mishnah 6

מ״ן המליך אות ג׳ וקשר לו כתר וצר בו
צדק בעולם יום שני בשנה ועין שמאל
בנפש :

He made the letter *Gimel* the king and tied a crown to it. He formed Jupiter with it in the world, Monday in the year, and the left eye in the soul.

The Mishnah according to the Vilna Gaon

He made the letter *Gimel* the king with riches and tied a crown to it. He combined them [the letters] with each other and formed with them Mars in the world, Monday in the year, and the right ear in the soul, male and female.

Until this chapter, the differences between the texts were minor. Here they assume major proportions. The Gaon's version is much easier to understand, as it is more in accord with the usual symbolism of the *Zohar*.

The *Mishnah* is telling us of the creation that resulted from the letter *Gimel* being placed before the other letters of *Beged Kafarta*. The texts differ on which planet and which organ resulted. In the previous *Mishnah* we saw the Gaon differ not only on these, but on the associated attribute as well. The Gaon there said that the attribute was *Wisdom* rather than *Life*. In this *Mishnah* the Gaon says the attribute connected with *Gimel* is *riches*, whereas the standard text fails to mention this attribute at all. This is particularly strange, since in the previous *Mishnah* the standard text did mention the associated attribute, *life*. The Gaon's version of the *Mishnayot* is more consistent with not only the *Zohar*'s symbolism, but with each other as well.

Nonetheless, one cannot easily dismiss the standard text, for the Raivad bases his commentary upon it. The most famous Kabbalist of them all, the Ari (Isaac Luria), is said to have favored the Raivad's commentary. In *Etz Chaim*, Chaim Vital quotes his famous mentor, the Ari, as saying that most commentaries on *Sefer Yetzirah* are flawed, but that of the Raivad is true and correct. This, despite the fact that the Ari acknowledges that the Raivad's commentary was not written by the historical Raivad but by an unknown Askenazi rabbi.[25]

Each letter of *Beged Kafarta* is associated with one of the seven lower *Sefirot*. According to the Vilna Gaon, the first letter is paired with the first *Sefirah* (*Chesed*), the second letter, *Gimel*, is associated with the second of the seven lower *Sefirot* (*Gevurah*), and so on. The Raivad, however, has a different order. The Vilna Gaon's method seems logical. The association in this *Mishnah* of Monday, riches, and *Gevurah* is supported by the common symbolism of the *Zohar*. *Gevurah* is associated throughout Kabbalah with Strict Laws. Fire is associated with it. Gold often has a red tint. In addition, the Scripture says, "From the north gold will come" (Job 37:22). *Gevurah* is located on the left side of the Heavenly Man, which is the northern side. This is like the setup in the Tabernacle, where the table with the twelve breads was in the north. It represents sustenance and wealth. Gold's reddish tint is similar to Mars, which is, therefore, also grouped with *Gevurah*.

The Gaon says that the associated body part is the right ear. He explains that the first three of the lower seven *Sefirot* are *Chesed*, *Gevurah*, and *Tiferet*, and corresponding are the right eye, ear, and nostril. The next three, *Netzach*, *Hod*, and *Yisod*, correspond to the left eye, ear, and nostril. The mouth is *Malchut*. The order of the standard text is right eye, left eye, right ear, left ear, right nostril, left nostril, and mouth. It is more difficult to explain than the Gaon's system.

The Gaon puts it as follows:

> The eyes are the *Yud* in the Tetragrammaton and the ears are the *Hey*. The nose is the *Vav* and the mouth the [final] *Hey*. So are the four senses they contain, as is known from several sources. They [the organs] are double, except for the mouth, for they form two groups. The first is *Chesed*, *Gevurah*, and *Tiferet*, [associated with] *Yud*, *Hey*, and *Vav*, and *Malchut* is *Hey* that completes the name. Similarly, *Netzach*, *Hod*, and *Yisod*—*Yud*, *Hey*, *Vav*—and *Malchut*—*Hey*—complete the name. This is what is written in the *Tikunim* (part of the *Zohar*), "*Malchut* is in the middle, between *Chesed-Gevurah-Tiferet* and *Netzach-Hod-Malchut*." So they are ordered here: right eye, ear, and nostril associated with *Chesed-Gevurah-Tiferet*, *Yud Hey Vav*, and left eye, ear, nostril associated with *Netzach*, *Hod*, and *Yisod*—*Yud Hey Vav*. The mouth is in the middle, between the right and left sides—*Hey*. The eyes and ears are separated in two places since the body separates between *Chesed* and *Netzach*, as it does also between *Hod* and *Gevurah*. However, between the body and the *brit* [penis] there is no separation, and so the rabbis said "the body and *brit* are considered as one." Therefore, there is no separation between the nostrils.[26]

The Gaon's words are fairly self-explanatory. In kabbalistic imagery, the right side is superior to the left and the top is superior to the bottom. The three higher *Sefirot* (of the seven) are therefore associated with the right side of the face. It would have been possible to associate *Gevurah* with the left eye, since *Gevurah* is on the left. This is what the standard text does. However, this results in a problem, because the next *Sefirah*, *Tiferet*, is in the middle, but the next part of the body, the ears, are to the sides and do not correspond. The Gaon's scheme is a cleaner fit than the standard text.

The mouth alone is a single unit and is in the middle. It naturally goes with both the right and left side. Thus, each group of three *Sefirot* represents the first three letters of God's name, but the final *Hey* combines with each group to complete the name.

This *Mishnah* would be incomplete without some of the Raivad's comments. He is the main commentator on the rest of the chapter. Most of the others, including the Vilna Gaon and the *Pree Yitzchak*, have no comments from here until the last *Mishnah* of this chapter.

The Raivad's commentary in Chapter 4 is heavily astrological. Although some of what he says is based on religious literature and known sources, much is of unknown origin, probably gleaned in part from the astrology current in his time. It is, nonetheless, interesting in its own right, though some seems at best tangentially related to the text of *Sefer Yetzirah*.

He says as follows:

He raised the letter *Gimel* to be the head, through the power of the high *Keter* and Wisdom. From the power of Kindness He gave it the power of peace, and gave it the attributes of kindness, honesty, justice, humility, good deeds, good reputation, and so on. To it belong peace, security from fear, help with kindness, love of the loyal, beautiful living places and houses, for it is the beginning of the creation, the palaces of kingship, and the worship of the King of Kings, God.[27]

DALET AND MARS, TUESDAY, AND THE RIGHT EAR

Sefer Yetzirah, Chapter 4, Mishnah 7

מ"ז המליך אות ד' וקשר לו כתר וצר בו
מאדים בעולם ויום ג' בשנה ואוזן ימין
בנפש:

He made the letter *Dalet* king, and tied a crown to it, and formed Mars with it in the universe, Tuesday in the year, and the right ear in the soul.

Gaon's text of the Mishnah

He made *Dalet* king of Seed, and tied a crown to it, and combined them [the letters] with each other. He formed the Sun with them in the world, Tuesday in the year, and the right nostril in the soul, male and female.

Both the standard version and the Vilna Gaon's version agree that Sunday was created with the first letter of *Beged Kafarta*, Monday with the second, and so forth. The *Dalet* is the third letter and is thus responsible for the creation of Tuesday. It is common in Kabbalah for the seven lower *Sefirot* to be associated with the seven days of the week in their normal order—*Chesed, Gevurah, Tiferet, Netzach, Hod, Yisod,* and *Malchut.*

This is exactly what the Vilna Gaon's text does. The standard text, as explained by the Raivad, however, associates Sunday with *Malchut* rather than *Chesed.* Then Monday is grouped with *Chesed,* Tuesday with *Gevurah,* and so on, until Sabbath is grouped with *Yisod.* There is a rationale to the Raivad's approach, however, as strange as it may seem.

In Chapter 1 we were told by *Sefer Yetzirah,* "Insert their end in their beginning and their beginning in their end."[28] We said there that the last *Sefirah* of the higher world is the material from which the first *Sefirah* of the lower is made. This ties the worlds together and emphasizes that all are directly related and none is independent of the Infinite first cause. While this is true of the big picture with the ten *Sefirot,* it is also true of the smaller groups. In the group of seven, the last *Sefirah,* *Malchut,* is tied in a sense to *Chesed,* the first. The *Sefirah* directly above *Chesed* is *Binah.* *Binah* and *Malchut* represent practically the same concept. *Binah* is called the upper *Shechinah,* *Malchut* the lower. They both are often considered feminine, *Binah* the mother, *Malchut* the daughter. *Malchut* is the mother of the lower worlds, just as *Binah* is mother to *Zair Anpin.* Both are represented by the same letter in the Tetragrammaton, the *Hey.* Thus, the concept of *Malchut* can be said to be the cause of *Chesed.*

Each *Sefirah* is caused (emanated) by its predecessor—*Gevurah* is caused by *Chesed,* *Tiferet* is caused by *Gevurah,* and so on. Thus, unlike the Gaon's version, which pairs the days and their associated *Sefirot,* the Raivad's version associates the days and the *Sefirot* that *cause* them. After all, the cause is present in the result. Remember the kabbalistic principal, "*The effect does not refute the cause.*" This is similar to the important principal of Hegelian philosophy, "The blossom does not refute the bud."

The standard version of this *Mishnah,* therefore, has Mars as the associated planet, for it represents *Gevurah* (Courage, War, Strict Law). While *Gevurah* is the second of the seven lower *Sefirot,* it is the direct cause of the third. It is therefore associated with *Dalet*, the third of the letters of *Beged Kafarta*.

There are not very many commentaries on this *Mishnah*. Saadia Gaon sums it up as follows:

> He made *Dalet* king and tied a crown to it. He combined the letters together and made them into a single utterance. He built it into "*Degev Kafarta*" [*Dalet, Gimel, Bet, Kaf, Peh, Resh* and *Tav*]. He formed Mars with it in the world, Monday in the week in the year, and the left eye in the soul, and wisdom and its replacement, foolishness.[29]

This quote of Saadia contains two major surprises. He associates the third letter of *Beged Kafarta* with Monday rather than Tuesday. He also associates it with the left eye. This is in contrast to the standard text which says the right ear, and the Vilna Gaon's text, which says the right nostril. There is no way of escaping the fact that at least three versions of *Sefer Yetzirah* seriously differ from each other. Yet, despite the differences, the versions reflect upon each other in a way that can be used to better understand the various underlying theories. The explanations of kabbalistic theories show the methodology that constitutes Kabbalah. This methodology defines Kabbalah much more than any conclusion it may reach. Kabbalah is a process much more than it is a body of dogma.

We end this *Mishnah* with the Raivad's commentary. It says as follows:

> It [*Gevurah*, the *Sefirah* associated with the *Mishnah*] points to strength of heart, stubbornness, cruelty, anger, ire, slayings, and wars, for such are the laws of *Gevurah*. Also included are the military officers and the spillers of the blood of wild animals and man. Also, any labor involving fire is related to it, for to it belongs the great fire. To it also belong the gold and the reddish pearls and all that is red. Also, in partnership with *Binah*, it is in charge of the nullifying and the withholding of goods. To it belong all types of fear and drunkardness, and the places where cooking is done. To it belong meat and blood and spice and red wine. It arouses, from the perspective of law, the desire for sex and intercourse and the first conjugal blood of virgins. To it belong jealousy and hate. . . . It is responsible for avenging false oaths and false witnesses and baseless hope. To it the insane relate from the standpoint of lost knowledge. To it belong falling from high places and fire and sulphur

and burning water and the place of the slaughter of sheep; therefore, they are slaughtered by the north side of the altar in the Temple. Also, war and stoves and baths, scorpions and bad animals belong to it. In its domain is also the second watch, barking dogs, wolves, and red clothing, as well as sharp drinks.[30]

This is a strange paragraph. In many ways it defies explanation. While the theory behind some of the points is clear, many are left unexplained. *Gevurah* is generally associated with harshness, law, fire, and blood in Kabbalah. These items have positive aspects. They encompass justice and the protection of the innocent. Curing the sick is also traditionally *Gevurah*'s domain, since it has dominion over things related to blood and fire (fever). In the Amidah prayer, the second blessing is that of *Gevurah*, and it includes a prayer for the sick. Certain functions are not of any one *Sefirah* alone. Thus, both *Gevurah* and *Binah* are involved in nullifying. *Gevurah* burns with its fire that which should be burnt. We nullify the unleavened bread Passover eve by burning it. *Gevurah* likewise nullifies the unleavened pride of the arrogant with its spiritual fire. *Binah* also nullifies, since *Binah* stands for the power of renewal. Renewal means change, and change implies that the old, in a sense, is nullified.

The great fire is not only a reference to God's creative fire. It is also the source of hell fire. However, what is meant is that it is its remote cause. *Gevurah* itself is a positive, not a negative, entity. Even though the worlds of the "side of darkness" *nurse from it*, that is, cling to it for their life power, it in itself is all good.

Gevurah is associated with fire, and so lust is thought to be somehow related to it, especially the lust for virgins, since the first intercourse usually involves virginal blood, and blood is red and is associated with *Gevurah*. The Raivad says that *Gevurah* arouses the sexual desire from "the perspective of law." This means desire from the fire of the left side (law). This is lust rather than love, which is from the middle or right.

The Raivad speaks of the slaughter of sheep. In the Temple, the *Mishnah* in Tractate *Zevachim* tells us that the holiest sacrifices were always slaughtered on the north side of the altar.[31] This law is based on the scriptural commandment, "Thou shalt slaughter it on the side of the altar that is northern" (Leviticus 1:11). The Raivad is supplying a kabbalistic reason for this law not mentioned in the Bible or Talmud.

It must be slaughtered on the northern side, because that is the side where the *Sefirah* of *Gevurah* is in the Heavenly Man. The sacrificing of animals is a function in its domain.

As to the Raivad's allusion to the second watch being associated with *Gevurah*, we find the following statement in the Talmud: "The night has three watches. In the first, donkeys bray; in the second, dogs bark; and in the third, infants nurse from their mothers' breasts and wives converse with their husbands."[32] Dogs barking, of course, is *Gevurah*-like. The Raivad already explained that anger is associated with *Gevurah*. Therefore, its domain includes the second watch.

KAF AND THE SUN, WEDNESDAY, AND THE LEFT EAR

Sefer Yetzirah, Chapter 4, Mishnah 8

מ"ח המליך אות כ' וקשר לו כתר וצר בו
חמה בעולם ויום ד' בשנה ואזן שמאל
בנפש :

He made the letter *Kaf* king and tied a crown to it. He formed the Sun with it in the universe, Wednesday in the year, and the left ear in the soul.

Vilna Gaon's version

He made the letter *Kaf* king with life and tied a crown to it. He combined them [the letters] each with each and formed Venus with them in the universe, Wednesday in the year, and the left eye in the soul, male and female.

This *Mishnah* continues the pattern described in the previous *Mishnayot*. The Gaon's version differs as to the identity of the *star* and *body part*

associated with the letter that was made king. It also differs as to the
attribute. The standard version neglects to mention the attribute at all.
Only in *Mishnah* 5 did the standard version speak of the attribute, and
from there we know that the standard text's association of attributes
with letters is different than the Gaon's.

The Torah tells us that the sun was created on the *fourth* day. This
adds support to the standard version of the text, which associates it
with the *fourth* letter of *Beged Kafarta*. On the other hand, the sun is
generally associated with the *third Sefirah* (of the seven lower ones), the
Sefirah of *Tiferet*, throughout the *Zohar*. As was mentioned previously,
one of the most common symbols representing the *Tiferet–Malchut*
pair are the *sun* and the *moon*. Consequently, the Gaon's version is
more what a Kabbalist would expect.

The Gaon's text adds the phrase "male and female" after naming the
associated body part. When we discussed *Emesh*, we learned that the
first letter did not determine the gender. It was rather the order of the
remaining letters. The same is true here with the letters of *Beged
Kafarta*. The order of the remaining letters, rather than *the letter that was
made king*, determines the sex. Therefore, the Gaon's version states that
the left eyes for both male and female were created with the letter *Kaf*
first. He does not, however, explicitly state the order of the remaining
letters.

As we found before, the text of Saadia Gaon differs from both the
standard text and that of the Vilna Gaon. Saadia states as follows: "He
made the letter *Kaf* king and tied a crown to it and built it into '*Kafarta
Beged*' [*Kaf, Peh, Resh, Tav, Bet, Gimel*, and *Dalet*]. He formed with it
the Sun in the universe, Tuesday in the week in the year, and the right
nose in the soul, as well as wealth and its replacement, poverty."[33]

Saadia, unlike the other commentators, provides the order of all the
letters of *Beged Kafarta*. However, he only provides one arrangement,
not separate ones for male and female. As we have seen before, the
associated day in his text is different from that which we find in the
other versions. It has been pointed out previously that each version has
its own logic. Saadia's version is similar to the Vilna Gaon's in that the
Sun is paired with Tuesday. This is the usual *Zohar* symbolism.
However, in Saadia's version, the associated letter is *Kaf*, while in the
Vilna Gaon's it is *Dalet*.

The Raivad's comments on this *Mishnah* are of the same type as we
have seen in the past three *Mishnayot*. He seems to jump from idea to

idea and speaks of many things that at first seem unrelated. Sometimes supporting arguments are presented, sometimes not. It is very difficult to determine exactly what point he is making. He begins by describing the qualities that belong to *Tiferet*, the *Sefirah* he associates with the *Mishnah*. According to him, the *letter*, the *star*, and the other items mentioned in the *Mishnah* all have a special relationship to this *Sefirah*. He puts it as follows:

> To it [*Tiferet*] belong grace, honor, and rule, and the unification of God's name in writing and orally. It points to hidden lights and the service of kings, for it [*Tiferet*] serves *Binah*. Also, it is clear that it relates to the companionship of those who are kind and righteous. Also, it is very clear that its domain is the wisdom of nature, since it [*Tiferet*] is [the result of] the combination of the letters of *Emesh*. It is over wealth, silver from the right side, gold from its left. Also, success is in its domain. To it belong strength from the side of *Gevurah* and many helpers from the side of unity. To it belongs all business involving silver and gold and all that has to do with the produce of the earth. All precious stones belong to its domain. Also, the twelve stones of the High Priest's breastplate [*Choshen*] and the stones of his apron [*Ephod*]. From what it [*Tiferet*] gets from the side of *Gevurah* it relates to damage and toil in business and hatred from officials. Since it makes peace between the fire and the water, therefore, it tells of peace from fear, quiet, and health. To travel by land is very good but to travel by sea and on all types of waters is very bad, for all the animals of the land cannot survive in the water by themselves. It subdues the enemy through the power of courage, and its hand is at the neck of its enemies and those who look to do harm. It testifies on the freeing of slaves, in accord with the secret of the seventh year (*Shemitah*). Also, on the release of prisoners from jail, according to the principal of exchange. It frees those under attack from the enemy, for "The Lord of hosts is a sun and shield" (Psalms 84:12) upon them. He returns to them the good will of man and will cause them to find grace in the eyes of God and man. It [*Tiferet*] testifies on arrogance and loftiness, and through it the sick will be cured, for it is intermediate between hot and moist and cold and dry."[34]

Clarification of some of the points in the above quote may be helpful.

1. The Raivad speaks of "unification" belonging to *Tiferet*. This is because *Tiferet* is positioned between the two opposing

Sefirot of *Chesed* and *Gevurah*, and serves to unify them. The *Sefirot*, as you know, are associated with the names of God. Thus, this process is sometimes called "the unification of the name." *Tiferet* is known as the *written Torah*, *Malchut* the *oral* one. The unification process happens with both, which is why the Raivad speaks of "the unification of God's name *in writing* and *orally*."

2. *Binah* is the "mother" of the Six Extremes, that is, their cause. *Tiferet* is the main *Sefirah* of the Extremes. It serves *Binah* in the sense that one must obey one's parent.

3. *Tiferet* is associated with good companionship, since its function is to unite the Six Extremes.

4. It is associated with the wisdom of nature. Nature is the product of *Emesh*. *Emesh*, you will recall, stands for air, water, and fire. These are the elements of nature. The diverse elements are incorporated in *Tiferet*, and it is, in a sense, the sum of these three.

5. Silver is associated with *Chesed*, Gold with *Gevurah*. The Scripture says, "Gold will come from the north" (Job 37:22). In the world of the *Sefirot*, north is left.

6. The number twelve is associated with *Tiferet*. In the next chapter we will learn that the twelve "single" letters of the alphabet belong to *Tiferet*. The twelve tribes, the twelve unique combinations of the letters of the Tetragrammaton, and the twelve diagonals, which we will discuss later, all belong to her. So do the twelve stones in the High Priest's vestment.

7. The Torah states, "If thou take a Hebrew slave, he shall work six years but on the seventh thou shall send him free" (Exodus 21:2). Seven is thus related to freedom.

8. The *principal of exchange* is that everything changes. Things constantly enter existence and go out of existence. Creatures come into being and die, are imprisoned and are freed. Nothing remains the same. Life is *exchanged* for death and death for life, freedom for slavery and slavery for freedom, and so on.

9. *Curing* is in *Tiferet*'s domain since it is a mediator. It is positioned between the Extremes and modifies them. Sickness is when there is too much heat (fever) or cold or moisture. *Tiferet* modifies and thus *cures* the Extremes.

It is not at all clear whether the Raivad intended his ideas to be put to practical use. None of the commentaries on *Sefer Yetzirah* provide formulas for magical uses. Nor do they even include instructions for meditative use.

Aside from the question of how the ideas are intended to be used, there is also the question of how they developed in the first place. It has been suggested that perhaps some of the ideas were developed during trancelike states or during some type of special meditation. Prophets, such as Ezekiel, tell that prior to prophecy they lost strength and fell to the ground. It was necessary that the physical body be disabled so as not to interfere with the purely spiritual, prophetic event. Except for Moses, prophesy is said to have occurred only during sleep. Some have suggested that prophesy can occur not only during *normal* sleep but also during meditative, dreamlike states.

It seems reasonable to assume that since the commentators do not speak of the use to which the information in *Sefer Yetzirah* is to be put, they feel that it is primarily provided for its own intrinsic spiritual value, and not for any practical use.

This is not to deny, of course, the possibility of practical uses. However, it is not the *primary* purpose of the book.

PEH AND VENUS, THURSDAY, AND THE RIGHT NOSTRIL

Sefer Yetzirah, Chapter 4, Mishnah 9

מ"ט המליך אות פ' וקשר לו כתר וצר בו
נוגה בעולם ויום ה' בשנה ונחיר ימין
בנפש:

He made the letter *Peh* king and tied a crown to it. He formed Venus with it in the universe, Thursday in the year, and the right nostril in the soul.

Vilna Gaon's text

He made the letter *Peh* king with kingdom and tied a crown to it. He combined them [the letters] each with each and formed with them Mercury in the universe, Thursday in the year, and the right ear in the soul, male and female.

The textual versions continue to vary according to the systematic approaches described in the previous *Mishnayot*. Saadia says as follows: "He made *Peh* king and built it into '*Parat Begdach*' (*Peh, Resh, Tav, Bet, Gimel, Dalet,* and *Kaf*). He formed with it Venus in the universe, Wednesday in the week in the year, the left nostril in the soul, and seed and its replacement, desolation."

Thus, as in the past *Mishnayot*, at least three versions of the text differ significantly from each other.

Most of the commentators say little or nothing about this *Mishnah*. The Raivad, on the other hand, says quite a lot. His commentary seems fragmented, and some of his sentences seem incomplete. I suspect that perhaps our version is faulty. In any case, I have translated it as best as I can. As many of the Raivad's statements need explanation, I have provided some information that may help in understanding him. Nevertheless, he remains difficult to fully comprehend.

The Raivad says as follows:

He made the letter *Peh* king and tied a crown to it. He formed Venus with it in the universe through the power of "*Hakav Tenei*" and Thursday in the year and the right nostril in the soul. He put Seed in its [the *Sefirah* of *Netzach*'s] power, and mating and the attraction of women. Also, the attraction of beauty, and achieving one's will with women, as it is written, "His right hand will embrace me" (Song of Songs 2:6), and it is also written, "Sweetness is in your right hand eternally [the word for *eternally* is *Netzach,* just as the name of the fourth *Sefirah* of the seven under discussion] (Psalms 16:11). [Also, in its power is] peace from fear through its contact with *Tiferet.* It has helpers from the side of *Chesed* (Kindness), as well as those who love it and work for its benefit from the side of *Tiferet.* It has [in its domain] desire for women and sex as well as musical instruments and happiness and engagement and jewelry and gardens and orchards and all sorts of pleasure. It points to pleasures that come from the side of *Chesed* (Kindness) to *Malchut* and peace from enemies, since it is victorious (*Netzach* also means *victory* in

Hebrew). Since it receives [influence] from the side of *Gevurah*, its appearance is like gold mixed with white silver. It testifies as to the purifiers of metals and silk and embroidery and types of drawings, and every type of pleasure and peace. To it belong news and tidings from the side of good (*Chesed*), and kind acts and mercy and benefaction and help and pretty houses and beautiful sights. To it belongs the power of pregnancy, for it has the wind of life and heat and moisture, since it leans toward moisture. It has the boys and girls, sons and daughters. Its color is yellow with a tint of red, since the "pipe" that comes from *Gevurah* mixes it with all sorts of mixtures. Fine acts are related to it. In its domain is the gathering of woman for good causes, though sometimes [the gatherings are] from the side of strict law for bad. From it grow compounders and mountains of spice and good smells and all the jewelry of women and merchandise, although sometimes disagreement from the side of the fire.[35]

1. "*Hakav Tenei*" (*Hey, Kuf, Bet, Tet, Nun, Ayin*) is one of the seven components of "the name of forty-two" letters. It is the fifth name, thus associated with the fifth day, Thursday. Each component has six letters, hence forty-two all together.
2. The *Sefirah* that is associated with this *Mishnah* is *Netzach*. It has several meanings in Hebrew, including eternity, victory, and blood. This explains some of the Raivad's associations.
3. Seed and sex are related to perpetuation of the species. It is, thus, related to *Netzach* (eternity).
4. The relationship of *Netzach* to beauty, pleasure, and so on, is all derived from it representing eternity.
5. While *Sefer Yetzirah* does not mention the concept of "pipes" between the *Sefirot*, this concept is well established in later Kabbalah. Pipes (*Tzinorot*) convey the heavenly "material" from one *Sefirah* to another. This material is referred to in various manners. It is sometimes called *influence, abundance,* or *light*. Material coming through pipes carries the traits of the source *Sefirah*. If it comes from *Gevurah*, it brings *Gevurah*'s characteristics. One can say that the pipes help mix the spiritual matter. The Raivad states that the color of *Netzach* is tinted red due to the matter arriving in the pipe from *Gevurah*.
6. One's neighborhood is important, even for the *Sefirot*. *Sefirot* are affected by which *Sefirot* are around them and influence them.

7. *Gevurah* is what the Raivad calls, in the last line, "the side of
   fire." This is because it is instrumental in the punishment of
   the wicked, as was explained in the previous *Mishnayot*.

RESH AND MERCURY, FRIDAY, AND THE LEFT NOSTRIL

Sefer Yetzirah, Chapter 4, Mishnah 10

מ"י המליך אות ר' וקשר לו כתר וצר בו
כוכב בעולם ויום ששי בשנה ונחיר
שמאל בנפש :

He made the letter *Resh* king and tied a crown to
it. He formed Mercury with it in the universe,
Friday in the year, and the left nostril in the soul.

Vilna Gaon's text

He made the letter *Resh* king with peace and tied
a crown to it. He combined them [the letters]
each with each and formed with them Saturn in
the universe, Friday in the year, and the left
nostril in the soul, male and female.

As in the previous *Mishnayot*, Saadia's text differs from the two
versions presented above. Saadia says as follows: "He made the letter
Resh king and built it into 'Retbag Dekaf' (*Resh, Tav, Bet, Gimel, Dalet,
Kaf,* and *Peh*). He formed with it Mercury in the world, Thursday in
the week in the year, the right ear in the soul, and grace and its
replacement, ugliness."[36]

Incidentally, another famous tenth-century Kabbalist, Shabbetai
Donnolo, seems to have had the same version as Saadia. Donnolo
states as follows: "In the beginning, before all the days of the week,
Sabbath was created with the letter *Bet*, since before God began to

create the world it was Sabbath."[37] Thus he, like Saadia, associates the Sabbath with the first letter of *Beged Kafarta*. As they are the earliest of the commentators, one suspects that perhaps their text is closer to the original than that of the later rabbis.

One of the main differences between the texts of this *Mishnah* concerns the identity of the associated planet. The Vilna Gaon's version states that the associated planet is Saturn. The other versions have Saturn related either to Sunday or to the Sabbath. Saturn has special significance, and there are reasons to associate it more with certain days than with others. One obvious reason to associate it with the Sabbath is its name. Saturn in Hebrew is *Shabbetai*, which has the same root as *Shabbat* (Sabbath). In the Raivad's commentary on *Mishnah* 5, he associates Saturn with quiet, rest, and desolation. The lack of activity is reminiscent of the Sabbath. The apparent movement of Saturn, of course, is the least of the seven heavenly bodies. This, too, leads to its association with the Sabbath and rest.

Saturn has an interesting place in Jewish theology for an additional reason. The other heavenly bodies are said to be hung from it! The Talmud Bavli tells us that a special blessing must be made by one who "sees the sun in its season."[38] It continues, "When is the season? Abaye says, every twenty-eight years."[39] Upon this Rashi comments, "Every twenty-eight years—of the season of *Nissan*. At the end of twenty-eight years, when the great cycle of the sun returns, so that the [hour that the season begins] falls on the hour that the heavenly lights were hung *onto* Saturn. This is the hour of the beginning of the night of the fourth day."[40]

It should be noted that Torah tells us that the sun, moon, and stars were created on day four of the genesis (Genesis 1:1). Also note that it takes Saturn approximately twenty-eight years to revolve around the sun. Thus, the association of Saturn with Wednesday would have been logical, but it is not found in any of the texts. As it is the first planet if we count from the most distant inward, its association with the first day, Sunday, is not surprising. The Gaon's text associates it with Friday, which has no obvious special significance for the sun.

This discussion would not be complete without the Raivad's commentary. As he did in the previous *Mishnayot* of this chapter, the Raivad tells of the various items associated with the *Mishnah*. The *Sefirah* that relates to this *Mishnah*, according to the Raivad, is *Hod* (Beauty). The Raivad says as follows:

He made the letter *Resh* king and tied a crown to it. He formed Mercury with it in the universe through the power of *"Yigel Pazak"* as well as Friday in the year and the right nostril in the soul. In its domain are books and wisdom and writing from the written Torah and knowledge and speech and counsel and reason. Since it has a pipe from the side of *Gevurah*, it has the strength of argumentation and joins [in disputes]. To it belong all types of crafts, for it is *Hod* [Beauty]. Therefore, it will join with all men. To it belong drawing, embroidery, and writing. It unites the enemies, whether for peace from the side of *Tiferet*, or for war, from the side of the fire. Sometimes errors reach it due to its great heat and anger. It has cunning, for it is learned in war through the side of *Gevurah*. It has sweet lips from the side of *Tiferet*. It has playfulness and song from the power of the natural heat of *Gevurah*. It has involvement with numerous affairs through the power of fire and *Tiferet*. It has a multitude of people through the twelve tribes of Israel that come to it through the power of *Tiferet*. It has dispute through the power of the wisdom of fire. Since it fights with the enemies of God it needs to have power in order to nullify their opinion on many matters. . . . To it belong the supplications and the prayers, for from it they descend. It is like the representative of the congregation and prays for Israel and the children of *Malchut*. To it come false rumors from the side of the replacements. However, "the eternity of Israel will not lie" (1 Samuel 15:29) as well.[41]

As usual, the Raivad's remarks are difficult and purposely secretive. He says in several places in his commentary that he provides only "chapter headings" but not the details.

A few clarifications follow:

1. *"Yigel Pazak"* is the sixth part of "the name of forty-two." It is, therefore, related to Friday (the sixth day).
2. The sixth *Sefirah* is *Yisod* and is between *Tiferet* and *Malchut*. *Tiferet* is known as the written Torah, *Malchut* the oral law. *Yisod*, being in between, gets from both. Therefore, both speech and written knowledge are in its domain.
3. Pipes, you will recall, refer to conduits of the spiritual matter between the *Sefirot*.
4. The side of fire refers to *Gevurah*, Strict Law.
5. The idea of *errors* reaching *Yisod* needs clarification. As it is part of the world of divinity (the emanations), there can be no error

within it. Only those influenced by it sometimes fall into error due to excessive heat (i.e., a hot temperament).

6. The number *twelve*, we shall see later, is related to *Tiferet*. As *Yisod* receives directly from *Tiferet*, it inherits its attributes.

7. *Yisod*'s relation to prayers comes from being between *Tiferet* and *Malchut*. Just as there is prayer below, there is also prayer above, in the world of the *Sefirot*. *Malchut* prays to *Tiferet*. As *Yisod* is in between, it is the channel through which the prayers must flow. Thus it is the *representative* of *Malchut*. *Malchut*, in turn, is known as *Knesset Yisroel*, the *Congregation of Israel*.

8. The last line is a reference to the *Sefirah* of *Netzach*. It, like *Yisod*, is associated with life and truth. Replacements, such as false rumors and lies, "*come* to *Yisod* and *Netzach*." This is to say, they are *related* to them. It is the same relation that lies and truth have, namely, an *inverse* relation. However, despite the *relation* to lies, the *Sefirot* themselves contain no lies, only truth.

TAV AND THE MOON, SABBATH, AND THE MOUTH

Sefer Yitzirah, Chapter 4, Mishnah 11

מי"א המליך אות ת' וקשר לו כתר וצר
בו לבנה בעולם ויום שבת בשנה
ופה בנפש :

He made the letter *Tav* king and tied a crown to it. He formed the moon with it in the universe, Sabbath in the year, and the mouth in the soul.

Vilna Gaon's text

He made the letter *Tav* king with grace and tied a crown to it. He combined them [the letters] each with each and formed with them Jupiter in the universe, Sabbath in the year, and the mouth in the soul, male and female.

The standard text of this *Mishnah* fits in perfectly with the usual kabbalistic symbolism for the *Sefirah* of *Malchut*. In the *Zohar*, *Malchut* is often referred to as the moon. It is commonly also referred to as the Sabbath.

In anatomical symbolism, of all the body parts, the mouth is the most strongly associated with *Malchut*. This is, perhaps, because *Malchut* is female. The mouth is the source of speech, about which the Talmud says, "Ten measures of speech descended into the world, and nine were taken by women."[42] Thus, mouths and women were forever bound together in Jewish thought, justly or otherwise.

Of the seven letters of *Beged Kafarta*, *Tav* is the natural candidate to be assigned to the feminine *Malchut*. This is because in Hebrew grammar, *Tav* signifies the feminine ending of words.

The Vilna Gaon clearly states that this *Mishnah* is associated with *Malchut*, although in his version the related planet (Jupiter) seems somewhat problematic. The Raivad's approach, on the other hand, is rather strange. He has this *Mishnah* representing *Yisod*, even though his commentary is based on the standard text, which strongly suggests *Malchut*. The Raivad's remarks, in a rather difficult style, follow:

He made the letter *Tav* king and tied a crown to it. He formed the moon with it in the universe through the power of "*Shaku Tzeit*," in conjunction with the *foundations of the world* (*Yisod*), the Sabbath in the year, and the mouth in the soul. He put in it the power of walking, moving, companionship, and travel in the ocean of wisdom. Also, the gathering of people, for there [in *Yisod*] gather all the heavenly visions. The forms of *Malchut* are suppressed there by the higher forms, according to what is written [in Genesis], "and conquer her" (Genesis 1:28). Therefore, it points to submission and requesting the consent of higher authority. Since it expands, it refers to movement and lack of rest. Since at times it brings close and at times pushes away, it refers at times to redemption and at times to exile, but it will obtain its desires. It gets news and correspondence from *Tiferet*, and to it belong messengers and those who relate good about others. Since it is sometimes in a state of extinguished light, it points to dangerous sickness and weeping. It also sometimes points to the shrouds of the dead in accord with the secret that the clothing of the slain and the sword that killed him are similarly ritually unclean. At times it points to health, in accord with its uniting with life [the right side] or death [the left]. To it belongs the rain, from Kindness [*Chesed*] that is in heaven. Also, the snow, the hail, the streams, the seas, and the water troughs. To it belong the gardens and orchards, for it is the actual Garden of Eden. Rule belongs to it, for it is kingdom. To it belongs working for the king, and war and peace and crossing bodies of water. In its domain are the cold and the merchandise, for to it the seventy kings will bring a tribute and a present to God. To it belong cold from *Chesed* and merchandise from *Tiferet*, argumentation from Fire and joy and honor.[43]

The following will help explain the above quotation:

1. "*Shaku Tzeit*" (*Shin, Kuf, Vav, Tzadi, Yud,* and *Tav*) is the last of the six-letter component names that comprise "the name of forty-two." It is the component associated with this *Mishnah* and the last letter of *Beged Kafarta*.
2. *Yisod* is frequently referred to in the *Zohar* as the "*foundation of the world.*" It is the *Sefirah* related to this *Mishnah*, according to the Raivad.
3. *Yisod* is a key *Sefirah* in its role of uniting the *Sefirot* of the Six Extremes and *Malchut*. It receives *spiritual flows* from both, and thus gathering and uniting are in its sphere. The *influence* and *forms* of the upper world are dominant over those from *Malchut* and thus *conquer* them, analogous to a man "conquering" a woman.
4. The reference to the *secret of the clothing of the dead and the sword* is a bit complicated. To understand this, you must know that *Yisod* (which is a mediator) is like a sword. *Sefer Yetzirah* calls the mediating function "a tongue of decree"[44] because it cuts a decision like a sword. It is also called *brit*, as it is associated with the cutting of circumcision.

    According to the Talmud, a sword is ritually unclean like the corpse it slew (Numbers 19:16).[45] So is the corpse's clothing. Since the sword is like the clothing in uncleanliness, they are considered related. Thus, *Yisod*, the sword, is related to the clothes of the dead.
5. Most of this quote can be understood by the position of *Yisod* among the *Sefirot* and the inter-*Sefirah* flows of heavenly substance. It is influenced by the *Sefirot* with which it interacts.
6. The seventy Kings refer to the seven lower *Sefirot*. Each *Sefirah* is said to be composed of all the rest, and thus they have all ten

within them. Seven *Sefirot* of ten each total seventy. As all seven provide *spiritual flows* into *Yisod* (including *Yisod* itself), it is as if these *spiritual flows* constitute presents to it.

The Raivad sums up all the seven *Mishnayot* that deal with *Beged Kafarta* as follows:

> With these seven levels you will find all the power of the "seven moving stars," how the powers spread to them from the power of the Tetragrammaton and ten *Sefirot*, from the power of the *name of forty-two*. They [the seven levels] are like chapter headings [without the details]. If you search in the Scriptures, you will find for each of them applicable verses from the Torah. These are the general headings of the powers, and should always be in front of your eyes. With them all the future will be known through the names of God, "*Yud Hey Vav Hey*" and "*Adonai*," may He be blessed and exalted.[46]

Thus, while we are not given the details of how to apply the knowledge of *Sefer Yetzirah*, we are told that the information is in the Torah and can be found. It is certainly beyond the scope of this book.

Finally, Saadia Gaon sums up his version of this *Mishnah* as follows: "He made *Tav* king and built it into '*Tabar Dichfar*' (*Tav, Bet, Gimel, Dalet, Kaf, Peh,* and *Resh*). He formed the moon with it in the universe, Friday in the week in the year, and the right ear in the soul, and rule and its replacement, slavery." Saadia proceeds to sum up as follows: "God split the three witnesses up to testify that He alone is the Living God and there is no other—the world separately, the year separately, and the soul separately. All three testify that He is One and there is no second to Him and no other, blessed be He and blessed be His name."[47]

The idea of inanimate objects testifying is based on an old biblical tradition. Moses teaches Israel in Deuteronomy, "Listen heavens and I will speak, and hear earth the words of my mouth" (Deuteronomy 32:1). Rashi states there that this verse implies that God made the heavens and the earth *witnesses*. Rashi continues: "Why did he make the heavens and earth witnesses? Moses said, 'I am flesh and blood. Tomorrow I die. If Israel says we did not accept the covenant, who will come and counter them?' Therefore, He made the heavens and the earth witnesses, for they last forever."[48]

LETTERS AS THE BUILDING BLOCKS
OF THE UNIVERSE

Sefer Yetzirah, Chapter 4, Mishnah 12

מ"ב שבע כפולות כיצד צרפן . שתי
אבנים בונות שני בתים . שלש
בונות ששה בתים . ארבע בונות ארבעה
ועשרים בתים . חמש בונות מאה ועשרים
בתים . שש בונות שבע מאות ועשרים בתים .
שבע בונות חמשת אלפים וארבעים בתים .
מכאן ואילך צא וחשוב מה שאין הפה יכול
לדבר ואין האוזן יכולה לשמוע . ואלו הן
שבעה כוכבים בעולם חמה נוגה כוכב לבנה
שבתאי צדק מאדים . ואלו הן ז' ימים בשנה
שבעה ימי בראשית . ושבעה שערים בנפש
שתי עינים שתי אזנים ושני נקבי האף והפה .
ובהן נחקקו שבעה רקיעים ושבע ארצות
ושבע שעות . לפיכך חבב שביעי לכל חפץ
תחת השמים :

The seven double letters, how were they combined? Two stones build two houses. Three
build six houses. Four build twenty-four houses.
Five build 120 houses. Six build 720 houses.
Seven build 5,040 houses. From here on, go and
figure that which the mouth is unable to utter
and the ear cannot hear. These are the seven
stars in the universe: the Sun, Venus, Mercury,
the Moon, Saturn, Jupiter, and Mars. These are
the seven days in the year: the seven days of
creation. These are the seven gates of the soul:
the two eyes, the two ears, the two nostrils of the
nose, and the mouth. With them were engraved
the seven firmaments, the seven lands, and the
seven hours. Therefore, He made seven beloved
for every item under the heavens.

The first part of the *Mishnah* is identical in the Vilna Gaon's version. The second part is as follows in the Gaon's text:

> **The seven doubles, *Beged Kafarta*, with them were engraved the seven worlds, the seven firmaments, the seven lands, the seven seas, the seven rivers, the seven deserts, the seven days, the seven weeks, the seven years, the seven *Shemitot* (seven-year cycles), the seven Jubilees, and the Holy Palace. Therefore, He made the sevens beloved under the whole heavens.**

To understand the first part of the *Mishnah*, you must understand the mathematical concept of a *factorial*. In addition, you must realize that while the *Mishnah* speaks in terms of stones and houses, it means letters and words.

The *Pree Yitzchak* explains it as follows: "The letters were called by the term *stones* since, just as stones are excavated from a rock mountain, so are the letters hewn and cut from the name of God, my rock and boulder (see Psalms 18:3). Through all twenty-two letters of the Torah, all things were shaped in all of the worlds."[49]

The Vilna Gaon was not only a famous Talmudist and Kabbalist, but a mathematician of some renown. In his commentary, he explains the concept of factorial and how factorial differs from combinations based on taking several items at a time from a larger number. To determine all the possible combinations of a collection of different letters, you multiply the number of letters, n, by $(n-1)$ then $(n-2)$, and so on, until 1. This yields the number of all the combinations, backward and forward. The *Mishnah* is telling us here that seven letters (*Beged Kafarta*) have 5,040 combinations. On the other hand, says the Gaon, to determine all the two-letter combinations that can be formed with the twenty-two letters, you must multiply n with $(n-1)$ only (22×21). This was done in Chapter 2 when we discussed the 231 gates. (Remember $22 \times 21 = 462$. Half of this is 231.) Likewise, all the combinations of three letters at a time taken from the twenty-two letters, with order counting, is equal to $22 \times 21 \times 20$.[50] Our *Mishnah*, of course, is discussing specifically the seven letters of *Beged Kafarta*, and thus only goes up to seven factorial.

The Raivad's comments are very interesting. He explains the similarity between people, letters, *Sefirot*, animal, vegetable, and mineral. In other words, everything!

He states as follows:

> The meaning of stones is letters, and so is it stated in the Scriptures "Among stones of fire did you walk" (Ezekiel 28:14), which means angels. It is also written "From there he pastored the stone of Israel" (Genesis 49:24). The letters are called stones because, just as the stone is cut from the rock, so are the letters cut and hewed from the name of God, "my rock and boulder" (see Psalms 18:3). Since houses and cities are built from stones, therefore buildings of stones are called houses. Without doubt, it has walls and a ceiling and a floor, as was explained earlier. All creatures are like houses, since a person's walls are the ribs and his insides are like the empty room. So is the head—the space in the head is like a house. So is it with all living things as well as inanimate objects. Even though they look solid, it is not so, but rather they contain chambers [houses], and so with things that grow [vegetation] and so with the entire world and so with the stars, and so with the letters and so with the ten *Sefirot*.[51]

There are several interesting aspects of Raivad's statement. The similarity between people and letters is not a chance occurrence. They are related in nature. All things in the world were produced through the natural forces that we call the letters of the *Aleph Bet* and are thus related. The world is one, and all bears the stamp of the one creator. Since all things were created with the letters, everything resembles them in some way.

The Raivad goes to the extent of saying that even angels are called stones, which is to say that they are similar to letters. This he proves from a verse that refers to "stones of fire." People are also spoken of as stones, as in the verse that speaks of "the stone of Israel." As strange as the analogy between stones, letters, and angels may seem, there is a basis for it in Jewish tradition. In the prayers on Rosh Hashana we speak of "angels coming from the sound of the *Shofar*."[52] Letters also produce sounds. In Hebrew, the word for angel, *Malach*, also means representative. Angels and words are all related in that they represent their issuer. People also represent their issuer, God, in a manner similar to that in which the stones of a house represent its builder.

The end of this *Mishnah* serves to sums up Chapter 4. It provides a list of items that were created in sets of sevens. The Raivad explains

that the combinations of *Beged Kafarta* start with each of its seven
letters and represent the six thousand years of the world's existence,
plus one thousand years that the world will be desolate.[53] The Raivad
continues:

> This is the gate to [understand] *Shemitot* [seven-year cycles] and Jubilees
> as well as the secret of the seven days of the week, the seven weeks that
> constitute the forty-nine days between Passover and Shavuot, the seven
> months between the holidays of Passover and Tabernacles. Also, the
> secret of the [lunar] year and the fifty-three portions of the Torah. They
> are the secret of the *Shemitot* and Jubilees.[54]

This *Mishnah* comes to teach us that just as there are seven days
beneath, so are there days and weeks and years and *Shemitot* and
Jubilees on high. This is the secret of leap months and the secret of "the
Sabbath of the Lord thy God" (Exodus 20:10) and is "the great and
terrible day of God" (Malachi 3:23).

All the meaningful sets of sevens stem from *Beged Kafarta*. Fifty has
special significance, as it directly follows seven times seven. The
fiftieth year is called the Jubilee in the Torah and is associated in
Kabbalah with the *Sefirah* of *Binah*, which is directly above the lower
seven *Sefirot*. *Binah* is their source and cause, and they are said to return
to it to be renewed. It is thus called *return* and *repentance*, as well as
shofar, which calls for *return* to God. *Binah* is said to have fifty gates of
understanding, seven times seven and one that transcends. Seven
repeats in small and large cycles. Even the entire span of the world's
existence (seven thousand years) is in units of sevens.

I have already explained that the seven lower *Sefirot* are called days,
and represent time in the world above. *Binah* is the Jubilee above. The
several verses the Raivad quotes refer to "days of God," which means
days that belong to God, that is, *Sefirot*.

As far as the secret of leap months, that remains a secret.

The commentaries go into the details of the elements that constitute
each set of seven. The Vilna Gaon says as follows:

> The seven worlds are the seven palaces that are called the young
> maidens of the Queen (*Malchut*), as the verse states, "*Alamot* [young
> woman] love you" (Song of Songs 1:3). Do not read it as *Alamot* [young
> women] but as *Olamot* [Worlds]. [These are the worlds] from lowest to
> highest: The whiteness of sapphire, the essence of heaven, shining,

merit, love, will, and holy of holies. They are double, male palaces and female. So are there seven blessings made over the *Shema* [a portion from the Torah] morning and evening. So is it in the replacements—the seven palaces of the side of uncleanliness correspond to them. As it says in *Tikun* 70,[55] "There are seven gates of hell and seven palaces."[56]

The Gaon continues to provide the details of the sets of sevens as follows: The seven heavens—*Vilon, Rakiya, Shechakim, Zevul, Ma'on, Mechon,* and *Aravot.* The seven lands—*Eretz, Adamah, Gei, Neshiyah, Tziyah, Arkah,* and *Tevel.* The seven seas—Of Tiberias, of Sodom, of Chaylot, of Chulta, of Sivchay, of Spain, and the great sea. The Altantic Ocean, says the Gaon, is not included, for it includes all the others and is not counted separately. It is at the level of *Binah,* that includes all seven [*Sefirot*] and so is it with every seven. The seven rivers—Jordan, Yarmok, Kirmiyon, Puga, Pishon, Gichot, and the Euphrates. They do not include the Tigris, which includes them all. The seven deserts, in which Israel walked when they left Egypt— Aytam, Shur, Sin, Sinai, Paran, Tzin, and Kedaymot. The desert of Matana includes them all. The seven weeks—Of the counting of the Omer (between Passover and Shavuot). The seven Jubilees—The first temple stood 410 years. In these years there were seven full Jubilees. The temple was destroyed in the thirty-sixth year of the eighth Jubilee.

The Gaon proceeds to say that the seventh in all these categories was the most beloved by God. Sinai was the seventh desert, and, therefore, the Torah was given there. The seventh palace is the "Holy of Holies," which, the *Zohar* says, "God set aside for Himself." *Aravot,* the seventh heaven, is where the Throne of Honor is. Yitzchak Ibn Giktallia points out that the *Targum*[57] translates "The children of Te'arovet" (2 Kings 14:14) (same root as *Aravot*) as "the children of the *important ones.*"

Moshe Botarel quotes *Sefer HaTarshish,* which points out that the first verse in the Bible (Hebrew text, of course) and the first verse in the ten commandments both have exactly seven words. The implication is that this was done purposely, to represent the infusion of sevens in nature (Genesis) and in spirituality (ten commandments).[58]

This *Mishnah* concludes the fourth chapter of *Sefer Yetzirah.* We now proceed to the next to last chapter, which discusses the third group of letters, that of the twelve singles.

5

The Twelve Single
Letters

TWELVE ATTRIBUTES AND TWELVE
SPATIAL BOUNDARIES

Sefer Yetzirah, Chapter 5, Mishnah 1

פ"ה מ"א שתים עשרה פשוטות ה"ו ז"ח
ט"י ל"נ ס"ע צ"ק יסודן ראיה,
שמיעה, ריחה, שיחה, לעיטה, תשמיש,
מעשה, הלוך, רוגז, שחוק, הרהור, שינה.
מדתן שתים עשרה גבולים באלכסונן. גבול
מזרחית צפונית, גבול מזרחית דרומית, גבול
מזרחית רומית, גבול מזרחית תחתית, גבול
צפונית רומית, גבול צפונית תחתית, גבול
מערבית דרומית, גבול מערבית צפונית,
נבול מערבית רומית, גבול מערבית תחתית,
גבול דרומית רומית, גבול דרומית תחתית.
ומרחיבין והולכין עד עדי עד והם זרועות
עולם :

The twelve single letters, *Hey, Vav, Zayin, Chet,*
Tet, Yud, Lamed, Nun, Samech, Ayin, Tzadi, Kuf—
their foundation is seeing, hearing, smelling,
speaking, eating, intercourse, action, walking,

**anger, laughter, thought, and sleep. Their mea-
sure is the twelve borders in their diagonal. The
northeastern border, the southeastern border,
the top eastern border, the bottom eastern border, the northern top border, the northern
bottom border, the southwestern border, the
northwestern border, the top western border,
the bottom western border, the southern top
border, and the southern bottom border. They
spread out and continue forever and ever and
they are the arms of the world.**

This chapter discusses the third major letter group, the twelve single
letters. These letters are all associated with the *Sefirah* of *Tiferet*, the
central *Sefirah* of the Six Extremes. The lower group of *Sefirot*, you will
recall, are composed of two sets of three and of *Malchut*. The first set
contains the *Sefirot* of *Chesed*, *Gevurah*, and *Tiferet*, which throughout
the *Zohar* represent the attributes of the three forefathers, Abraham,
Isaac, and Jacob. Jacob had twelve sons, and so twelve is associated
with him.

In the world we find several important sets of twelve. These include
the number of zodiacal constellations and the number of months in the
year. These are all associated with Jacob's *Sefirah*, *Tiferet*.

It might be helpful to begin with the last part of the *Mishnah* first. It
speaks of *twelve diagonal boundaries*. These, it turns out, are merely the
meeting points of all the pairs of directions. Every material object has
the twelve boundaries mentioned in the *Mishnah*. This can best be seen
when considering cubes. Every six-sided cube has twelve edges. It has
a northeastern edge, a southeastern edge, and so on. It is a property of
nature.

Another property is that all matter in this world is three-dimen-
sional, which corresponds to the three letters of *Emesh*. Also, all matter
has six sides and a middle (top, bottom, north, east, south, west, and a
center). This corresponds to the seven letters of *Beged Kafarta*. Kabbalah considers the letter groups as basic properties of nature. In a
similar manner, the effects caused as a consequence of their existence
result in the laws of nature. The forces that the letters represent
establish the properties of physical space. The Infinite God, being the
cause of these letters, is consequently the ultimate law of the universe.

So *Sefer Yetzirah*, which at first appears to be a book about letters and language, turns out to be a work about the creation of nature itself. In addition, the holy tongue is not considered *plain* language like all the rest, but is thought of as *natural* language in the sense that it is the language that created *nature* and represents its basic structure.

Let us return to the details of the *Mishnah*. The twelve boundaries are called diagonals for they radiate out from the center of *Tiferet* endlessly in all directions. The word the *Mishnah* uses for diagonal, "Alecson," really means the longest line of a triangle, the hypotenuse. For example, if a line is drawn north from a point, and another line east, the line connecting the ends of these two lines is called the "Alecson," the diagonal. Using the six directions (north, south, east, west, up, and down), there are twelve such diagonals. These are enumerated in the *Mishnah*.

The Vilna Gaon puts it as follows:

> Every house that has six planes [Six Extremes, as explained earlier], wherever two edges meet is called a boundary, because it is the boundary of the edges. There are four [edges] in each plane. Since there are six planes, there should be twenty-four boundaries, but since one boundary serves two planes, therefore, there are twelve. . . . Every line that is bigger [than the others] is called "Alecson," as if to say the longest line.[1]

The Raivad begins his explanation of this *Mishnah* as follows:

> After it has been explained that the Wisdom of the *Sefirot* and their Life, Peace, Grace, Wealth, Seed, and Rule are emanated from *Beged Kafarta* to the "face of the man that is in them" [the Heavenly Man, the *Sefirot*], *Sefer Yetzirah* returns and explains in this chapter that the power of feeling and the power of movement and the power of soul all are extended to the ten *Sefirot* through the power of the twelve single letters, which are *Hey, Vav, Zayin, Chet, Tet, Yud, Lamed, Nun, Samech, Ayin, Tzadi,* and *Kuf.* From them extend the power of

1. Vision
2. Hearing
3. Smell
4. Speech
5. Eating
6. Sex
7. Action
8. Anger
9. Walking

10. Laughter
11. Thought
12. Sleep

from the power of the twelve letters of God's name of twelve letters and
from them to the name of twelve Tetragrammatons and from them to
the twelve "pipes" and from them to the twelve tribes of Israel.[2]

The following might help to understand the Raivad:

1. The letters, it will be remembered, are said to constitute the
   body of the *Sefirot*, the vessels. "The man that is in them" is the
   inner essence of the *Sefirot*. The seven attributes of *Beged
   Kafarta* color the essence of their respective *Sefirot* and give
   them their distinctiveness.
2. The twelve letters represent three different types of activities.
   Some are sense activities, like feeling and hearing. Some involve movement, like walking. Others are just "soul" activities, like thought and sleep.
3. The name of twelve letters probably refers to the three four-
   letter names of God that encompass all the worlds. They are
   Aleph, Hey, Yud, Hey, which represent *Keter, Chachmah*, and
   Binah; *Yud, Hey, Vav, Hey*, which represent the middle *Sefirot*;
   and *Aleph, Dalet, Nun, Yud*, which represents *Malchut*. The
   Vilna Gaon points out that not only do these three names
   together contain twelve letters, but the numeric value of their
   respective first letters totals twelve as well.[3]
4. The name of twelve names refers to the twelve unique combinations of the four letters of the Tetragrammaton.
5. The twelve pipes are the twelve connections between the
   Sefirot. There are actually twenty-two connections, but only
   twelve are diagonal (the twelve single letters represent the
   twelve diagonals). (See Appendix A.)
6. The direction of the propagation of these powers is downward.
   The twelve tribes are the most physical, the most earthly.

The Raivad proceeds to match each attribute with the corresponding tribe of Israel. He then continues:

With all of these twelve attributes God's actions are described, sight—
"God saw" (Genesis 1:4), [hearing] "God heard" (Exodus 2:24),
[smelling] "God smelled" (Genesis 8:21), and so on. When you find one

of these descriptions in the Bible applying to God, know that it is needed for the handed-down [kabbalistic] explanation but should *not* be understood to apply to the cause of causes (the Infinite), for God forbid that He should be described by these descriptions."[4]

The *Sefirot* serve to insulate the Infinite from the world, so that He is in no way dividable, nor can He be said to have multiple traits or spiritual parts.

Saadia Gaon has several comments on this *Mishnah*. He states that the reason these twelve letters are called singles and not doubles is that "when they are alone they are not weak and not emphasized [dotted]. However, when they are combined with the other letters, they have replacements like the letters of *Beged Kafarta*."[5] He proceeds to name their twelve replacements, for instance, the replacement of seeing is blindness, and so on.

Incidentally, the Vilna Gaon disagrees with Saadia. He states that these twelve powers (seeing, etc.) are *always* present, even when they cannot be actualized. Therefore, blindness, for example, is only due to organ deficiencies. The potential to see is always present in the soul. In the Vilna Gaon's words: "These twelve letters have *no* replacements. All have all twelve powers. Even though there are deaf and blind people, the deficit is in the *vessel* through which the power is actualized, for these twelve powers are not dependent on their particular organ."[6] Saadia continues by associating the twelve single letters with the Egyptian exile of the children of Israel:

> The twelve letters represent the exile of Israel in Egypt. . . . The sum of numeric values of the twelve letters equals the period of the settlement of Egypt. How? In the generation of the Tower of Babel the city of Hebron was built and the Bible says "Hebron was built seven years before Tzoan in Egypt" (Numbers 13:22). From the Tower of Babel until the Egyptians were smitten was 452 years. Subtract the 7 from 452 and 445 remain. Thus, it turns out that the settlement of Egypt was 445 years. This is what the numerical value of the twelve single letters equals.[7] [See Appendix B.]

Saadia proceeds to list the relationship of the letters to the twelve constellations of the Zodiac, and tells how each represents an aspect of the Egyptian exile.

One may object that Saadia is making several assumptions that are not necessarily well founded. For instance, he assumes that the building of Tzoan is the beginning of Egyptian civilization. His historic accuracy is not the point, but rather his kabbalistic approach is. The attributes of the twelve letters filter not only through the different levels of creation, but through history itself. History and nature and language are all aspects of a common source. The unity of all things is a central theme in most types of mysticism and metaphysics. It is often thought to define mysticism, and it is certainly what most mystical systems have in common.

The Vilna Gaon makes some interesting comments about the difference between the three letters of *Emesh*, the seven of *Beged Kafarta*, and the twelve single letters.

> The difference between the establishment of *Emesh* in the soul, and between the doubles, and between the singles is that the establishment of *Emesh* is in the *essence* of the soul, but the establishment of the twelve senses is [the fact that they are] contingencies attached to essence, for it is impossible to exist without them. The establishment of the seven doubles [which are Wisdom, and so on] is that they are contingencies not attached [to essence], for it is possible to exist without them.[8]

This sums up for the Gaon the basic differences between the letter groups. *Emesh* represents essence, that which constitutes a creature's very self. The twelve singles represent attributes that do not define a creature, but yet are always present. Thus, while these traits are not usually what define a person, they are, nevertheless, "attached to essence" and, as a result, are always present. Finally, the seven letters of *Beged Kafarta* represent attributes that may or may not exist.

THE ZODIAC, MONTHS, AND LEADERS OF THE SOUL

Sefer Yetzirah, Chapter 5, Mishnah 2

מ"ב שתים עשרה פשוטות ה"ו ז"ח ט"י ל"נ
ס"ע צ"ק חקקן חצבן שקלן צרפן
המירן וצר בהם שנים עשר מזלות בעולם
סימן טש"ת סא"ב טע"ק גד"ד . ואלו הן שנים

עשר חדשים בשנה ניסן אייר סיון תמוז אב
אלול תשרי מרחשון כסלו טבת שבט אדר .
ואלו הן שנים עשר מנהינין בנפש שתי ידים
ושתי רגלים שתי כליות טחול כבד מרה
המסס קיבה קרקבן [שתי לועזים ושתי עליזים
שתי יועצים ושתי יעוצים שתי טורפין ושתי
ציידים]. עשאן כמין (מדינה) [מריבה] וערכן
כמין מלחמה גם את זה לעומת זה עשה
האלהים :

כיצד צרפן . המליך אות ה' וקשר לו כתר וצר בו
טלה בעולם וניסן בשנה ויד ימין בנפש זכר
ונקבה . המליך אות ו' וקשר לו כתר וצר בו שור
בעולם ואייר בשנה ויד שמאל בנפש . המליך אות ז'
וקשר לו כתר וצר בו תאומים בעולם וסיון בשנה ורגל
ימין בנפש . המליך אות ח' וקשר לו כתר וצר בו סרטן
בעולם ותמוז בשנה ורגל שמאל בנפש . המליך אות ט'
וקשר לו כתר וצר בו אריה בעולם ואב בשנה וכוליא
ימין בנפש . המליך אות י' וקשר לו כתר וצר בו
בתולה בעולם ואלול בשנה וכוליא שמאל בנפש .
המליך אות ל' וקשר לו כתר וצר בו מאזנים בעולם
ותשרי בשנה וכבד בנפש . המליך אות נ' וקשר לו
כתר וצר בו עקרב בעולם ומרחשוון בשנה וטחול
בנפש . המליך אות ס' וקשר לו כתר וצר בו קשת
בעולם וכסלו בשנה ומרה בנפש . המליך אות ע'
וקשר לו כתר וצר בו גדי בעולם וטבת בשנה והמסס
בנפש . המליך אות צ' וקשר לו כתר וצר בו דלי
בעולם ושבט בשנה וקיבה בנפש . המליך אות ק'
וקשר לו כתר וצר בו דגים בעולם ואדר בשנה
וקרקבן בנפש :

The twelve single letters, *Hey, Vav, Zayin, Chet,
Tet, Yud, Lamed, Nun, Samech, Ayin, Tzadi, Kuf,*
He engraved them and hewed them, weighed
them and combined them and substituted them.
He formed with them twelve constellations in

the universe. The sign [mnemonic to remember them] is "*Teshat Saab Maak Gedad.*" These are the twelve months in the year: *Nissan, Iyar, Sivan, Tamuz, Av, Elul, Tishrei, MarCheshvan, Kislev, Tevet, Shevat,* and *Adar.* These are the twelve leaders in the soul: two hands, two feet, two kidneys, the spleen, the liver, the gall bladder, the additional stomach [of an animal that chews its cud], the [regular] stomach, and the gizzard. [This list contains] two falsifiers, two happy ones, two advisors, two advised, two attackers, and two hunters. He made them like a conflict, he stationed them like [in] a war, for "God made each to the level of each" [Ecclesiastes 7:14].

How did He combine them? He made the *Hey* king and tied a crown to it. He formed with it Aries in the universe, *Nissan* in the year, and the right hand in the soul, male and female. He made the letter *Vav* king and tied a crown to it. He formed with it Taurus in the universe, *Iyar* in the year, and the left hand in the soul. He made the letter *Zayin* king and tied a crown to it. He formed Gemini with it in the universe, *Sivan* in the year, and the right leg in the soul. He made the letter *Chet* king and tied a crown to it. He formed Cancer with it in the universe, *Tamuz* in the year, and the left foot in the soul. He made the letter *Tet* king and tied a crown to it. He formed with it Leo in the universe, *Av* in the year, and the right kidney in the soul. He made the letter *Yud* king and tied a crown to it. He formed with it Virgo in the universe, *Elul* in the year, and the left kidney in the soul. He made the letter *Lamed* king and tied a crown to it. He formed with it Libra in the universe, *Tishrei* in the year, and the liver in the soul. He made the letter *Nun* king and tied a crown to it. He formed with it Scorpio in the universe, *MarCheshvan* in the year, and the spleen in the soul. He made the letter *Samech* king and tied a crown to it. He formed with it Sagittarius in the universe, *Kislev* in the year, and the gall bladder in the soul. He made the letter *Ayin* king and tied a crown to it. He formed with it Capricorn in the universe, *Tevet* in the year, and the additional stomach in the soul. He made the letter *Tzadi* king and tied a crown to it. He formed with it Aquarius in the universe, *Shevat* in the year, and the stomach in the soul. He made the letter *Kuf* king and tied a crown to it. He formed Pisces with it in the universe, *Adar* in the year, and the gizzard in the soul.

The twelve letters were first cut in *Chachmah* and then took on a definite form in *Binah*. This is the same process as was already described for the other two letter groups, *Emesh* and *Beged Kafarta*. Each letter has a *weight*, that is, a numerical value. Each was combined with the other letters and were made first in the order of the letters, but in turn were replaced in their position by each of the others. The five terms the *Mishnah* uses—engraved, hewed, weighed, combined, and substituted—are meant to convey these events.

Each of the twelve letters is associated with a constellation. The mnemonic to remember the Hebrew names of the constellations is "*TeShaT SaAB MaAK GeDaD.*" These words are formed by the first letter of each of the constellations as follows:

1. *Tleh*—Aries
2. *Shor*—Taurus
3. *Teomim*—Gemini
4. *Sartan*—Cancer
5. *Aryeh*—Leo
6. *Betulah*—Virgo
7. *Moznayim*—Libra
8. *Akrav*—Scorpio
9. *Keshet*—Sagittarius
10. *Gedi*—Capricorn
11. *Deli*—Aquarius
12. *Dagim*—Pisces

The *Otzar HaShem* comments:

> The names of the twelve constellations were established in ancient times according to the shape formed by the stars in the eighth sphere. For instance, the Ram [Aries] is called so because it is shaped like a Ram, and similarly the rest. As far as the twelve months are concerned, we do not know the reasons for their names. A few of them are mentioned in the Scriptures, like *Adar*, *Nissan*, *Sivan*, and *Kislev*. Perhaps in Abraham's time they were well known among the *Casdim* and on the far side of the Jordan, so he [Abraham, who came from Ur Casdim] used them [in *Sefer Yetzirah*].[9]

The origin of the names of the constellations is not Jewish, and most are thought to have been named by the early Greeks. Apparently, the *Otzar HaShem* thinks the shapes actually resemble the objects for which they are named, which is not surprising, for the Greeks did, too. The implication is that the names are natural rather than arbitrary.

It is generally accepted that the names of the months were adopted from the Babylonians [*Casdim*] during the exile after the First Temple was destroyed. Several appear in the Bible in addition to the ones mentioned. However, the others are not commonly used, and appear to be of Hebrew rather than Babylonian origin. For instance, the "month of *Ziv* (brightness)" is mentioned in the Scriptures (1 Kings 6:1). This is a Hebrew term, yet the Babylonian name for this month, *Iyar*, is the name that is commonly used.

By twelve leaders in the soul is meant things that affect behavior. The Rokeach states:

> The falsifiers are the gall bladder and the kidneys, which excite a person and cause him falseness. The two happy ones are the stomach and the spleen, which gladden people—the stomach with eating and drinking and the spleen with laughter. The two advisors are the two kidneys, as it is said, "I will bless God who advised me, even at night my kidneys admonished me" (Psalms 16:7).[10]

The Rokeach goes on to describe the rest of the leaders, but our version of his text appears to be corrupted. In any case, the idea is that the twelve organs have specific functions. Some of these functions are similar, as in the case of the gall bladder and kidneys. These organs work in unison. Others, the *Mishnah* tells us, function as if in a conflict.

This part of the *Mishnah* is rather mysterious. The *Otzar HaShem*, based on the Raivad, explains as follows:

[*Sefer Yetzirah*] says that the Infinite made the world, the year, and the soul like a war. What is meant is that each of the twelve leaders in the world, year, and soul appear to be in conflict with each other. Aries, Leo, and Capricorn are fire. Taurus, Virgo, and Sagittarius are air. Gemini, Libra, and Aquarius are wind. Cancer, Scorpio, and Pisces are water. Those of water fight with those of fire. Those of air fight with those of wind. Some acquit and some convict. Some kill and some make live. Some are hot and wet and some cold and dry. . . . So is it with the [leaders of the] soul. Some are active, some passive. So is it in the year— He made four opposite seasons. After the heat He always puts the moderate temperature. After the summer, which is hot and dry, He brought the fall, which is cold and wet. Likewise, the spring, which is warm and wet, comes after the winter, which is cold and dry. He did so in order to avoid going from extreme to extreme and causing great change and thus bad happenings. Therefore, in His great wisdom, He made them like a fight and stationed them like in a war. *Sefer Yetzirah* says "like" a war, for these things are not [conflicts] with words or with physical swords but rather result from the combinations and their reflections one on the other. That is what is meant by "God made each to the level of the each" (Ecclesiastes 7:14).[11]

War is an integral property of the very nature of the universe! The elements of nature are in opposition, and this enables the proper functioning of nature. Conflict can be beneficial. The *Otzar HaShem* concludes that the verse cited in the last line of the *Mishnah* means that the elements are in equal opposition to each other. That is what is meant by their being "at war." The verse cited is commonly used in Kabbalah to prove that for everything that is in the world of holiness, there exists an equivalent object that belongs to the side of uncleanliness (the devil's domain). That use of the verse is not very different from the way it is used in this *Mishnah*, for it represents *war* also, that between good and evil.

The Vilna Gaon says:

All twelve are according to the secret of the twelve combinations of the Tetragrammaton. The first is in its usual order (*Yud, Hey, Vav, Hey*) and the others in the various orders of the combinations. The spring season

contains all the Tetragrammatons that begin with *Yud*, the summer with
Hey, fall with *Vav*, and winter with *Hey*, for they are divided into four
times three. So are the months and the constellations. So is it with the
name of *Aleph-Hey-Yud-Hey*, but this refers to the surrounding light and
the former to the inner light. And so is it with the twelve tribes.[12]

The Gaon concludes by telling us that the talmudic rabbis said that
each of the twelve senses is associated with each of the twelve tribes of
Israel. Verses are brought to show which sense is paired with which
tribe.

A few comments are in order. It was noted previously that the
power of all creation is the Infinite essence that flows through the
Sefirot. This inner essence, as seen through the *Sefirot*, is that to which
the Tetragrammaton refers. (Unbounded essence, known as *Ein Sof*,
has no name to describe it, for it is totally unknowable.) Time and
again the commentaries refer to it as the power supply of the world. In
the *Zohar* it is commonly referred to as "*Shaku DeIlna*"—the water of
the tree (of *Sefirot*).

The various names of God refer to different things. Both names
mentioned by the Gaon are *Shemot HaEtzem*, names that refer to
God's essence. However, there is a difference between the two. The
Tetragrammaton refers to the essence that dwells within the *Sefirot*.
The extra essence, that which was too great to be held inside, remained
as surrounding light around the *Sefirot*. It is to this that the Gaon says
the term *Aleph-Hey-Yud-Hey* refers. The different types of light are a
major topic in later Kabbalah, and are analyzed not only in terms of
inner and outer light, but *forward* and *backward* light as well.

One might wonder what it means that each tribe has an associated
"sense." It would appear to imply that those from the tribe of Reuben,
for instance, which is associated with sight,[13] would have a natural
tendency to be visionary and serve as "the eyes of the congregation."

The second part of the *Mishnah* has the same form as the *Mishnayot*
that dealt with the permutations of *Beged Kafarta* in Chapter 4 (*Mishnayot* 5–11). Each of the twelve letters is made king (i.e., put first) in
turn, and each is associated with a constellation in the world, a month
in the year, and a body part in the soul. Some of the Raivad's comments are particularly interesting and illustrate his approach to this
Mishnah.

From the power of the *Hey* flows a stream to extract the strength of the Tetragrammaton of the constellation Aries. These are Tetragrammatons grouped according to the shape of Aries (Ram). So is it with all twelve constellations and all that is on the land—they are all from the Tetragrammatons grouped in accord with their shape. Those beneath are called according to the upper name with the power of the *Hey*.[14]

The Raivad seems to be saying that all nature is empowered by the powers represented by the four letters of the name of God, *Yud, Hey, Vav, Hey*. The shapes of nature and the shapes that these names of God (powers) assume are necessarily identical. The lower powers (names) are "called" according to the higher name, since the main denotation of the name of God is in the divine sphere above nature and refers to higher spiritual aspects. Each of the unique Tetragrammatons is associated with one of the twelve single letters, in this example, the *Hey*.

The Raivad continues: "*Nissan in the year*—since during the period when the *upper* moon (*Malchut*) receives from that Tetragrammaton [the Tetragrammaton of *Nissan*] those particular days will be called *Nissan*, as it is written, 'In the first month, which is the month of *Nissan*' (Esther 3:7)."[15]

The months differ not only in when they occur but in the source that fuels them. The upper moon is *Malchut*. It receives the light of the upper *Sefirot*. When *Tiferet* (Sun) shines with the light of *Nissan* (i.e., the light of the letter *Hey* from the twelve single letters that it possesses), this gives the month of *Nissan* its particular attributes. Remember, *Tiferet* is symbolized by the sun, *Malchut* by the moon.

The Raivad continues: "He made *Vav* king—Taurus, the face of the ox, is through the strength of the *Vav* of the letters *Hey, Vav, Zayin, Chet, Tet, Yud, Lamed, Nun, Samech, Ayin, Tzadi*, and *Kuf*. It is associated with the left hand for 'The face of the ox is to the left of the four of them' (Ezekiel 1:10). In the year it is associated with *Iyar*."[16] The quoted verse is from Ezekiel's description of the four-faced angels in the first chapter of Ezekiel. The ox's face is toward the left.

The Raivad goes on:

He made *Zayin* king . . . and formed Gemini (twins) with it in the world and *Sivan* in the year and the right leg in the soul. Gemini is like two faces, male and female, that are attached, according to the secret of "twins of the doe," (Song of Songs 7:4), from the power of the *Zayin*. It is associated with the right leg and wisdom; therefore the Torah was given to Israel in this month and with this Tetragrammaton, as is written, "In the third month" (Exodus 19:1). It was not given with a shape other than twins, for sense and wisdom and understanding and knowledge were given to mankind only [Gemini represents *human* twins. Most of the other constellations represent animals].[17]

The concept of two-faced twins is very important in Kabbalah. Adam and Eve were said to have been created as Siamese twins, back to back. God had to cut them apart to allow them to propagate. This is known as "the secret of the cutting" (*Sod HaNasirah*). In Kabbalah, the reference is not only to the earthly Adam and Eve, but to the *Sefirot* of *Tiferet* and *Malchut*. Their recombining is a major objective of creation. They represent God and Israel being one. In the Song of Songs, which is said to represent the courtship of God and Israel, there is a reference to "twins of the doe." The Raivad understands the twins to represent *Tiferet* and *Malchut*, and what is basically the same thing, God and the Congregation of Israel. The giving of the Torah also represents the uniting of God and Israel. Thus *Sivan*, the month when the sun is in Gemini, is the perfect time for this to occur.

THE MOTHERS, FATHERS, AND THREE BASIC ELEMENTS

Sefer Yetzirah, Chapter 5, Mishnah 3

מ"ג שלש אמות שהם שלשה אבות שמהם
יצא אש ורוח ומים , שלש אמות ושבע
כפולות ושנים עשר פשוטות:

The three mothers are the three fathers from which emerged fire and wind and water. Three mothers, seven double letters, and twelve single letters.

The standard text of this *Mishnah* appears to identify the three mothers with the three fathers. However, even the commentators who base their analysis on the standard text do not understand the fathers to be identical to the mothers. In addition, the other textual versions of the *Mishnah* clearly differentiate between the two.

The *Otzar HaShem*, expanding upon the comments of the Raivad, explains these terms as follows:

> From the three mothers, *Emesh*, which symbolize the ten *Sefirot*, emerged the three fathers of the separate entities. Some of these are in the likeness of air, water, and fire. Of a nature parallel to the seven double and the twelve single letters, which symbolize the seven *Sefirot* of the building and the twelve diagonal borders, are the seven moving stars and the twelve constellations.[18]

"The separate entities" in the above passage refers to all that is not part of the world of divinity. Remember, of the four worlds of Kabbalah (*Atzilut*, *Briyah*, *Yetzirah*, and *Asiyah*), only the world of the *Atzilut* is considered part of the divine sphere. The *Sefirot* of this world constitute divinity in the sense that the undifferentiated Infinite light is present in them in a pure form. That is not to say that the light has the same intensity as the light of the *Ein Sof*, which is not confined in any way. But even though the light in the World of the *Sefirot* is somewhat diminished, it is basically unchanged. This is not the case in the lower worlds, where the character of the light itself is changed. This passage of the light into the lower world is through a filtering process. The light passes through a *curtain* (*Masach*) and is thus altered as it descends into the lower spheres. The *Sefirot* of the World of *Atzilut*, however, receive light that is unfiltered through *curtains*. Chaim Vital, in his book *Etz Chaim*, treats this subject at length.[19]

In the above quote, the *Otzar HaShem* is stressing that the physical world is in the image of the spiritual. *Sefer Yetzirah* did not concentrate on the lower worlds until this chapter. Therefore, the "fathers" were not mentioned until now, for by "fathers" is meant "the *cause* of the nondivine, *separate* entities."

The Vilna Gaon's version of *Sefer Yetzirah* contains this *Mishnah* as part of the sixth chapter. Its wording is slightly different, and explicitly differentiates between "mothers" and "fathers":

These are the three mothers, *Emesh*, and from them emerged three fathers, and they are air, water, and fire, and from the fathers (emerged) offspring.

The three mothers are the first three *Sefirot*. The fathers are the derivatives produced by the mothers. That which is found in the lower worlds, the worlds separated from the sphere of divinity, descend from the fathers. This version clearly states that the fathers are air, water, and fire. However, this is not necessarily meant to refer to the *material* elements.

The *Pree Yitzchak* says as follows: "The first three *Sefirot* are mothers [foundations] to air, water, and fire, which are rooted in them in potential. From them emerged *Chesed*, *Gevurah*, and *Tiferet* [the next lower three], which are the three fathers, and they are air, water, and fire."[20] The *Pree Yitzchak* thus understands the "fathers" to be *Sefirot* also. The "offspring" mentioned in the *Mishnah* consist of the remaining four lowest *Sefirot*. A simpler interpretion of this version of the text, however, suggests that the term *fathers* merely means the basic elements of the physical world.

The Vilna Gaon seems to hold a hybrid view, incorporating both physical and spiritual meanings simultaneously. He states: "In the soul, the three letters of *Emesh* are the roots. In man they are air, water, and fire, as well as head, stomach, and body. This is because from every one item, two items came into being, one spiritual and one physical."[21] The Gaon agrees that air, fire, and water in the *Mishnah* are spiritual quantities, but they also have physical counterparts, like man's head, stomach, and body. Both are meant by the *Mishnah*'s reference to air, water, and fire.

The above illustrates one of the main difficulties with Kabbalah. It can be understood on many levels. Sometimes several meanings are intended, sometimes one specific meaning. It is not always possible to reach a conclusion based on reason alone. This is why this field of study is known as Kabbalah. "Kabbalah" comes from the root "to receive" and stresses that one may not rely on one's own wisdom but only upon that "which is received," that is, that which is passed down from scholar to scholar.

THE LETTERS AND THE NAMES
OF GOD

Sefer Yetzirah, Chapter 5, Mishnah 4

מ"ד אלו עשרים ושתים אותיות שבהם יסד
הקב"ה יה יהוה צבאות אלהים חיים
אלהי ישראל רם ונשא שוכן עד וקדוש שמו
מרום וקדוש הוא:

**These are the twenty-two letters with which the
Holy One, Blessed be He, established *Yah*, the
Tetragrammaton, *Tzvaot*, the living God, the
God of Israel, high and uplifted, who dwells for-
ever and holy is His name, exalted and holy is He.**

This was a difficult *Mishnah* to translate, as the Hebrew text appears to
be somewhat incomplete. The translation above states that the Holy
One, Blessed be He, established the various names of God. While this
might be correct, other translations are possible.

An alternative interpretation of the mishnaic text is that God (referred to by all ten names in the *Mishnah*) established something, but
what that something is the *Mishnah* fails to say. A look at a different
version of the text will be helpful.

The Vilna Gaon's version of this *Mishnah*, while grammatically
difficult, is more complete. It is found in the sixth chapter of his text,
Mishnah 6. It reads as follows:

> **These are the twenty-two letters with which
> "*Aleph-Hey-Yud-Hey*," "*Yah*," "*Tetragramma-
> ton Elohim*," "*Elohim* Tetragrammaton," "Te-
> tragrammaton *Tzvaot*," "*Elohim*," "*Tzvaot*," "*El
> Shaddai*," "Tetragrammaton," "*Adonai*," en-
> graved and made from them three books, and
> created His entire universe from them, and
> formed with them all that was created and all
> that is to be created in the future.**

In this version, it is clear that the *Mishnah*'s intent is that God engraved the letters and made the books. The names of God are usually associated with particular *Sefirot* and represent God's "essence" as seen through the vessels of the *Sefirot*. This *Mishnah* is concerned with the creation of the lower worlds, however, and the names of God appear to be presented as the subject (the engraver) rather than the object (the engraved).

The Vilna Gaon,[22] Meir Rotenburg,[23] and Moshe Botarel[24] all point out that there are ten names mentioned in this *Mishnah*, and they represent the ten *Sefirot*. Meir Rotenburg and the Vilna Gaon both list God's names and the corresponding *Sefirot*. While their lists conflict, they nevertheless agree that each name corresponds to a *Sefirah*. In the first *Mishnah* of *Sefer Yetzirah*, names of God were also mentioned. Twenty-two words were used there, which the Gaon says represents the twenty-two Hebrew letters. The ten mentioned here, together with the twenty-two of the first *Mishnah*, equal thirty-two. Thus, this *Mishnah* completes the main part of the book begun in Chapter 1, the discussion of the thirty-two paths of wisdom in the spiritual world, namely, the ten *Sefirot* and the twenty-two letters. The last chapter of *Sefer Yetzirah*, in contrast, deals with the lower world, namely, the manifestations of the "fathers" in the physical sphere.

The *Mishnah* is explained by *Otzar HaShem*, who bases his remarks on the Raivad's commentary as follows:

This *Beraita*[25] was [basically] explained already in Chapter 1. However, it is repeated here to inform us how the ten *Sefirot* hinted at in this *Beraita* [by the ten names of God] do not include the things that are separated and apart. They also do not include those items that received abundance and existence from separated objects, which receive it originally from the *Sefirot*. For the ten *Sefirot* are Divinity, and the Infinite *Ein Sof*, blessed be He, is always within them. Therefore, all the multitude of things found in the world, year, and soul were descended from separated objects that receive their abundance from the ten *Sefirot*. That is what the verse says, "I fill the heavens and the earth" (Jeremiah 23:24), for actions reflect on he who does the act. I am [God] who speaks [and creates the world]. Know that the heavens and earth being referred to here are physical and perceivable.[26]

"*That which is separate and apart*" means that which is not part of divinity. This was explained in the last *Mishnah*. God literally fills the world of the *Sefirot* since He "*is always within them.*" However, He also is said to fill the physical heavens and earth. This is, however, in the sense that it was His actions that created them, and the created always reflects on the Creator. In contradistinction to the *Sefirot*, the separated items are not part of divinity (*Elohut*). They receive "abundance" from the *Sefirot*, but it is abundance filtered through the curtain between the worlds. Abundance (*Shefa*) denotes the influence of the higher on the lower, the nourishment that is passed down. It is called "blessing" and in the upper worlds is described as "light." The *Otzar HaShem* concludes by telling us to understand that he is speaking of the physical heavens and earth. This is because the *Sefirot* of *Tiferet* and *Malchut* are also known as heaven and earth, respectively. He is not referring to them, as they are in the realm of divinity.

The end of the Gaon's text is interesting. It says that the three books (which were discussed at length in Chapter 1, *Mishnah* 1) were formed from the letters, as well as all that was created and all that will be created in the future.

The idea is that all of the creation took place during the original genesis. There is a tradition that during the first day of creation everything was created, but was not put in place until the appropriate day of the week. Thus, Rashi says in his biblical commentary on the creation of the celestial bodies: "They were created on the first day, but on the fourth He commanded that they be hung in the firmament. So were all the offspring of the heavens and earth created on the first day, and each was set in place on the day that God decreed for it."[27]

According to this, even things destined to appear at a future time were created in the very beginning. Ecclesiastes tells us that "there is nothing new under the sun" (Ecclesiastes 1:9). Before the sun was placed in the heavens, however, the earth was not under the sun. Therefore, there was something new, namely, the original matter, which arose from nonbeing. Since then, however, there was not much new. That original matter, however, was formed and placed in its proper location. It was converted into the universe and all its inhabitants.

6

The Controlling Elements of Space, Time, and the Soul

THE RULERS AND THE ELEMENTS

Sefer Yetzirah, Chapter 6, Mishnah 1

פ״ן מ״א שלשה אבות ותולדותיהן ושבעה
כוכבים וצבאותיהן ושנים עשר
נבולי אלכסונין וראיה לדבר עדים נאמנין
עולם שנה נפש חק שנים עשר ושבעה
ושלשה ופקידן בתלי וגלגל ולב. שלשה אש
ומים ורוח אש למעלה ומים למטה ורוח חק
מכריע בינתים וסימן לדבר האש נושא את
המים. מ״ם דוממת שי״ן שורקת אל״ף חוק
מכריע בינתים:

The three fathers and their offspring, the seven
stars and their hosts, and the twelve diagonal
boundaries. Proof of the matter are the trustworthy witnesses—world, year, and soul. He
decreed twelve, seven, and three, and assigned
them to *Tlee*, sphere, and heart. Three—fire,
water, and wind—fire is above, water is below,
and wind is the decree that mediates between
them. This matter is symbolized by "fire carrying water." *Mem* is quiet, *Shin* screeches, and
Aleph is the decree that mediates between them.

This is a difficult *Mishnah* due to its fragmented style. It is composed of phrases, some of which are not incorporated into complete sentences. Much of the difficulty in understanding *Sefer Yetzirah* is due to this type of difficult syntax.

The *Mishnah* speaks of three witnesses: world, year, and soul. It does not explicitly state to what these witnesses testify, nor does it say how the testimony is given. The purpose of the *Mishnah*'s first line is also left unclear.

There are at least two opinions as to the testimony that these witnesses provide:

1. They testify to God's unity.
2. They testify to the threefold nature of creation.

These two theories do not necessarily conflict. The latter part of the *Mishnah* attempts to show that all of creation is from a single source. The proof is based on the fact that there is a strong parallelism in the three levels of nature (world, year, and soul). Thus, the three ultimately testify that all is from the One.

According to the first opinion above, the *Mishnah* is attempting to convey the idea that the world, year, and soul act as witnesses by giving testimony to affirm God's unity. The Raivad puts it as follows: "Proving the matter are the reliable witnesses of world, year, and soul. For all that is in the soul can be found in the year and the world, and similarly with each of the others. These are reliable witnesses that they are all derived from one source."[1]

The Raivad goes on to say that the unity of the different aspects of creation is seen from the operation of the "*Tlee*, sphere, and heart." These three are said to control the three aspects of creation—the spatial world, time, and the soul, respectively. What these are, and how they show that all is from one source, follow below.

The *Pree Yitzchak* discusses these three witnesses in a little more detail than the Raivad. He explains, in a difficult, mystic style, as follows:

All of this is to testify as to God's unity, praised be He, since all that is in the soul you will find in the year in the world, that is, in each one of them. This is because He decreed twelve and seven and three in each one of them. That is to say, He decreed twelve, which constitutes the secret of the twelve diagonal boundaries, and the twelve constellations and the twelve months and the twelve leaders in the world, year, and soul. And so with seven: seven stars, seven days, seven gates, which are in the world, year, and soul [respectively]. So is it with three: the three of *Emesh*—air, water, fire—are in the world, year, and soul. This is what is meant by "they are trustworthy witnesses," that all emerged from a single source.[2]

Several points can use some clarification. *Pree Yitzchak* says that "all that is in the soul you will find in the year in the world." He does not say in the year *and* in the world, but rather "in the year in the world." The world contains the year. It also contains the soul. Similarly, the soul contains the world and the year. Likewise, the year contains the other two.

The *Pree Yitzchak* is conveying the idea that each of these three aspects of creation contains the others. Even the contained aspects themselves contain the others in endless subdivision. This is similar to how we described the *Sefirot*. Each *Sefirah* is composed of all the others. Each minute dot of each *Sefirah* contains all that is found in the entire set of *Sefirot*. Thus, every particular entity is intimately related to the whole, and this reflects God's unity.

This principle works on both the micro and macro levels. The three numbers—three, seven, and twelve—are important in the big universe, but also in each granule and cell. Thus in the macro universe there are twelve constellations, seven moving stars, and the three elements. Within each particular element in the universe these three numbers are also prominent. Thus, every physical item has *twelve* diagonal boundaries, six planes and a center, and is composed of the *three* elements. Likewise, in time, we find these three numbers prominent. On the macro level, we find twelve months, seven days, and three seasonal temperature levels (hot, cold, moderate). However, we can find these elements on the micro level, too. For instance, days can be divided into twelve hours of day, twelve of night. I will omit the details, but three and seven can be found (with some ingenuity) to be elements of time on the micro level as well. The same pattern can be found on the level of Soul. The twelve leaders, seven gates, and three temperaments (hot, cold, and temperate) repeat in each of the various subdivisions.

All this implies that the different aspects of existence emerged from a single source, for all levels of creation are similarly structured. It is this that comprises their testimony. Speech is unnecessary for this testimony, for it is constituted by their very nature.

The Vilna Gaon explains the witnesses somewhat differently. He states they arc witnesses because they testify "that everything is in groups of three, whether in width or in length, in world-year-soul, in *Emesh* (the three mothers), and [even the groups of] seven and twelve [are composed of threes], in all of them [three is the basic number], and they themselves are divided also into groups of three, as was said earlier, 'the three mothers, *Emesh*.' "[3]

The Gaon is saying that the testimony the witnesses give is that *the nature of creation is based on three*. Width and length both have *three* parts, a beginning, a middle, and an end. The basic groups of *Emesh* and world-year-soul are both triples. Even the groups of seven and twelve mentioned in previous *Mishnayot* break down into groups of three. This is explained later in this chapter (*Mishnah* 3), where it says that seven is composed of *three verses three and one in the middle* and twelve subdivides into four groups of three. The groups of three ultimately testify that they all have but a single source, the *One* God.

The *Mishnah* continues by telling us that God assigned twelve, seven, and three to "*Tlee*, sphere, and heart." This needs explanation.

We have said that *Sefer Yetzirah* is interested in the three major dimensions of existence—world, year, and soul. Each of these has a boss, a prime mover. In the soul, the heart is the central organ, the seat of the emotions. In time, it is the movement of the spheres that dominates. In the world, it is *Tlee*.

Ancient astrology believed that the Zodiac did not move by itself. There was a power that moved it, and this power was known as the *Tlee*. This is described in detail by Shabbetai Donnolo, who claims to have received his astrological education from the most prominent Arabic astrologer of his time. He describes *Tlee* as a great crooked snake that turns the constellations.[4] Moshe Botarel quotes Joseph Ashkenazi as follows: "*Tlee*'s place is in the fourth heaven; it extends from one side to the other, and all the orbs of the stars, lights, and constellations are attached and united and tied to it. It is invisible, but it leads and rules and sustains them all."[5]

A more scientific approach is taken by the *Otzar HaShem*. He says the head and tail of *Tlee* correspond to the intersections of the celestial equator and the ecliptic. The head, thus, is what is known in modern astrology as the first point of Aries. When the sun is near it, the spring begins. The tail is six constellations away, and when the sun enters it, fall begins. It was thought that the entire Zodiac was anchored to these points, and moved by them. In his worlds, *"Tlee* is the snake mentioned in the words of the astrologers and is the place where the circle of the equator is cut by the circle of the Zodiac. The first cut is called *head*, and the second *tail.*"[6]

The *Mishnah* says that each of the main movers of creation—the mover of time, of soul, and of the physical world—all were assigned three, seven, and twelve. Thus, all of nature is of uniform form. This points to the fact that all is from the same source. The three aspects of creation all point to their single source, the one God.

The *Mishnah* concludes that fire is above, water below, and wind mediates. This has been taken to mean that the lower world is a mirror image of the upper. In the world of the *Sefirot*, water (*Chesed*) comes before fire (*Gevurah*). On earth it is reversed. Fire evaporates the water and it rises, as if the fire is "carrying" the water. The basic structure of the upper and lower worlds is the same, but sometimes things are inverted. There is always a correspondence. But as in a mirror, some things are opposite, some are the same. Top remains top and bottom bottom, but left and right are switched. In the world, comparing the various levels, we find certain things the same, certain things switched. But there is always a similarity, for the lower worlds proceed from the upper.

The last line of the *Mishnah* is another example of a similar structure existing in the different aspects of creation. The three letters of *Emesh* represent two opposites and a mediator, not only in their material nature, but in their sound qualities as well. The letter *Mem*, we said, represents water. Still water makes no sound and the pronunciation of the letter *Mem* is a quiet hum. *Shin* represents fire, which hisses, and so does the *Shin* when it is pronounced. Air is in between, and so is *Aleph*, which can assume various sounds based on the associated vowel. The letters, the elements they represent, and the sounds the letters make and the sounds the elements themselves make, all share the same structure and reflect the unity of the world and its One source.

TLEE, THE SPHERE, AND THE HEART

Sefer Yetzirah, Chapter 6, Mishnah 2

מ"ב תלי בעולם כמלך על כסאו. גלגל בשנה
כמלך במדינה . לב בנפש כמלך
במלחמה . גם את כל חפץ זה לעומת זה
עשה האלהים . טוב לעומת רע . טוב מטוב
ורע מרע. הטוב מבחין את הרע והרע מבחין
את הטוב . טובה שמורה לטובים ורעה
שמורה לרעים :

**Tlee in the world is like a king on his throne. The
sphere in the year is like a king in his kingdom.
The heart in the soul is like a king in war. Also,
every desire, "this to the level of this God made"
(Ecclesiastes 7:14). Good to the level of evil.
Good from good and evil from evil. The good
tests the evil and the evil tests the good. Goodness is put aside for the good, and evil is put
aside for the evil.**

The *Mishnah* is describing the functioning of the *controllers* of world,
year, and soul. We said in the last *Mishnah* that the controlling element
of the world is *Tlee*, of the year is the sphere, and of the soul is the
heart. We are being told here of their functions on each of these levels.
The *Otzar HaShem* describes it in the following manner:

Tlee is like a king on his throne who is totally unafraid. Sphere is like a
king in his kingdom who has to be occupied with judging the nation.
His mind is not completely at ease. The heart is like a king who must
wage war on his enemies, to kill or be killed, or to suffer. This is the
plain meaning of the *Mishnah*. However, its hidden meaning is as
follows: *Tlee*, which is *Binah*, is on top of *Tiferet* like a king on his
throne. There is no temptation and no evil occurrences, like an old man
filled with mercy. The sphere in the year is *Tiferet*, which contains the
twelve diagonal boundaries. *Tiferet* is "like a king in his kingdom," who
judges *Malchut*. The heart in the soul is *Malchut*, as *Malchut* is called

"heart." She is "like a king at war," for she fights and avenges the revenge of God and His Torah. "In the soul" means all that is beneath the unity (divinity); angels, those that prevent and cause, and the intelligences in general. These are all together called "soul."[7]

There is the most peace on the level of the physical universe. Planets and stars do not get upset. The year can be turbulent, as it brings good seasons and bad, based on God's judgment. The most turbulence is in the soul, however. Man's soul often is like a war, with conflicting passions fighting each other.

The *Otzar HaShem* says that, on a deeper level, *Tlee* symbolizes *Binah*, sphere symbolizes *Tiferet*, and *Malchut* symbolizes the heart. *Binah* is situated on top of *Tiferet* like a king on his throne. *Binah* is above time, where all is placid. *Tiferet*, in turn, is atop *Malchut*, but this relationship is judgmental. This is within time, where there are the opposites of kindness and strict law. The most agitation is in the lower level, that of *Malchut*. It interacts with the lower worlds. This is reminiscent of Isaiah's statement, "The wicked are chased as the (turbulent) ocean, for rest is impossible, and its waters are agitated with dirt and mud" (Isaiah 57:20). He also said, "There is no peace for the wicked" (Isaiah 57:21). Of course, there is no real wickedness in the *Sefirot*, or even among the angels, but the higher you get, the greater the peace.

The final statement of the *Otzar HaShem* says that the soul refers to that which is below the unity. This is quite strange, since the soul is generally associated in the *Zohar* with the *Sefirah* of *Malchut*, which is part of the unity. Perhaps the *Otzar HaShem* is referring to the aspect of *Malchut* that serves as the *Keter* of the world beneath, *Briyah*. This aspect of *Malchut* (and soul) is below the unity.

The Vilna Gaon has a similar approach. He says as follows:

There are three types (of relationships described here). The first is that the king and the kingdom dwell in peace and quiet and he sits on his throne. The second is that he watches the kingdom and makes sure its needs are met. The third, that he takes the kingdom to war, and must fight to protect himself. The world, year, and soul are associated with *Emesh*. The world, which is the heavens, is all peaceful and quiet, with no need for protection, for nothing changes there. The second is the year, [associated with] air. In the year exist the changes of the seasons, winter and summer and the various periods. This requires supervision of their behavior. The third, land, there is the soul of all the reversals and changes and wars and bad occurrences. Similarly, in the soul are the passions and anger and the four biles and sickness. But to none does pain come like to the heart, which is the king, and all the wars are on its behalf.[8]

One might well ask, "Is there no peace in the soul or turbulence in the physical world?" The above is not meant to deny this. What can be found in each level can also be found in the others. The Gaon describes it as follows:

> Each of the levels is included in the other levels. For even in the world and year there is like a war, as we said in a previous *Mishnah* (about the world), "three lovers, three haters, three that give life, and three killers." So all are included one in the other, for the heart is also like a king on his throne, for from it all the organs get life and they all come to it, since at night during sleep they all gather to it. Nevertheless, it is mainly at war and must protect itself that the enemies and killers should not overpower it.[9]

The heavens are mainly at peace, the soul at war. Sometimes peace comes to the soul. Sometimes stars explode.

The *Mishnah* continues with the verse from Ecclesiastes, which tells us that God made every desire "this to the level of this" (Ecclesiastes 7:14). It is speaking of balance in nature, balance between peace and turbulence, kindness and law, good and evil. The *Pree Yitzchak* comments that this verse is meant to convey that "other side (evil) was created in contrast to the holy side." The two sides are structured similarly, but are in opposition, one against the other. This approach to evil is frequently found in Kabbalah.

The Vilna Gaon discussed the similarity of the two sides. The evil side has ten *Sefirot* also, as well as thirty-two paths. The ten *Sefirot* are composed of two groups, a group of three and a group of seven, just like the holy *Sefirot*. The group of three is represented by a goat, slave, and maid and the group of seven are the seven gates of hell.

The Gaon understands this verse on an additional level as well. He says that "this to the level of this" can also refer to *Zair Anpin* and *Malchut*. He puts it as follows: "As there are twelve constellations in the male, so in the female there are the twelve cattle. *Zair Anpin* has twelve combinations of the Tetragrammaton and *Malchut* has twenty-four combinations of the letters of *Adonai*, for she has both his and hers, twenty-four books. That is what is meant by '*Zeh LeUmat Zeh*' (this to the level of this)."[10]

Do not be surprised that he speaks of constellations rather than diagonal boundaries in *Zair Anpin*. He does not mean physical constellations. He expects the reader to understand that when discussing *Sefirot*, nothing physical is meant, and he therefore feels free to call the group of twelve in *Zair Anpin* constellations.

The twelve cattle is what is described in 1 Kings. It tells of Solomon building the Holy Temple and constructing a basin upon twelve statues of cattle. The Temple represents *Malchut*, which thus has twelve associated items, similar to her husband, *Zair Anpin*. The male gives the seed to the female, and thus she obtains both his twelve and hers. The name of God associated with *Malchut* is *Adonai*, which has four different letters and thus twenty-four combinations. This is the same as the traditional number of books in the Bible, twenty-four. (This differs from most Jewish Bibles in use today, which use the Christian division of the Old Testament.)

Incidentally, the Hebrew for the biblical phrase, "this to the level of this" is "*Zeh LeUmat Zeh.*" The Hebrew word for *this* is *Zeh*. It is composed of a *Zayin* and a *Hey*. Check the numeric chart (Appendix B) and you will find that these letters sum to twelve. Thus the Gaon concludes that the verse is really saying the twelve of the female was made in parallel to the twelve of the male; they are in balance.

The *Mishnah* continues by telling us that good was created from good and evil from evil. The *Otzar HaShem* explains: " '*Good from good*' means (the *Sefirah*) *Netzach* from (the *Sefirah*) *Chesed*. '*Evil from evil*' refers to *Hod* from *Gevurah*." Although *Chesed* is the fourth *Sefirah* and *Gevurah* the fifth, *Chesed*'s influence is felt more strongly in *Netzach* (the seventh *Sefirah*) because it, like *Chesed*, is positioned on the right, the side of kindness (see Appendix A). What requires explanation is the use of the word "evil" in regard to the *Sefirot*. The *Pree Yitzchak* explains as follows: "Holiness is from the side of good and *Chesed*. The bad, the evil side, is from the side of strict law, which is positioned opposite the good side of the lower three worlds, for 'around them the wicked go,' but in the world of Emanations the verse states, 'Evil will not dwell with you.' "[11]

There is no evil in the Emanations. However, they are the root of all below. Evil must come from somewhere. In the above paragraph the *Pree Yitzchak* is saying that it springs from the left, the side of law. He goes on to say that even the "good" part of the lower worlds is surrounded by evil, for they are associated with the side of strict law above. Of the emanations themselves, however, it is written "evil will not dwell with you" (Psalms 5:5).

The Vilna Gaon, in a particularly interesting section, explains as follows:

> [The *Mishnah* is calling] *Chesed* "good" and *Gevurah* "evil" even though there is no evil above, for despite this lack of evil above, beneath evil is aroused. So is it that *Tiferet*, "good from good," is drawn from *Chesed*. *Malchut*, evil, on the side of *Gevurah*, bad. God made "this to the level of this" in mating face to face, for then his [*Zair Anpin*'s] *Chesed* is opposite her [*Malchut*'s] *Gevurah*, which is what is meant by "evil to the level of good." This is the secret of sweetening the *Gevurot* through mating.[12]

Tiferet's main influence is *Chesed*, and *Malchut*'s is *Gevurah*. Although both are in the middle line of *Sefirot*, *Tiferet* "leans" toward the right, *Malchut* toward the left. This is what the Gaon thinks is meant by "good from good" and "evil from evil."

Furthermore, when *Tiferet* (*Zair Anpin*) and *Malchut* are facing each other, his *Chesed* is opposite her *Gevurah*. They mix in mating, and thus the strength of the strict law is "sweetened" (diluted) by *Chesed*. That is what the *Mishnah* means by "the good test the bad." The Gaon goes on to explain: "Her good tests his bad and her bad tests his good because just as they cannot get too much bad, so they cannot get too much good."[13] That is, kindness and strictness moderate each other. The world needs a mixture of both. As the *Pree Yitzchak* explains:

> "The good tests the bad" means that it knows that evil is needed in the world to exact judgment against the wicked. "The evil tests the good" means that it knows that kindness is needed in the world so anger should not come too rapidly in order to give the evil a chance to repent. For this reason, God made mercy and strict law partners so that the world could be maintained through them.[14]

The Vilna Gaon goes on to say that in this world, "good is tested by bad and bad by good," but in the next world, "good is put aside for the good and bad for the bad." In this world God punishes the good so that they can enter the next world clean. He also rewards the good deeds of the evil, so they can be destroyed afterward. However, in the next world, the good get good, the evil, evil.

This is symbolized, says the Gaon, by two rearrangements of the alphabet, *AtBash* and *AlBag*. These have been traditionally used by Hebrew poets in many of their liturgical poems. *AtBash* is the alphabet ordered as follows: the first letter, *Aleph*, comes first, then the last letter, *Tav*, then the next to first (*Bet*) and the next to last (*Shin*), etc.

AlBag, on the other hand, is ordered the first and the twelfth, the second and thirteenth, etc. This world uses the method of *AtBash*! The best and worst are often associated, the bad getting reward, and the good suffering. In the next world, however, the first (best) of this world (symbolized by the first eleven letters of the alphabet) is associated with the first in the next (the second half of the alphabet).

The *Pree Yitzchak* explains as follows:

> The true "good and bad" are kept for the future, for today is for the purpose of doing good and evil and tomorrow is for receiving their rewards. The good and evil in this world is not good and evil in essence, for good that befalls the wicked is to enable them to be paid fully for their evil later, and the bad to the righteous is to atone for their sins.[15]

The *Otzar HaShem* concludes: "Know that there is no change in the will above. It is only from the view of those that receive below. The ways of a person will find him."[16]

God's will is eternal and does not change. A good person automatically gets good in the end. It appears to us below that God changes His will. However, in reality, He always wants the same thing. What actually happens is a result of man's deeds.

THE RELATIONSHIPS BETWEEN THE LETTERS

Sefer Yetzirah, Chapter 6, Mishnah 3

מ"ג שלשה כל אחד לבדו עומד . ז' חלוקין
שלשה מול שלשה וחק מכו"יע בינתים .
שנים עשר עומדין במלחמה שלשה אוהבים
שלשה שונאים שלשה מחיים שלשה ממיתים.
שלשה אוהבים הלב והאזנים והפה . שלשה
שונאים הכבד והמרה והלשון. ואל מלך נאמן
מושל בכולן , אחד על גבי שלשה שלשה
על גבי שבעה שבעה על גבי שנים עשר
וכולן אדוקין זה בזה :

> **Three, each one stands alone. Seven is split three against three and the decree mediates in between. Twelve stand in war—three lovers, three haters, three that make live, and three that kill. The three lovers are the heart, the ears, and the mouth. The three haters are the liver, the gall bladder, and the tongue. God, the faithful King, rules over all of them. One is over three, three is over seven, and seven is over twelve, and they all cling one to another.**

This *Mishnah* describes the relationships between the items of the various groups—three, seven, and twelve. The group of three is composed of three individual items. The group of seven is composed of two groups of three and a mediator. The group of twelve is subdivided into four groups of three. Three is the key number, for it represents the three basic lines—kindness, strict law, and the mediator, mercy.

Each group, it will be remembered, represents more than one set of objects. Each represents items in space, time, and soul, as well as in the upper world of the *Sefirot*. All the levels are structured similarly, and the relationships described by the *Mishnah* are meant to apply to all the levels.

The *Mishnah* in Vilna Gaon's version of the text is similar to the standard text above, but contains more details. It reads as follows:

> **Three, each one stands alone; one finds merit, one finds guilty, and one mediates in between. Seven, three against three, and the decree mediates in between. Twelve stand in war—three lovers, three haters, three that make live, and three that kill. The three lovers are the heart and the ears. The three haters are the liver, the gall bladder, and the tongue. The three that give life are the two nostrils and the spleen. The three that kill are two orifices and the mouth. God, the faithful King, rules over all of them, from His holy place until forever and ever. One is over three, three is over seven, and seven is over twelve, and they all cling one to another.**

The *Mishnah* begins by telling us that each of the three stands alone. The Gaon's version goes on to say that each has a separate function; one finds merit, one finds guilt, and the third mediates. This is true not only of the first group of three *Sefirot—Keter, Chachmah*, and *Binah—* but of the two groups of three that compose the group of seven as well. The commentaries refer us back to the first *Mishnah* of Chapter 3, where the group of three is discussed in regard to *Emesh*.

The *Mishnah* tells us that the group of seven is composed of two groups of three, with a seventh element mediating. The *Otzar HaShem*[17] states that the *Sefirot* of the two group of three are: (1) *Chesed, Gevurah*, and *Tiferet*, and (2) *Netzach, Hod*, and *Yisod*. The mediator is *Malchut*. According to this configuration, each group of three has a *Sefirah* from the right, one from the left, and one in the middle. Thus, in addition to the overall mediator, *Malchut*, each group is mediated by its *Sefirah* from the middle (*Tiferet* and *Yisod*).

One might wonder how *Malchut* can be the overall mediator, as it is the last *Sefirah*. However, as we mentioned before, *Malchut* at times rises to the level of *her husband, Tiferet*. In this position she is between the two groups of three *Sefirot*. In addition, we have said previously that *Malchut* also represents the space in the middle of the six planes of all objects in space. The six planes are represented by the six *Sefirot* (i.e., the two groups of three). *Malchut* is in the middle, which allows her to mediate.

The Vilna Gaon disagrees with the *Otzar HaShem*. He states that each of the two groups does not consist of a *Sefirah* from the right, middle, and left, but rather one group is composed of three *Sefirot* from the right and the other group of the three to the left. He agrees with *Otzar HaShem* only on the fact that *Malchut* is the mediator.

The Gaon goes on to say that on the anatomical level, the one group is represented by the right eye, ear, and nostril, and the other by the left eye, ear, and nostril. The mouth, which represents *Malchut*, is, of course, in the middle.[18] The Gaon's approach has the advantage that there is only one mediator, which is how the *Mishnah* reads. The horizontal grouping of the *Otzar HaShem*, however, is the more usual way the *Sefirot* are grouped in the *Zohar*.

The *Mishnah* continues, telling us that twelve stand in war. The *Otzar HaShem* comments as follows: " 'Twelve stand in war' refers to the diagonal boundaries, which we have already said influence the constellations of the Zodiac. Three are of fire, three from earth, three of water, and three of air. The warmth is beloved by nature, and the cold is hated, and the air saturates nature, and so does water."[19]

"Saturates" here means an intermediary trait, as opposed to an extreme. This strange use of the word was seen previously in *Sefer Yetzirah* (see the discussion in Chapter 3, *Mishnah* 4).

The above quote implies that the four elements are of opposing natures and so are the constellations. After all, each constellation is aligned with a particular element.

The Vilna Gaon analyzes the twelve based on the four letters of the Tetragrammaton. The three lovers are associated with the first letter, *Yud*, which represents *Chachmah* (Wisdom). *Chachmah* is on the right side and represents the creative power of "loving" kindness. The three haters are associated with the letter *Hey*, which represents *Binah*, the first *Sefirah* of the left side, the side of strict law. Therefore, since strictness arises from the left and the "side of uncleanliness" gets its nourishment from it, the three "haters" are also connected there. The last two letters of the Tetragrammaton are the *Vav* and *Hey*, which, we mentioned previously, stand for *Tiferet* and *Malchut*. *Tiferet* is known as the "Tree of Life" and *Malchut* as the "Tree of Knowledge." The Tree of Knowledge, however, turns out to be the "Tree of Death," for when Adam and Eve ate from it, death was decreed in the world. The *Zohar* says that *Malchut* is called *Callah* (bride) because it destroys all that is beneath it (*Mechalleh* means destroys and is from from the same root as *Kallah* [bride]—*Kaf, Lamed, Hey*). Thus, "*the three that make live and the three that kill*" are associated with the *Vav* and *Hey* of the Tetragrammaton—the trees of life and death.

The Gaon goes on as follows: "The three lovers are the heart and the ears, which are the tools to acquire Torah." While the standard version of the text also includes the mouth as one of the lovers, the Gaon's version has it as a "killer." It seems to me that the mouth indeed serves in both capacities, and either view can be justified. As the verse says, "Death and life are in the hands of the tongue" (Proverbs 18:21).

About the "haters" the Gaon says, "The three haters are the liver, gall bladder, and tongue, for all the desires are in the liver, as is known from *Midrash Ne'elam*.[20] All jealousy is in the gall bladder, as is written in *Bava Metzia* 107b, "*Machalah* [the name of Esau's wife, which literally means sickness] is the gall; why is it called *Machalah*, for it makes all of the body ill.' The rot of the bones, jealousy, that is *Machalah*."

The last hater, continues the Gaon, is the tongue, in which all pride is bound, as in praise of oneself and degradation of others. The three killers are the two orifices for excrement and the mouth. If these are too closed or too opened, they can cause death. Finally, the three that give life are the spleen and the nostrils. Obviously the nostrils give life because the breath of life is through them. The spleen is a little harder to understand. We said previously that laughter is associated with the spleen, so perhaps it is because some laughter is needed to live.

The Gaon associates the spleen with the pleasures of this world. In a difficult passage, he says as follows:

> All of this world is entirely in the spleen, as the expression goes, "The world laughs for him"[21] in the spleen. It laughs for the evil in this world, [the world] where all the animals prowl, that is, the wicked. The spleen is night, which is for the wicked, but for the righteous it is the happiness of good deeds, which is the flame of observing commandments at night and in the day. The Torah is light.[22]

The spleen laughs, but there are two kinds of laughter, of good and evil. The same organ functions for both, depending on its host. Each of the twelve items have *Temurot*—replacements of an opposite nature. Light travels in two directions, both forward and backward. Similarly, things like laughter can be either positive or negative.

The *Mishnah* concludes, "One is over three, three is over seven, and seven is over twelve, and they all cling one to another." The *Pree Yitzchak* says as follows:

> This means the aspect of the Infinite (*Ein Sof*) is over the three, *Keter*, *Chachmah*, and *Binah*. Three on seven means *Keter*, *Chachmah*, and *Binah* are over the seven lower *Sefirot*. Seven on top of twelve are the seven lower *Sefirot* of forward and backward light of the Six Extremes, which are incorporated into *Tiferet*, which are their roots. They are also the secret of the twelve cattle that the upper sea stands on.[23]

Twelve is associated with *Tiferet*. *Tiferet* is the central *Sefirah* of the Six Extremes. The *Sefirot* both send and receive light, spirituality. This is known in Kabbalah as forward and backward light. Thus, each of the Six Extremes has these two aspects of light, totaling twelve aspects in all. This light is why the various sets of twelve are associated with *Tiferet*. The twelve cattle was a structure in Solomon's temple. Upon these statues was a great basin, known as the *Sea* of Solomon. This is described in 1 Kings. The *Pree Yitzchak* says it symbolized the sets of twelve discussed in *Sefer Yetzirah*.

The Vilna Gaon concludes that the three items, *Tlee*, Sphere, and heart, discussed in the previous *Mishnah*, are the "rod of Moses" with which God does miracles. Each, you will recall, is said to control its level of existence. This, he concludes, is what the *Mishnah* meant by "One is over three."

ABRAHAM, GOD, AND *SEFER YETZIRAH*

Sefer Yetzirah, Chapter 6, Mishnah 4

מ"ד וכיון שצפה אברהם אבינו ע"ה והביט
וראה וחקר והבין וחקק וחצב וצרף וצר
ועלתה בידו אז נגלה עליו אדון הכל ב"ה
והושיבהו בחיקו ונשקו על ראשו וקראו
אוהבי וכרת לו ברית ולזרעו והאמין בה'
ויחשבה לו צדקה . וכרת לו ברית בין עשר
אצבעות רגליו והיא ברית המילה, ועשר
אצבעות ידיו והוא הלשון . וקשר לו עשרים
ושתים אותיות בלשונו וגלה לו את יסודן .
משכן במים דלקם באש רעשן ברוח בערן
בשבעה נהגם בשנים עשר מזלות:

Once Abraham, may he rest in peace, observed, and looked and saw and investigated and understood and engraved and hewed and combined and formed and was successful, then the Master of All, blessed be He, revealed Himself to him. He sat him in His lap and kissed him on his head and called him "He who loves Me." He cut with

> him a covenant between the ten toes of his feet—
> this is the covenant of circumcision. Also, [a
> covenant] between the ten fingers of his hands,
> and this is the tongue. He tied twenty-two let-
> ters in his tongue and revealed to him their
> foundation. He pulled them in water, He burnt
> them in fire, He made them tumultuous in the
> wind, He ignited them in seven and led them in
> the twelve constellations [of the Zodiac].

This *Mishnah* speaks of Abraham, the traditional author of *Sefer Yetzi-rah*, in third person. While it seems strange that one would write of himself using third person, this is not without precedent. In fact, we find the same situation in the Torah itself. The last chapter in the Torah speaks of the death of Moses. The question arises of how Moses could have written these lines. Two answers are given in the Talmud. One opinion says Joshua wrote the last few lines of the Torah. Rabbi Meir, however, says that Moses himself, weeping, wrote them, as God dictated.[24]

In *Sefer Yetzirah* the same two possibilities exist. It is possible that Rabbi Akiva wrote this last *Mishnah* as a postscript to the already existing *Sefer Yetzirah*. It is also possible that Abraham wrote about himself in third person. Of course, there are many other possibilities as well, and the question of the creation of the "Book of Creation" remains a mystery, like many of the hidden meanings within the book.

This *Mishnah* tells of Abraham's "observing, looking, seeing, inves-tigating, understanding, engraving, hewing, combining, forming, and being successful." These terms in the *Mishnah* fall into two groups, contemplative and active. The first group tells of his discovery of God and His attributes (the *Sefirot*). This is not surprising, as he is tradition-ally acknowledged to be the person who formulated the Judaic con-cept of monotheism. The second group of terms is a little more difficult. *Sefer Yetzirah* used these terms previously to refer to *God's* actions, but how do they apply to Abraham's?

The Raivad addresses this question by quoting a portion of the Talmud in Tractate *Sanhedrin*. It states as follows: "Rabba created a man and sent him to Rabbi Zeyra. Rabbi Zeyra spoke to him, but he did not reply. Rabbi Zeyra then said, 'This man was created by the scholars. Return to your dust!' "[25] Rashi comments on this, "He created the man using *Sefer Yetzirah*, where he learned how to combine the letters of the name of God."[26]

In other words, *Sefer Yetzirah* was not thought of as a purely speculative work, but also a practical handbook. According to legend, Abraham used it to create life. Of course, man can never match God. The creation of Rabbi Zeyra couldn't talk. In the famous legend of the Golem (artificial man) of the Maharal of Prague, the Golem, too, had its shortcomings.

The problem is, *Sefer Yetzirah* does not explicitly explain how to combine the letters of God's name. I have read it more than once, and I have not the vaguest idea how to make a Golem. Either our version of *Sefer Yetzirah* is incomplete, or what is meant is that *Sefer Yetzirah* provides the principles but not the details.

Genesis states, "Abraham took Sari, his wife, and Lot, the son of his brother, and all their wealth, and *the souls that he made* in Haran" (Genesis 12:5). While the usual explanation of "souls that he made" has to do with conversions to the faith, some Kabbalists take this phrase literally, that is, as meaning souls Abraham made using *Sefer Yetzirah*.

Another place where a similar legend appears is in the commentary of the *Malbum* on Genesis.[27] The Scriptures state that Abraham gave the three angels who visited him beef, cakes, milk, and butter (Genesis 18:6–8). Although Abraham lived before the Torah was given, the Talmud states that he observed all the laws of the Torah, which include not eating meat and milk together. How was it that he served them both meat and milk? He offers an astounding Rabbinic legend. The beef was not from a natural animal, but rather from one created using *Sefer Yetzirah*. Artificial animals do not come under the prohibition of meat and milk, only natural ones.

To sum up, the *Mishnah* is saying that Abraham discovered the principles upon which *Sefer Yetzirah* is based and he used them as well. The number of descriptive verbs used in detailing Abraham's actions is a matter of debate among the various commentators. Moses Botarel quotes "Rabbi Aaron, the head of the Yeshiva of Babylonia, the great Kabbalist" as follows:

> The author of *Sefer Yetzirah* "took, gazed, looked, saw, understood, investigated, engraved, concentrated, combined, and formed success-fully." These ten terms are representative of the ten *Sefirot*, five on each

side. They are hinted at by the secret of the covenant of circumcision, for it is between the two sets of five toes. So are there five on each side of the covenant of the heart [i.e., fingers].[28]

In contrast to this are the words of the Vilna Gaon, "The seven descriptive terms represent the seven lower *Sefirot*."[29] The textual version of the Gaon did, in fact, have seven verbs. The standard version has ten, though they differ somewhat from those cited by Rabbi Aaron of Babylonia.

The *Mishnah* continues to tell us of God's love for Abraham. It tells us that He revealed Himself to him, sat him in His lap, and kissed him on his head and called him "He who loves Me." God hides, but nevertheless wants to be found. It is like a game of hide and seek, which is no fun if no one comes looking.

The Torah tells us that ritual circumcision began with Abraham. It represents an agreement between him and God, but not the only one. There are agreements on various levels. The heart has its own covenant. The tongue, too, must be controlled, not only the libido. Remember, there are three groups of three *Sefirot*, each with its mediator. One represents reason, one emotion, and one physical functions. There are, likewise, three covenants with Abraham. The lower one, says the Vilna Gaon, is described in Genesis as the *covenant between the parts* of the animals (*Brit bein HaBetarim*) (Genesis 15). The second is circumcision. The highest one is what is called "the secret of God to those who fear him" (Psalms 25:14).

The *Mishnah* continues, "He tied twenty-two letters in his tongue and revealed to him their foundation." This, says the *Pree Yitzchak*, means that God taught Abraham the secret of combining the letters of His name.[30]

It should be noted that while this *Mishnah* speaks of the person Abraham, on another level it also refers to his counterpart in the *Sefirot*, the *Sefirah* of *Chesed* (Kindness). The Bible speaks of Abraham's kindness, for example, his welcoming guests and his sacrifices for Lot. Whenever the Torah speaks of him, Kabbalists automatically think of the *Sefirah* of *Chesed* as well. This *Sefirah* is the first of the seven lower *Sefirot*. The lower *Sefirot* are known also as *the world*. *Chesed* is thus the beginning of the world, as it is written, "*Olam chesed yibaneh*" (the world will be built with Kindness) (Psalms 89:3). The linking of Abraham and creation is consequently quite appropriate.

The book ends, "He pulled them in water, He burnt them in fire, He made them tumultuous in the wind, He ignited them in seven and led them in the twelve constellations [of the Zodiac]."

The beginning of *Sefer Yetzirah* was about the thirty-two paths comprised of letters and *Sefirot*, and so is its end. These thirty-two elements were formulated in God's Will (*Keter*), and wind through all levels of creation, until they manifest in the lower world in the very heart of man. It is not by accident that the Hebrew word for heart is *Lev*, which has a numerical value of thirty-two.

This concludes our analysis of *Sefer Yetzirah*. We traced the powers of creation through the *Sefirot* and letters. In the *Sefirot* there exists the basic antithesis of kindness and harshness, fire and water. In the alphabet this opposition exists as well. The Torah's letters are like water, as is written, "My teaching will drip like rain" (Deuteronomy 32:2) and like fire, as it is written, "From his right hand is the law of fire for them" (Deuteronomy 33:2).

Thus, *Sefer Yetzirah* teaches that the source for all that we find below is in the spiritual spheres above. The three basic elements have as their root the spiritual forces known as *Emesh*. The seven *moving stars* and the days of the week are related to the letters of *Beged Kafarta*. The twelve zodiacal constellations and the twelve months of the year are rooted in the twelve single letters.

More important than knowing the source of any of these, however, is knowing one's own root in God. Then, if one becomes lost, he merely has to follow his own *path* back home.

APPENDIX A

Structure of the Sefirot in the Shape of Man

Following is the structure of the *Sefirot* in the shape of man, including the twenty-two connecting pipes. It is based on a diagram from *Paamon VeRimon,* by Mordechai ben Jacob, written in 1708. The thirty-two Paths of Wisdom are comprised of the ten *Sefirot* and the twenty-two pipes.

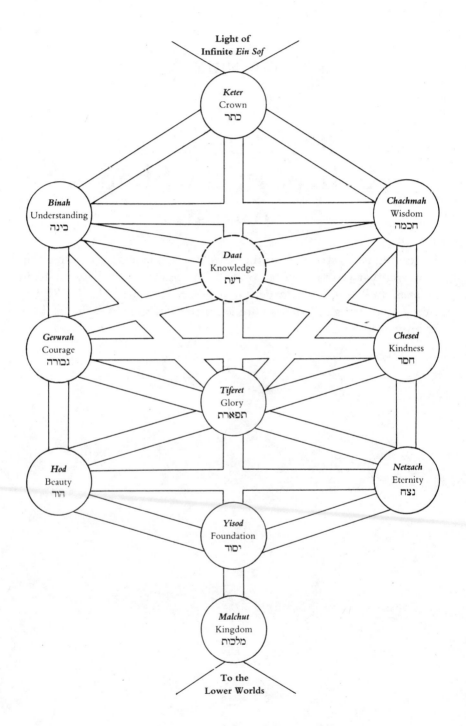

Light of
Infinite *Ein Sof*

Keter
Crown
כתר

Binah
Understanding
בינה

Chachmah
Wisdom
חכמה

Daat
Knowledge
דעת

Gevurah
Courage
גבורה

Chesed
Kindness
חסד

Tiferet
Glory
תפארת

Hod
Beauty
הוד

Netzach
Eternity
נצח

Yisod
Foundation
יסוד

Malchut
Kingdom
מלכות

To the
Lower Worlds

212

APPENDIX B

Numerical Values of Letters

THE REGULAR METHOD

LETTER	NAME	VALUE
א	Aleph	1
ב	Bet	2
ג	Gimel	3
ד	Dalet	4
ה	Hey	5
ו	Vav	6
ז	Zayin	7
ח	Chet	8
ט	Tet	9
י	Yud	10
כ	Kaf	20
ל	Lamed	30
מ	Mem	40
נ	Nun	50
ס	Samech	60
ע	Ayin	70
פ	Peh	80
צ	Tzadi	90
ק	Kuf	100
ר	Resh	200
ש	Shin	300
ת	Tav	400

Examples

אב = 1 + 2 = 3

בגד = 2 + 3 + 4 = 9

בית = 2 + 10 + 400 = 412

PRAT KATAN—THE SMALL METHOD

In this method, all zeroes are removed from the "Value" column above. Thus, *Kaf* equals 2, not 20, as does *Resh*. *Shin* equals 3, not 300. This alternative method is occasionally used by the Kabbalists.

Appendix C

Vowels and Letters
Associated with Sefirot

The *Sefirot* are associated with letters as well as vowels. The letters make up the body of the *Sefirot*; the vowels are their soul. Names of God have a special place in Kabbalah. The Tetragrammaton, for instance, sometimes refers to the inner life of the "tree of *Sefirot*" and is called by the *Zohar* "*Shaku DeIlna*"—the liquid of the tree. Each letter of the Tetragrammaton is associated with one or more different *Sefirot*.

Keter—The associated vowel is the *Kamatz*, which means "closed." *Keter* is the highest *Sefirah*, and the least understood. It is closed to us and is thus assigned the *Kamatz*. As far as letters are concerned, it is only assigned the little thorn at the end of the first *Yud* in the Tetragrammaton, since it is so hidden.

Chachmah—This *Sefirah* is considered the beginning of the creation and is thus assigned the vowel *Patach*, which means "to open" or "to begin." The first letter of the Tetragrammaton, *Yud*, is associated with *Chachmah*.

Binah—The vowel of *Binah* is the *Tzeirei*, which comes from the word *Tzurah* (form) in Hebrew. It is here where the primal matter of *Chachmah* takes "form." This includes the formation of the letters themselves. The second letter of the Tetragrammaton, *Hey*, is associated with *Binah*.

The Six Extremes—all share the letter *Vav*, which has the numeric value of six (see Appendix B). The vowels vary.

Malchut—Its letter is the last *Hey* in the Tetragrammaton. It and *Binah* are usually thought of as feminine, and *Hey* denotes a feminine ending in Hebrew. There is some question as to whether *Malchut* has a vowel at all, for it is like the moon, whose light is not its own but rather that of the sun.

In addition to being part of the overall Tetragrammaton, each *Sefirah* has separate names of God associated with it (see Appendix D). Also, each of the twenty-two letters of the *Aleph Bet* is associated with one of the twenty-two pipes connecting the *Sefirot* (see Appendix A).

APPENDIX D

The Names
of God

The names of God that are associated with the various *Sefirot* are listed below. This list is based on commonly found associations, but many variations exist. Differences are mainly due to divergent opinions among the Kabbalists. Also, at different levels, different names may apply.

Keter—Aleph Hey Yud Hey (EhHehYeh)
Chachmah—Yud-Hey (Yah)
Binah—Yud-Hey-Vav-Hey Elohim
Chesed—El
Gevurah—Elohim
Tiferet—Yud-Hey-Vav-Hey
Netzach—Tzvaot (shared with *Hod*)
Hod—Tzvaot (shared with *Netzach*)
Yisod—Shaddai
Malchut—Aleph-Dalet-Nun-Yud (Adonai)

Computations of Numeric Values of God's Names

The Tetragrammaton equals 26 as follows: *Yud* (10) *Hey* (5) *Vav* (6) *Hey* (5).

There are four first expansions of the Name *(Milui)*. *An expansion takes the value of the name* of each letter. The first letter in the Tetragrammaton is *Yud*. It is spelled *Yud Vav Dalet*. The second letter is *Hey*, which is spelled *Hey Aleph*. The third, *Vav*, is spelled *Vav Aleph Vav*. The last, *Hey*, is *Hey Aleph*. This results in the original four letters expanding to ten, with a total numerical value of 45. That ten is also the number of *Sefirot* is not a fact that is lost on the Kabbalists. Nor is the fact that forty-five is also the value of the Hebrew word *Adam*—man.

We said that *Hey* is spelled *Hey Aleph*. Sometimes, however, it is spelled *Hey Hey* and sometimes *Hey Yud*. *Vav* also has alternative spellings, namely *Vav Vav* and *Vav Yud Vav*. The names of God that are known as *The Name of seventy-two*, *The name of sixty-three*, and *The name of fifty-two* are constructed using these alternate spellings. Each has specific meaning, especially in Lurian Kabbalah.

A second expansion of the ten letters yields twenty-eight letters, known as the "Name of *Koach* (strength)." The numerical value of *Koach* (strength) is 28. It is said to be the name with which the world was created.

Other interesting variations are sometimes used. One is called "the squaring of the name." The first letter of the name is taken alone, then the first two letters together, then the first three, and finally all four. This yields ten letters. Their sum is called the square of the name (*ribua*) and is said to represent the "back" of the *Sefirot*.

Names of God constitute a major topic in Kabbalah and cannot be fully treated here. It is important to understand that God's names are considered descriptive of His actions as far as we can know them. The highest aspect of God, the infinite *Ein Sof*, has no name attached, for we can know nothing about it.

Of God's names, only three address His essence at all. These are known as the "Names of essence." According to Avraham Ibn Ezra, they are the Tetragrammaton, *Yah*, and *EhHehYeh*. We know little about God's essence, but we do know it is eternal—past, present, and future. This fact is what the "names of essence" stress.

The Thirty-Two Paths According to the Raivad

1. Wondrous reason
2. Radiating reason
3. Holy reason
4. Established reason
5. Rooted reason
6. Abundant separated reason
7. Hidden reason
8. Complete reason
9. Pure reason
10. Sparkling reason
11. Shining reason
12. Bright reason
13. Reason leading the unity
14. Light giving reason
15. Establishing reason
16. Eternal reason
17. The reason of feeling
18. Reason of the house of abundance
19. Reason that is the secret of all the spiritual actions
20. Reason of the will
21. Reason of the sought item
22. Faithful reason
23. Lasting reason
24. Reason of the imagination
25. Experiential reason

26. Renewed reason
27. Felt reason
28. Natural reason
29. Embodied reason
30. General reason
31. Constant reason
32. Worshiped wisdom

The Raivad provides short explanations for each. The items on this list, however, are not even alluded to in *Sefer Yetzirah* itself.

APPENDIX F

The Soul and the Five Partzufim

The ten *Sefirot* are associated with five *Partzufim*. A *Partzuf* is a full set of ten sub-*Sefirot*, structured to hold more light than "simple" *Sefirot*. It is said that the seven lower *Sefirot* in the World of *Tohu* broke because they were not able to stand the intense light. The restructuring is called "*Tikun*"—fixing—and the restructured world is known as "The World of *Tikun*." The *Partzufim* and the *Sefirot* they correspond to are as follows:

1. *Arich Anpin* —Keter
2. *Abba* —Chachmah
3. *Imma* —Binah
4. *Zair Anpin*—The Six Extremes
5. Female of *Zair Anpin*—Malchut

These five encompass the entire world of the *Sefirot*. Lurian Kabbalah has other *Partzufim* as well. *Atik*, for instance, is a second *Partzuf* associated with *Keter*. Nevertheless, these five are the basic ones constituting each particular world. Associated with each is a "level of soul."

THE SOUL

The soul's five parts correspond to the five *Partzufim* as follows:

1. *Yechidah*—corresponds to *Arich Anpin*
2. *Chayah*—corresponds to *Abba*
3. *Neshamah*—corresponds to *Imma*

4. *Ruach*—corresponds to *Zair Anpin*
5. *Nefesh* —corresponds to Female of *Zair Anpin*

The parts are hierarchical. *Nefesh*, the lowest part, resides in the liver. *Ruach* is in the heart. *Neshamah* is in the brain. *Yechidah* and *Chayah* are too great to be contained within the body. *Chayah* surrounds each of the three lower souls and is sometimes called "the soul's soul." *Yechidah* is the highest level and surrounds all the others. The light of each soul stems from the five *Partzufim*. Thus, man contains the divine light of the *Sefirot* (*Nefesh Eloha MiMaal*).

The 231 Gates According to Shabbetai Donnolo

The 462 letter pairs below represent the Gates forward and backward. According to Donnolo, each letter pair is a gate.

אב	בנ	גד	דה	הו	וז	זח	חט	טי	יך	כל
אג	בד	גה	דו	הז	וח	זט	חי	טך	יל	כם
אד	בה	גו	דז	הח	וט	זי	חך	טל	ים	כן
אה	בו	גז	דח	הט	וי	זך	חל	טם	ין	כם
או	בז	גח	דט	הי	וך	זל	חם	טן	ים	כע
אז	בח	גט	די	הך	ול	זם	חן	טס	יע	כף
אח	בט	גי	דך	הל	ום	זן	חם	טע	יף	כץ
אט	בי	גך	דל	הם	ון	זם	חע	טף	יץ	כק
אי	בך	גל	דם	הן	וס	זע	חף	טץ	יק	כר
אך	בל	גם	דן	הם	וע	זף	חץ	טק	יר	כש
אל	בם	גן	דם	הע	וף	זץ	חק	טר	יש	כת
אם	בן	גם	דע	דע	הף	וץ	זק	חר	מש	ית	כא
אן	בם	גם	נע	דף	הץ	וק	זר	חש	טת	יא	כב
אם	בע	גף	דץ	הק	ור	זש	חת	טא	יב	כג
אע	בף	גץ	דק	הר	וש	זת	חא	טב	יג	כד
אף	בץ	גק	דר	הש	ות	זא	חב	טג	יד	כה
אץ	בק	גר	דש	הת	וא	זב	חג	טד	יה	כו
אק	בר	גש	דת	הא	וב	זג	חד	טה	יו	כז
אר	בש	גת	דא	הב	וג	זד	חה	טו	יז	כח
אש	בת	גא	דב	הג	וד	זה	חו	טז	יח	כט
את	בא	גב	דג	הד	וה	זו	חז	טח	יט	כי

לם	מן	נם	סע	עף	פץ	צק	קר	רש	שת	תא
לן	מם	נע	סף	עץ	פק	צר	קש	רת	שא	תב
לם	מע	נף	סץ	עק	פר	צש	קת	רא	שב	תג
לע	מף	נץ	סק	ער	פש	צת	קא	רב	שג	תד
לף	מץ	נק	סר	עש	פת	צא	קב	רנ	שד	תה
לץ	מק	נר	סש	עת	פא	צב	קג	רד	שה	תו
לק	מר	נש	סת	עא	פב	צג	קד	רה	שו	תז
לר	מש	נת	סא	עב	פג	צד	קה	רו	שז	תח
לש	מת	נא	סב	עג	פד	צה	קו	רז	שח	תט
לת	מא	נב	סג	עד	פה	צו	קז	רח	שט	תי
לא	מב	נג	סד	עה	פו	צז	קח	רט	שי	תך
לב	מג	נד	סה	עו	פז	צח	קט	רי	שך	תל
לג	מד	נה	סו	עז	פח	צט	קי	רך	של	תם
לד	מה	נו	סז	עח	פט	צי	קך	רל	שם	תן
לה	מו	נז	סח	עט	פי	צך	קל	רם	שן	תם
לו	מז	נח	סט	עי	פך	צל	קם	רן	שם	תע
לז	מח	נט	סי	עך	פל	צם	קן	רם	שע	תף
לח	מט	ני	סך	על	פם	צן	קם	רע	שף	תץ
לט	מי	נך	סל	עם	פן	צם	קע	רף	שץ	תק
לי	מך	נל	סם	ען	פם	צע	קף	רץ	שק	תר
לך	מל	נם	סן	עם	פע	צף	קץ	רק	שר	תש

223

The 231 Gates According to Otzar HaShem

Each letter has 231 forward Gates and 231 backward Gates, according to *Otzar HaShem*. Below are the Gates associated with the letter *Aleph*. All the other letters of the *Aleph Bet* also have Gates.

אב גד הו זח טי כל מנ סע פצ קר שת
בא גד הו זח טי כל מנ סע פצ קר שת
אג דה וז חט יכ למ נס עפ צק רב תב
גא בד הו זח טי כל מנ סע פצ קר שת
אד הו זח טי כל מנ סע פצ קר שת בג
דא בג הו זח טי כל מנ סע פצ קר שת
אה בג דו זח טי כל מנ סע פצ קר שת
הא בג דו זח טי כל מנ סע פצ קר שת
או זח טי כל מנ סע פצ קר שת בג דה
וא בג ד הו זח טי כל מנ סע פצ קר שת
אז חט יכ למ נס עפ צק רב תב גד הו
זא בג דה וז חט יכ למ נס עפ צק רב שת
אח טי כל מנ סע פצ קר שת בג דה וז
הא בג דה וז חט יכ מנ סע פצ קר שת
אט יכ למ נס עפ צק רב תב גד הו זה
טא בג דה וז חט יכ למ נס עפ צק רב שת
אי כל מנ סע פצ קר שת בג דה וז חט
יא בג דה וז חט יכ למ נס עפ צק רב שת
אכ למ נס עפ צק רב תב גד הו זה טי
כא בג דה וז חט יכ מנ סע פצ קר שת
אל מנ סע פצ קר שת בג דה וז חט יכ

Endnotes

INTRODUCTION

1. David Hume, *Treatise on Human Nature*, 1739.

2. Rene Descartes (1596–1650), *Meditations.*

3. Moses Cordovero (1522–1570), *Pardes Rimonim* (originally published 1591 in Cracow), Gate 1, Chapter 1.

4. Traditionally attributed to the *Tanna* Nechunia ben Hakaneh, *Sefer HaBahir*, published originally in 1176, Provence. Some modern scholars claim this is a much later work, and they credit authorship to Isaac the Blind of the twelfth century.

5. See *Library of Biblical Studies*, Harry Orlinsky, 1968, for full text and discussion of *Masoret HaMesoret. Massoret HaMesoret* was originally published in 1538 in Venice. The author, Eliyahu Bachur, is known to the non-Jewish world as Elias Levitas.

6. *Pardes Rimonim,* Gate 1, Chapter 1.

7. There is some confusion as to the identity of the Raivad. Raivad is an abbreviation for Rabbi Avraham ben David. There are at least three famous rabbis for whom the term Raivad has been used. The most famous is the author of the Glosses on *Mishneh Torah*. It has been traditionally assumed that it was he who wrote this commentary. This association has been strengthened by the fact that his son was Isaac the Blind, a very famous Kabbalist. However, his authorship of this commentary has been widely disputed, not only by modern scholars, but even by the great Kabbalist, Yitzchak Luria, himself. Luria says that although the real author is not the Raivad but an unknown Ashkenazi scholar, the work is one of the few valuable, true commentaries on *Sefer Yetzirah*.

8. Moses ben Maimon (Maimonides), *Guide to the Perplexed* (completed 1190), Section 3, Chapter 10.

9. Attributed to Shimon bar Yochai, *The Zohar* appeared in Europe in manuscripts issued by Moses De Leon in the thirteenth century. For a fascinating discussion of the authorship of this book see *Mishnat HaZohar*, by Lechover and Tishbi (Mosad Bialik, 1949).

10. The term *Midrash* refers to rabbinic bible commentary. The earliest *Midrashim* were written by the authors of the *Mishnah*, such as the Sifri and Sifra. Other *Midrashim*, such as *Midrash Rabbah*, appeared much later. The period of the *Midrash* is spread over about 1,000 years.

11. Moses Cordovero (1522–1570), *Pardes Rimonim*, Gate of The Order of How They Stand (*Shaar Seder Amidatan*).

12. Chaim Vital, *Etz Chaim*, originally compiled by the author in 1594 and circulated in pieces until it was published in 1772 under the name *Etz Chaim*.

13. The scheme of right, meaning Kindness, and left, Strictness, is used universally in Kabbalah. It is based in part on *Sefer Yetzirah*, Chapter 2, *Mishnah* 1, which says, "Their foundation is the hand of innocence [of the scale of justice], the hand of guilt, and the tongue of decree that decides between them."

14. Raivad, *Glosses to Maimonides' Mishneh Torah*, Section *Yisodei HaTorah*.

15. Moses Cordovero (1522–1570), *Pardes Rimonim*, Gate of Essence and Vessels (*Atzmut VeCaylim*).

16. Maimonides, *Guide to the Perplexed* (Part 2, Chapter 1) and *Mishneh Torah*, Section *Yisodei HaTorah*.

17. Raivad, *Glosses to Maimonides' Mishneh* Torah, *Yisodei HaTorah*.

18. This idea is based on *Sefer Yetzirah*, Chapter 1, *Mishnah* 3. Rabbi Isaac Luria (Ari), in his *Maamar Kadishin*, greatly expands on the details. This is one of the few pieces the Ari himself wrote. It associates parts of the hand with specific *Sefirot* and letters.

19. Maimonides, *Guide to the Perplexed*, Part 2.

20. So states an often quoted *Midrash*. The wording of the statement is, "Only God and His Name (*Shemo*) existed." The Kabbalists were quick to point out that the numerical value of *Shemo* (His Name) is the same as *Ratzon* (Will). They concluded that what was meant is that only the *Ein Sof* and *Keter* existed. That is, the will to create necessarily pre-dated the creation. This association of the Infinite light (*Ein Sof*) with *Keter* led some to believe they are identical. Cordovero spends much time proving that they are, indeed, two distinct items.

21. *Pardes Rimonim*, Gate 4, Chapter 4.

22. Moses Chaim Luzzatto, *Maamar HaVikuach* (B'nei B'rak, Israel: Sifreyati Publishers). This same idea is expressed in *Chokar U'Mikubal* and

Milchemet Moshe, which are essentially other versions of *Maamar HaVikuach.* Luzzatto was a unique figure in Jewish history. He not only was a famous Kabbalist and *Mussar* teacher, but he wrote secular plays as well and is considered by some the father of modern Hebrew literature. He is not universally accepted, however, due to his messianic aspirations.

23. Rabbi Yehuda Leib Ashlag, *Talmud Esser Sefirot,* volume 1 (Jerusalem: M. Klor, 1955).

24. Aryeh Kaplan, *The Bahir* (New York: Samuel Weiser, Inc., 1979). See Introduction and n. 68 to the Introduction.

25. Cordovero, *Pardes Rimonim,* Gate 3.

26. Vital, *Etz Chaim,* the first few chapters.

27. *Sefer HaBahir,* paragraph 14.

28. See n. 5. Introduction to *Masoret HaMesoret.*

29. Hegel, *The Philosophy of History,* 1805. Translated by Carl Friedrich, 1953. Published by Modern World Library, *The Philosophy of Hegel.*

30. Ibid.

31. *Bereishit Rabbah,* Chapter 6. Brought by Rashi in his commentary on Genesis, fourth day.

32. Shabbetai Horowitz (son of the ShaLaH), *Shefa Tal (Abundance of Dew),* 17th century, Posen, Amsterdam.

33. *Sefer Yetzirah,* Chapter 1, *Mishnah* 8.

34. Ibid., *Mishnah* 6.

CHAPTER 1

1. Maimonides, *Guide to the Perplexed,* Part 1, Chapter 54.

2. *Pardes Rimonim,* Gate 1, Chapter 1.

3. Raivad, *Commentary on Sefer Yetzirah.*

4. *Pesachim,* Chapter 1.

5. See Introduction, n. 4, above.

6. That there are exactly ten vowels in Hebrew is not clear. There are basically nine. *Chataf-kamatz* is generally taken to be the tenth.

7. *Zohar,* page 280, side 1.

8. In *Pirke Avot* 5:1 it states, "With ten statements God created the world." Actually, if you count in the Torah, there are only nine. This has led to the

well-known explanation that the statement "In the beginning God created the heavens and the earth" constitutes the tenth.

9. Commentary of Rabbi Eliyahu of Vilna on *Sefer Yetzirah*, Chapter 1, *Mishnah*, 1, *Ofan* 5. Interestingly, this commentary is written in five different sections, each representing a different "level" of explanation. Each level is called an *Ofan* (Way).

10. Commentary of Abraham Ibn Ezra on *Shemot* 3:15.

11. Maimonides, *Mishneh Torah, Mada, Yesodei HaTorah*, Chapter 6.

12. The Talmud says the world started to expand unceasingly until God "said to His world, 'enough.'" The phrase "said to His world enough" in Hebrew shortens to name *Shaddai*.

13. Maimonides, *Guide to the Perplexed*, beginning Part 1, Chapter 51.

14. Ramban is short for Rabbi Moses ben Nachman, also known as Naimonides. He is among the greatest early rabbis. He wrote a widely used commentary on the Torah that is full of kabbalistic references. He is said to have seen a copy of the *Zohar* before its public appearance, although this is uncertain. Many ideas that appear in the *Zohar* are hinted at in his commentary on *Sefer Yetzirah*. He was familiar with *Sefer HaBahir* and valued it highly.

15. Commentary of Ramban on *Sefer Yetzirah*, Chapter 1, *Mishnah* 2.

16. *Tikunei HaZohar, Tikun* 27, page 71, side 2.

17. Rabbi Yitzchak Isaac, *Pree Yitzchak*, Chapter 1, *Mishnah* 2.

18. Ramban, commentary on *Sefer Yetzirah*, Chapter 1, *Mishnah* 2.

19. Eliyahu Gaon of Vilna, commentary on *Sefer Yetzirah*, Chapter 1, *Mishnah* 2, *Ofan* 2.

20. Quoted in *Pree Yitzchak*, Chapter 1, *Mishnah* 2, from Chaim Vital's *Etz Chaim*.

21. The quote is in reference to the creation of *Zair Anpin*, the child of the *Partzufim Abba* (Father) and *Imma* (Mother). The creation of a human child is supposedly similar. The Kabbalists never tire of saying, "From my own body will I see the Lord" (Job 19:26), that is, the human body parallels that of the Heavenly Man.

22. *Pree Yitzchak*, Chapter 1, *Mishnah* 3.

23. Ibid.

24. Eliyahu Gaon of Vilna, commentary on *Sefer Yetzirah*, Chapter 1, *Mishnah* 3, *Ofan* 1.

25. Ibid.

26. Ibid., *Mishnah* 4.

27. See n. 21.

28. Commentary of Ramban on *Sefer Yetzirah*, Chapter 1, *Mishnah 3*.

29. Commentary of Raivad on *Sefer Yetzirah*, Chapter 1, *Mishnah 3*.

30. *Pardes Rimonim, Shaar HaArachim, Daat.*

31. *Pree Yitzchak* in the name of the Ari, Chapter 1, *Mishnah 4*.

32. Ibid.

33. Eliyahu Gaon of Vilna, commentary on *Sefer Yetzirah*, Chapter 1, *Mishnah 4, Ofan 1*.

34. Shabbetai Horowitz was the son of the famous Kabbalist Isaiah Horowitz, known as the ShaLaH. They lived in the seventeenth century and were followers of Moses Cordovero.

35. Shabbetai Horowitz, *Shefa Tal*, "Hundred Year Old Introduction."

36. Meir Gabbai, *Avodat HaKodesh* (The Holy Service), early sixteenth century.

37. *Pree Yitzchak*, Chapter 1, *Mishnah 4*.

38. Ibid.

39. Clothing (*Hitlabshut*) in Kabbalah refers to a covering. The light is clothed in the vessels. Sometimes various *Sefirot* are clothed by others. For instance, *Etz Chaim* describes the arms of the *Partzuf Arich Anpin* as being clothed by the *Partzufim* of *Abba* and *Imma*. Clothing limits and diminishes the light. It makes it more bearable. Incidentally, the standard layers of covering from inner to outermost are generally ordered as follows: Root, Soul, Body, Clothing, and House.

40. Eliyahu Goan of Vilna, commentary on *Sefer Yetzirah*, Chapter 1, *Mishnah 5*.

41. Commentary of Ramban on *Sefer Yetzirah*, Chapter 1, *Mishnah 5*.

42. Interestingly, the *Sefirah* of *Gevurah* (Courage) is called *Pachad* (Fear) by the Ramban. This *Sefirah* is identified with Isaac. He was "courageous" in allowing Abraham to sacrifice him. The word *fear* here refers to fear of God and does not gainsay Isaac's courage. The Torah says that Jacob swore to Lavan by the "fear" of his father Isaac. This means that he swore by the God that Isaac feared. Based on this verse, the *Sefirah* of *Gevurah* is sometimes called *Pachad*.

43. Maimonides, *Guide to the Perplexed*, Section 3, Chapter 10.

44. Chaim Vital, *Etz Chaim, Shaar HaKlalim, Drush Seder HaTikun*.

45. Ibid.

46. *Hagiggah* 14b.

47. The Talmud uses the term *bazak* in the phrase "to spread olive waste in a stove." This usage is quoted by those who support this translation.

48. Moshe bar Yaakov HaGoleh mentions this possibility in his commentary *Otzar HaShem*.

49. Eliyahu Gaon of Vilna, commentary on *Sefer Yetzirah*, Chapter 1, *Mishnah* 6. Interestingly, it has been said that there is a basic difference between *Chasidut* and the Gaon on this point. The beginning of creation, according to Lurian Kabbalah, is the contraction of the Infinite light. The Gaon is reported to have taken this quite literally, saying that the contraction resulted in a true vacuum. The chasidic view disagrees. It feels that even the vacuum was not completely devoid of the Infinite's light. Nevertheless, here the Gaon states, "No place is devoid of God's presence." Perhaps he means now that the vacuum has been filled, after the emanations.

50. *Pree Yitzchak*, Chapter 1, *Mishnah* 6.

51. Saadia Gaon, commentary on *Sefer Yetzirah*, Chapter 1, *Mishnah* 6.

52. The Ramban uses the term *Tevunah* rather than the common term *Binah* for Understanding. In Lurian Kabbalah, *Tevunah* is a *Partzuf* composed of the bottom part of *Binah*. I am not sure the Ramban meant to imply this distinction.

53. Commentary of Ramban on *Sefer Yetzirah*, Chapter 1, *Mishnah* 7.

54. Moshe Botarel, commentary on *Sefer Yetzirah*, Chapter 1, *Mishnah* 7.

55. The term *Atik Yomin* appears in the Book of Daniel. There it means "ancient of days." *Atik* has two meanings in Hebrew, "ancient" and "moved." Kabbalah uses both. Since the days (*Sefirot*) are from the upper (senior) world, they are ancient. Since they are part of the lower world, it is as if they have moved.

56. Commentary of Raivad on *Sefer Yetzirah*, Chapter 1, *Mishnah* 7.

57. Eliyahu Gaon of Vilna, commentary on *Sefer Yetzirah*, Chapter 1, *Mishnah* 7.

58. *Pree Yitzchak*, Chapter 1, *Mishnah* 7.

59. Eliyahu Gaon of Vilna, commentary on *Sefer Yetzirah*, Chapter 1, *Mishnah* 8. Also, see Appendix F.

60. *Kiddushin* 49b.

61. Moshe Botarel, commentary on *Sefer Yetzirah*, Chapter 1, *Mishnah* 8.

62. Moshe bar Yaakov HaGoleh, *Otzar HaShem*, Chapter 1, *Mishnah* 8.

63. Eliyahu Gaon of Vilna, commentary on *Sefer Yetzirah,* Chapter 1, *Mishnah* 8.

64. Maimonides, *Guide to the Perplexed*, Section 2, Chapters 6–12 explain the author's theory of angels. Also, *Mishneh Torah*, *Yisodei HaTorah*, Chapter 2:2.

65. See the Ramban's commentary on Genesis and his treatment of the angels that appeared to Abraham. While Maimonides thought of this as a dream, Ramban takes a different approach.

66. Saadia Gaon, commentary on *Sefer Yetzirah*, Chapter 1, *Mishnah 8*.

67. Eliyahu Gaon of Vilna, commentary on *Sefer Yetzirah*, Chapter 1, *Mishnah 8*.

68. Ibid.

69. Ibid. See the commentaries of the Raivad and Ramban on *Sefer Yetzirah*, Chapter 1, *Mishnah 8*.

70. Commentary of Ramban on *Sefer Yetzirah*, Chapter 1, *Mishnah 9*.

71. Please remember that the Hebrew *"Bereishit"* is often translated by Kabbalists "with the beginning (*Chachmah*)" rather than "in the beginning."

72. *Pree Yitzchak*, Chapter 1, *Mishnah 9*.

73. Commentary of Raivad on *Sefer Yetzirah*, Chapter 1, *Mishnah 9*.

74. Eliyahu Gaon of Vilna, Commentary on *Sefer Yetzirah*, Chapter 1, *Mishnah 9*.

75. Commentary of Ramban on *Sefer Yetzirah*, Chapter 1, *Mishnah 9*.

76. Eliyahu Gaon of Vilna, commentary on *Sefer Yetzirah*, Chapter 1, *Mishnah 9*.

77. *Zohar* 135b on Exodus, *Parshat Trumah*.

78. Yehuda Leib Ashlag, *HaSulam*, *Parshat Trumah*, explanation of *Zohar* 135b.

79. Commentary of Ramban on *Sefer Yetzirah*, Chapter 1, *Mishnah 9*.

80. Ibid.

81. Raivad, Commentary on *Sefer Yetzirah*, Chapter 1, *Mishnah 10*.

82. Ibid.

83. Commentary of Ramban on *Sefer Yetzirah*, Chapter 1, *Mishnah 10*.

84. Eliyahu Gaon of Vilna, commentary on *Sefer Yetzirah*, Chapter 1, *Mishnah 10*.

85. Chaim Vital, *Etz Chaim*, Gate of Rules, Chapter 3.

86. Eliyahu Gaon of Vilna, commentary on *Sefer Yetzirah*, Chapter 1, *Mishnah 10*.

87. Commentary of Ramban on *Sefer Yetzirah*, Chapter 1, *Mishnah 10*.

88. Raivad, commentary on *Sefer Yetzirah*, Chapter 1, *Mishnah 10*.

89. Ibid.

90. Commentary of Ramban on *Sefer Yetzirah*, Chapter 1, *Mishnah 10*.

91. Ibid.

92. Refer to the discussion of the three mother letters (*Mishnah 2*).

93. Commentary of Ramban on *Sefer Yetzirah*, Chapter 1, *Mishnah 10*.

94. Raivad, commentary on *Sefer Yetzirah*, Chapter 1, *Mishnah 10*.

95. Sapphire has the same root in Hebrew as *Sefirah*. Some say the term *Sefirah* originated from *Sapir* (Sapphire). The Raivad is using this word intentionally here, as we are speaking of the origin of a *Sefirah*.

96. Raivad, commentary on *Sefer Yetzirah*, Chapter 1, *Mishnah* 11.

97. *Sefer HaBahir*, paragraph 2.

98. Commentary of Ramban on *Sefer Yetzirah*, Chapter 1, *Mishnah* 11.

99. Raivad, commentary on *Sefer Yetzirah*, Chapter 1, *Mishnah* 10.

100. Commentary of Ramban on *Sefer Yetzirah*, Chapter 1, *Mishnah* 11.

101. Eliyahu Gaon of Vilna, commentary on *Sefer Yetzirah*, Chapter 1, *Mishnah* 11.

102. Saadia Gaon, commentary on *Sefer Yetzirah*, Chapter 1, *Mishnah* 12.

103. Commentary of Ramban on *Sefer Yetzirah*, Chapter 1, *Mishnah* 12.

104. Saadia Gaon, commentary on *Sefer Yetzirah*, Chapter 1, *Mishnah* 12.

105. Eliyahu Gaon of Vilna, commentary on *Sefer Yetzirah*, Chapter 1, *Mishnah* 12.

106. Raivad, commentary on *Sefer Yetzirah*, Chapter 1, *Mishnah* 12.

107. Eliyahu Gaon of Vilna, commentary on *Sefer Yetzirah*, Chapter 1, *Mishnah* 12.

108. Rashi, commentary on Deuteronomy 18:6.

109. Raivad, commentary on *Sefer Yetzirah*, Chapter 1, *Mishnah* 13.

110. *Otzar HaShem*, Chapter 1, *Mishnah* 13.

111. Ibid.

112. *Pree Yitzchak*, Chapter 1, *Mishnah* 13.

113. Commentary of Ramban on *Sefer Yetzirah*, Chapter 1, *Mishnah* 13.

114. Eliyahu Gaon of Vilna, commentary on *Sefer Yetzirah*, Chapter 1, *Mishnah* 13.

115. Commentary of Ramban on *Sefer Yetzirah*, Chapter 1, *Mishnah* 13.

116. Eliyahu Gaon of Vilna, commentary on *Sefer Yetzirah*, Chapter 1, *Mishnah* 13.

117. The Gaon says that the Six Extremes are the Spirit (*Ruach*) of man. This is based on the kabbalistic notion that the soul has five aspects. The highest, *Yechidah*, is associated with *Keter*. The next, *Chayah*, is in *Chachmah*, followed by *Neshamah*, which is in *Binah*. Beneath *Neshamah* is *Ruach* (Spirit), which is associated with the next *Sefirah* group down, the Six Extremes. That is what the Gaon means when he says that the Extremes are the spirit of man. Finally, *Nefesh* is associated with *Malchut*.

118. Eliyahu Gaon of Vilna, commentary on *Sefer Yetzirah*, Chapter 1, *Mishnah* 13.

119. Commentary of Ramban on *Sefer Yetzirah*, Chapter 1, *Mishnah* 14.

120. Ibid.

121. *Otzar HaShem*, Chapter 1, *Mishnah* 14.

122. Raivad, commentary on *Sefer Yetzirah*, Chapter 1, *Mishnah* 14.

123. Eliyahu Gaon of Vilna, commentary on *Sefer Yetzirah*, Chapter 1, *Mishnah* 14.

CHAPTER 2

1. Eliyahu Gaon of Vilna, commentary on *Sefer Yetzirah*, Chapter 2, *Mishnah* 1.

2. *Otzar HaShem*, Chapter 2, *Mishnah* 1.

3. Commentary of Ramban on *Sefer Yetzirah*, Chapter 2, *Mishnah* 1.

4. Raivad, commentary on *Sefer Yetzirah*, Chapter 2, *Mishnah* 1.

5. *Otzar HaShem*, Chapter 2, *Mishnah* 1.

6. Commentary of Ramban on *Sefer Yetzirah*, Chapter 2, *Mishnah* 1.

7. Raivad, commentary on *Sefer Yetzirah*, Chapter 2, *Mishnah* 1.

8. *Targum* of Yonatan ben Uziel on Genesis 6:4.

9. *Pirke Avot* (Ethics of the Fathers), Chapter 2, *Mishnah* 12.

10. *Otzar HaShem*, Chapter 2, *Mishnah* 1.

11. *Pree Yitzchak*, Chapter 2, *Mishnah* 1.

12. Eliyahu Gaon of Vilna, commentary on *Sefer Yetzirah*, Chapter 2, *Mishnah* 1.

13. Commentary of Ramban on *Sefer Yetzirah*, Chapter 1, *Mishnah* 10.

14. Raivad, commentary on *Sefer Yetzirah*, Chapter 2, *Mishnah* 2.

15. Eliyahu Gaon of Vilna, commentary on *Sefer Yetzirah*, Chapter 2, *Mishnah* 2.

16. Ibid.

17. Commentary of Ramban on *Sefer Yetzirah*, Chapter 2, *Mishnah* 2.

18. *Pree Yitzchak*, Chapter 2, *Mishnah* 2.

19. Raivad, commentary on *Sefer Yetzirah*, Chapter 2, *Mishnah* 3.

20. *Pree Yitzchak*, Chapter 2, *Mishnah* 3.

21. Eliyahu Gaon of Vilna, commentary on *Sefer Yetzirah*, Chapter 2, *Mishnah* 3.

22. *Pree Yitzchak*, Chapter 2, *Mishnah* 3.

23. Commentary of Ramban on *Sefer Yetzirah*, Chapter 2, *Mishnah* 3.

24. Raivad, commentary on *Sefer Yetzirah*, Chapter 2, *Mishnah* 3.

25. Commentary of Ramban on *Sefer Yetzirah*, Chapter 7, *Mishnah* 3.

26. Eliyahu Gaon of Vilna, commentary on *Sefer Yetzirah*, Chapter 2, *Mishnah* 3.

27. *Otzar HaShem*, Chapter 2, *Mishnah* 4.

28. Ibid.

29. Ibid.

30. Raivad, commentary on *Sefer Yetzirah*, Chapter 2, *Mishnah* 4.

31. Ibid.

32. Eliyahu Gaon of Vilna, commentary on *Sefer Yetzirah*, Chapter 2, *Mishnah* 4.

33. *Otzar HaShem*, Chapter 2, *Mishnah* 5.

34. Commentary of Ramban on *Sefer Yetzirah*, Chapter 2, *Mishnah* 5.

35. Raivad, commentary on *Sefer Yetzirah*, Chapter 2, *Mishnah* 5.

36. Ibid.

37. *Pree Yitzchak*, Chapter 2, *Mishnah* 5.

38. Eliyahu Gaon of Vilna, commentary on *Sefer Yetzirah*, Chapter 2, *Mishnah* 5.

39. Commentary of Ramban on *Sefer Yetzirah*, Chapter 1, *Mishnah* 10.

40. *Otzar HaShem*, Chapter 1, *Mishnah* 11.

41. *Pree Yitzchak*, Chapter 2, *Mishnah* 6.

42. Commentary of Ramban on *Sefer Yetzirah*, Chapter 2, *Mishnah* 6.

43. Moshe Botarel, commentary on *Sefer Yetzirah*, Chapter 2, *Mishnah* 6.

44. *Pree Yitzchak*, Chapter 2, *Mishnah* 6.

45. Raivad, commentary on *Sefer Yetzirah*, Chapter 2, *Mishnah* 6.

46. Commentary of Ramban on *Sefer Yetzirah*, Chapter 2, *Mishnah* 6.

47. Ibid.

48. Ibid.

49. Raivad, commentary on *Sefer Yetzirah*, Chapter 2, *Mishnah* 6.

50. Eliyahu Gaon of Vilna, commentary on *Sefer Yetzirah*, Chapter 2, *Mishnah* 6.

CHAPTER 3

1. Raivad, commentary on *Sefer Yetzirah*, Chapter 3, *Mishnah* 1.

2. Ibid.

3. Saadia Gaon, commentary on *Sefer Yetzirah*, Chapter 3, *Mishnah* 1.

4. Raivad, commentary on *Sefer Yetzirah*, Chapter 3, *Mishnah* 2.

5. Commentary of Ramban on *Sefer Yetzirah*, Chapter 3, *Mishnah* 2.

6. Ibid.

7. Raivad, commentary on *Sefer Yetzirah*, Chapter 3, *Mishnah* 2.

8. Eliyahu Gaon of Vilna, commentary on *Sefer Yetzirah*, Chapter 3, *Mishnah* 2.

9. Commentary of Ramban on *Sefer Yetzirah*, Chapter 3, *Mishnah* 3.

10. Raivad, commentary on *Sefer Yetzirah*, Chapter 3, *Mishnah* 3.

11. Ibid.

12. Ibid.

13. Eliyahu Gaon of Vilna, commentary on *Sefer Yetzirah*, Chapter 3, *Mishnah* 6 (his *Mishnah* 6 is different than the standard version).

14. Commentary of Ramban on *Sefer Yetzirah*, Chapter 3, *Mishnah* 4.

15. Ibid.

16. Ibid, *Mishnah* 5.

17. Raivad, commentary on *Sefer Yetzirah*, Chapter 3, *Mishnah* 5.

18. Saadia Gaon, commentary on *Sefer Yetzirah*, Chapter 3, *Mishnah* 6.

19. Commentary of Ramban on *Sefer Yetzirah*, Chapter 3, *Mishnah* 6.

20. Eliyahu Gaon of Vilna, commentary on *Sefer Yetzirah*, Chapter 3, *Mishnah* 7.

21. Commentary of Ramban on *Sefer Yetzirah*, Chapter 3, *Mishnah* 7.

22. Ibid.

23. Eliyahu Gaon of Vilna, commentary on *Sefer Yetzirah*, Chapter 3, *Mishnah* 3.

24. Chaim Vital, *Etz Chaim*, Gate of *Tenta*, Chapter 7.

CHAPTER 4

1. Eliyahu Gaon of Vilna, commentary on *Sefer Yetzirah*, Chapter 4, *Mishnah* 1.

2. Rabbi Eliezer of Garmiza, a well-known early rabbi (*Rishon*) popularly called The Rokeach, commentary to *Sefer Yetzirah*, Chapter 4, *Mishnah* 1.

3. *Pree Yitzchak*, Chapter 4, *Mishnah* 1.

4. Ibid.

5. Ibid.

6. *Sefer HaBahir*, paragraph 14.

7. Eliyahu Gaon of Vilna, commentary on *Sefer Yetzirah*, Chapter 4, *Mishnah* 5. His *Mishnah* 5 is included in our *Mishnah* 2.

8. *Tikunei HaZohar*, *Tikun* 18.

9. Eliyahu Gaon of Vilna, commentary on *Sefer Yetzirah*, Chapter 4, *Mishnah* 4. His *Mishnah* 4 is included in our *Mishnah* 3.

10. It is called, in the *Shemoneh Esrei* prayer, "the most beautiful of days" and in the *Zemirah* "*Yom Zeh Mechubad*" "the most honored of days."

11. Rabbi Moses Cordovero, the great sixteenth-century Kabbalist, discusses these two aspects of *Shabbat* (before and after the week) in his classic *Pardes Rimonim*.

12. Raivad, commentary on *Sefer Yetzirah*, Chapter 4, *Mishnah* 3.

13. *Otzar HaShem*, Chapter 4, *Mishnah* 3.

14. *Pree Yitzchak*, Chapter 4, *Mishnah* 3.

15. Raivad, commentary on *Sefer Yetzirah*, Chapter 4, *Mishnah* 4.

16. Ibid.

17. Eliyahu Gaon of Vilna, commentary on *Sefer Yetzirah*, Chapter 4, *Mishnah* 6. His *Mishnah* 6 is included in our *Mishnah* 4.

18. Chaim Vital, *Etz Chaim, Shaar Tenta (The Gate of tones, dots, letter adornments, and letters)*.

19. *Pree Yitzchak*, Chapter 4, *Mishnah* 6. (His sixth *Mishnah* is our fourth.)

20. Raivad, commentary on *Sefer Yetzirah*, Chapter 4, *Mishnah* 5.

21. Ibid.

22. Eliyahu Gaon of Vilna, commentary on *Sefer Yetzirah*, Chapter 4, *Mishnah* 8. His *Mishnah* 8 is included in our *Mishnah* 5.

23. *Tikunei HaZohar*, *Tikun* 70.

24. Eliyahu Gaon of Vilna, commentary on *Sefer Yetzirah*, Chapter 4, *Mishnah* 8.

25. Chaim Vital's introduction to *Etz Chaim*.

26. Raivad, commentary on *Sefer Yetzirah*, Chapter 4, *Mishnah* 6.

27. *Sefer Yetzirah*, Chapter 1, *Mishnah* 7.

28. Saadia Gaon, commentary on *Sefer Yetzirah*, Chapter 4, *Mishnah* 7.

29. Raivad, commentary on *Sefer Yetzirah*, Chapter 4, *Mishnah* 7.

30. *Mishnah Zevachim*, Chapter 5, *Mishnah* 1.

31. *Berachot* 3a.

32. Saadia Gaon, commentary on *Sefer Yetzirah*, Chapter 4, *Mishnah* 8.

33. Raivad, commentary on *Sefer Yetzirah*, Chapter 4, *Mishnah* 8.

34. Raivad, commentary on *Sefer Yetzirah*, Chapter 4, *Mishnah* 9.

35. Saadia Gaon, commentary on *Sefer Yetzirah*, Chapter 4, *Mishnah* 10.

36. Shabbetai Donnolo, *Sefer Chachmoni*, Chapter 4.

37. *Berachot* 59b.

38. Based upon this, a special prayer is recited over the sun every twenty-eight years. This is known as "the blessing of the sun" (*Birkat HaChamah*). The twenty-eight years approximately corresponds to Saturn's orbit around the sun. While Abaye might not have thought that Saturn revolved about the sun, he certainly was aware that it returned to the same place every twenty-eight years.

39. Please note that there are two main cycles in the Jewish calendar, one known as the great cycle and the other as the little cycle. The former is the cycle of the sun in twenty-eight years. This is based on the belief that the sun returns to the same place it was in when it was originally put in the heavens on the fourth day of creation. The other cycle is that of the moon. This cycle is only nineteen years, and the cycle of leap years is set by it. Each little cycle of nineteen years has exactly seven leap years.

40. Raivad, commentary on *Sefer Yetzirah*, Chapter 4, *Mishnah* 10.

41. *Kiddushin* 49b.

42. Raivad, commentary on *Sefer Yetzirah*, Chapter 4, *Mishnah* 11.

43. *Sefer Yetzirah*, Chapter 2, *Mishnah* 1.

44. The Talmud learns from the phrase "killed by a sword" that the sword has the same uncleanliness as he who is killed.

45. Raivad, commentary on *Sefer Yetzirah*, Chapter 4, *Mishnah* 11.

46. Saadia Gaon, commentary on *Sefer Yetzirah*, Chapter 4, *Mishnah* 11.

47. Rashi's commentary to Deuteronomy 32:1.

48. *Pree Yitzchak*, Chapter 4, *Mishnah* 12.

49. Eliyahu Gaon of Vilna, commentary on *Sefer Yetzirah*, Chapter 4, *Mishnah* 16 (his *Mishnah* 16 corresponds to our *Mishnah* 12).

50. Raivad, commentary on *Sefer Yetzirah*, Chapter 4, *Mishnah* 12.

51. Ibid.

52. See prayer after the sounding of the *Shofar*. Because of its strangeness, some prayer books with translations omit it from translated section.

53. The Talmud tell us that the world will exist for six thousand years and will then become desolate. Thus, the seventh thousand will be, in a way, analogous to the Sabbath.

54. Raivad, commentary on *Sefer Yetzirah*, Chapter 4, *Mishnah* 12.

55. *Tikunei HaZohar*, *Tikun* 70.

56. Eliyahu Gaon of Vilna, commentary on *Sefer Yetzirah*, Chapter 4, *Mishnah* 16.

57. *Targum* of Yonatan ben Uziel on 2 Kings 14:14.

58. Moshe Botarel, commentary on *Sefer Yetzirah*, Chapter 4, *Mishnah* 12.

CHAPTER 5

1. Eliyahu Gaon of Vilna, commentary on *Sefer Yetzirah*, Chapter 5, *Mishnah* 1.

2. Raivad, commentary on *Sefer Yetzirah*, Chapter 5, *Mishnah* 1.

3. Eliyahu Gaon of Vilna, commentary on *Sefer Yetzirah*, Chapter 5, *Mishnah* 1.

4. Ibid.

5. Saadia Gaon, commentary on *Sefer Yetzirah*, Chapter 5, *Mishnah* 1.

6. Eliyahu Gaon of Vilna, commentary on *Sefer Yetzirah*, Chapter 5, *Mishnah* 1.

7. Saadia Gaon, commentary on *Sefer Yetzirah*, Chapter 5, *Mishnah* 1.

8. Eliyahu Gaon of Vilna, commentary on *Sefer Yetzirah*, Chapter 5, *Mishnah* 1.

9. *Otzar HaShem*, Chapter 5, *Mishnah* 2.

10. Rabbi Eliezer of Garmiza (Rokeach), commentary to *Sefer Yetzirah*, Chapter 5, *Mishnah* 2.

11. *Otzar HaShem*, Chapter 5, *Mishnah* 2.

12. Eliyahu Gaon of Vilna, commentary on *Sefer Yetzirah*, Chapter 5, *Mishnah* 2.

13. Genesis 29:32 states that Leah named her son Reuben because she said "God *saw* my suffering." Reuben is thus associated with *sight*.

14. Raivad, commentary on *Sefer Yetzirah*, Chapter 5, *Mishnah* 2.

15. Ibid.

16. Ibid.

17. Ibid.

18. *Otzar HaShem*, Chapter 5, *Mishnah* 3.

19. Chaim Vital, *Etz Chaim*, Gate of Rules (*Shaar HaKlalim*).

20. *Pree Yitzchak*, Chapter 6, *Mishnah* 1 (part of his *Mishnah* 1 of Chapter 6 corresponds to our Chapter 5, *Mishnah* 3).

21. Eliyahu Gaon of Vilna, commentary on *Sefer Yetzirah*, Chapter 6,

Mishnah 1 (part of his *Mishnah* 1 of Chapter 6 corresponds to our Chapter 5, *Mishnah* 3).

22. Ibid., Chapter 6, *Mishnah* 6, which corresponds to our Chapter 5, *Mishnah* 4.

23. Meir Rotenburg, as quoted by Moshe Botarel, commentary on *Sefer Yetzirah*, Chapter 5, *Mishnah* 4. Meir was the most prominent rabbi of thirteenth-century Germany and was known as "the light of the exile." The famous Rabbenu Asher was his student.

24. Moshe Botarel, commentary on *Sefer Yetzirah*, Chapter 5, *Mishnah* 4.

25. *Beraita* is a term for mishnaic material not included in the codification of the *Mishnah* by Rabbi Judah HaNasi.

26. *Otzar HaShem*, Chapter 5, *Mishnah* 4.

27. Rabbi Shlomo Yitzchaki (Rashi), commentary on Genesis 1:14.

CHAPTER 6

1. Raivad, commentary on *Sefer Yetzirah*, Chapter 6, *Mishnah* 1.

2. *Pree Yitzchak*, Chapter 6. Please note that his text is divided differently than the standard one.

3. Eliyahu Gaon of Vilna, commentary on *Sefer Yetzirah*, Chapter 6, *Mishnah* 1.

4. Shabbetai Donnolo, *Sefer Chachmoni*, Chapter 6.

5. Moshe Botarel, commentary on *Sefer Yetzirah*, Chapter 6, *Mishnah* 1.

6. *Otzar HaShem*, Chapter 6, *Mishnah* 1.

7. Ibid., *Mishnah* 2.

8. Eliyahu Gaon of Vilna, commentary on *Sefer Yetzirah*, Chapter 6, *Mishnah* 3. His *Mishnah* 3 is included in our *Mishnah* 2.

9. Ibid.

10. Ibid., *Mishnah* 4. His *Mishnah* 4 is included in our *Mishnah* 2.

11. *Pree Yitzchak,* Chapter 6. Please note that his text is divided differently than the standard one.

12. Eliyahu Gaon of Vilna, commentary on *Sefer Yetzirah*, Chapter 6, *Mishnah* 4.

13. Ibid.

14. *Pree Yitzchak*, Chapter 6.

15. Ibid.

16. *Otzar HaShem*, Chapter 6, *Mishnah* 2.

17. *Otzar HaShem*, Chapter 6, *Mishnah* 3.

18. Eliyahu Gaon of Vilna, commentary on *Sefer Yetzirah*, Chapter 6, *Mishnah* 5. His *Mishnah* 5 is our *Mishnah* 3.

19. *Otzar HaShem*, Chapter 6, *Mishnah* 3.

20. *Midrash Ne'elam* is one of the subdivisions of the *Zohar*.

21. The allusion is to a common Hebrew expression, "*HaShaah misacheket lo*"—the hour is laughing for him. It means "it is a favorable time for him."

22. Eliyahu Gaon of Vilna, commentary on *Sefer Yetzirah*, Chapter 6, *Mishnah* 5.

23. *Pree Yitzchak*, Chapter 6, *Mishnah* 5. Please note that his *Mishnah* 5 is our *Mishnah* 3.

24. *Bava Batra* 15a.

25. *Sanhedrin* 65b.

26. Rashi, *Sanhedrin* 65b.

27. Commentary of *Malbum*, Book of Genesis, Chapter 18.

28. Moshe Botarel, commentary on *Sefer Yetzirah*, Chapter 6, *Mishnah* 4.

29. Eliyahu Gaon of Vilna, commentary on *Sefer Yetzirah*, Chapter 6, last *Mishnah*.

30. *Pree Yitzchak*, Chapter 6, last *Mishnah*.

References

Ashlag, Yehuda Leib. *Talmud Esser Sefirot*. B'nai B'rak, Israel: M. Klor, 1946.

Cordovero, Moses. *Pardes Rimonim*. Jerusalem: Modachai Ateya, 1962.

Cottingham, J. *Descartes: Meditations on First Philosophy*. Cambridge, England: Cambridge University Press, 1986.

Friedrich, Carl. *The Philosophy of Hegel*. New York: Random House, 1953.

Gabbai, Meir. *Avodat HaKodesh*.

Horowitz, Shabbetai. *Shefa Tal*. Brooklyn: Rabbi Y. Amsel, 1960.

Hume, David. *A Treatise on Human Nature*. Harmondsworth, Middlesex, England: Penguin Books, 1985.

Kaplan, Aryeh. *Sefer HaBahir*. New York: Samual Weiser, Israel: 1979.

Luzzatto, Moshe Chaim. *Shaaray Ramachal*. B'nai B'rak, Israel: Sifriyati, 1989.

Maimonides, Moses. *Mishneh Torah*. New York: Otzar HaSefarim, 1946.

_____ . *Moreh Nevuchim* (Guide to the Perplexed). Jerusalem: A. Monson, 1960.

Midrash Rabbah. New York: Otzar HaSefarim, 1946.

Mikraot Gedolot Tanach. New York: Pardes, 1951.

Orlinsky, Harry. *Library of Biblical Studies—Mesoreth HaMessoreth*. New York: Ktav, 1968.

Sefer Yetzirah. Attributed to Abraham. Jerusalem: Modachai Ateya, 1962.

Talmud Bavli. New York: Otzar HaSefarim, 1957.

Tikunei HaZohar. Attributed to Rabbi Shimon bar Yochai. Israel, 1967.

Tishbi, Y. *Mishnat HaZohar*. Jerusalem: Mosad Bialik, 1949.

Vital, Chaim. *Etz Chaim*. Tel Aviv: The Arizal Publishing Society, 1960.

Zohar. Attributed to Rabbi Shimon bar Yochai. Jerusalem: Or HaZohar, 1954.

_____ . *Zohar with the Ladder*. Israel: Brody-Katz, 1975.

Index

ABOUT THE AUTHOR

Leonard R. Glotzer received a Bachelor of Arts degree in psychology from Brooklyn College and rabbinic ordination from Yeshivat Eretz Yisroel in New York. He served as rabbi of the New Springville Synagogue in Staten Island from 1976 to 1982. This book represents the culmination of his passion for Jewish philosophy and Kabbalah, which developed during his days in *yeshivah*. The author also has a strong interest in Hebrew poetry, which he writes in his spare time. A grandfather of two, he lives in Staten Island with his wife, Shirley.